CiTY·SMaRT™

Dallas/Fort Worth

Sharry Buckner

D1569210

**AVALON
TRAVEL**
publishing

Acknowledgements

Many thanks to the dozens of people who helped make this book as accurate as possible, to the members of DFW Writers' Workshop, and to my husband, Al, whose support is the wind beneath my wings.

CiTY·SMaRT: Dallas/Fort Worth
1st edition

Sharry Buckner

Published by
Avalon Travel Publishing
5855 Beaudry St.
Emeryville, CA 94608, USA

Printing History
First printing—September, 2000
5 4 3 2 1

Please send all comments, corrections, additions, amendments, and critiques to:

CiTY·SMaRT™
AVALON TRAVEL PUBLISHING
5855 BEAUDRY ST.
EMERYVILLE, CA 94608, USA
e-mail: info@travelmatters.com
www.travelmatters.com

ISBN: 1-56261-433-9
ISSN: 1531-0493

Editors: Angelique Clarke, Peg Goldstein, Suzanne Samuel
Copyeditor: Ginjer Clarke
Indexer: Vera Gross
Graphics Coordinator: Erika Howsare
Typesetter: Melissa Tandysh
Maps: Mike Ferguson, Mike Morgenfeld

Front cover photo: © Vladpans/Leo de Wys
Back cover photo: Fort Worth Convention & Visitors Bureau

Distributed in the United States and Canada by Publishers Group West

Printed in the United States by Publishers Press

CONTENTS

MAP CONTENTS

Restaurants, hotels, museums and other facilities marked by the
& symbol are wheelchair accessible.

See Dallas/Fort Worth the CiTY·SMaRT™ Way

The Guide for Dallas/Fort Worth Natives, New Residents, and Visitors

In *City•Smart: Dallas/Fort Worth*, local author Sharry Buckner tells it like it is. Residents will learn things they never knew about their city, new residents will get an insider's view of their new hometown, and visitors will be guided to the very best Dallas and Fort Worth, have to offer—whether they're on a weekend getaway or staying a week or more.

Opinionated Recommendations Save You Time and Money

From shopping to nightlife to museums, the author is opinionated about what she likes and dislikes. You'll learn the great and the not-so-great things about Dallas and Fort Worth's sights, restaurants, and accommodations. So you can decide what's worth your time and what's not; which hotel is worth the splurge and which is the best choice for budget travelers.

Easy-to-Use Format Makes Planning Your Trip a Cinch

City•Smart: Dallas/Fort Worth is user-friendly—you'll quickly find exactly what you're looking for. Chapters are organized by travelers' interests and needs, from Where to Stay and Where to Eat to Sights and Attractions, Kids' Stuff, Sports and Recreation, and even Day Trips from Dallas and Fort Worth.

Includes Maps and Quick Location-Finding Features

Every listing in this book is accompanied by a geographic zone designation (see the following pages for zone details) that helps you immediately find each location. Staying on Crescent Court and wondering about nearby sights and restaurants? Look for the Downtown Dallas zone label in the listings and you'll know that that statue or café is not far away. Or maybe you're looking for Fort Worth Water Gardens . Along with its address, you'll see a Downtown Fort Worth label, so you'll know just where to find it.

All That and Fun to Read, Too!

Every City•Smart chapter includes fun-to-read (and fun-to-use) tips to help you get more out of Dallas and Fort Worth, city trivia (did you know exterior shots of Southfork were of a real Texas home near Dallas?), and illuminating sidebars (for the best in Barbecue, for example, see page 75). And well-known local residents provide their personal "Top Ten" lists, guiding readers to the city's best sites for western heritage and more.

DALLAS/FORT WORTH ZONES

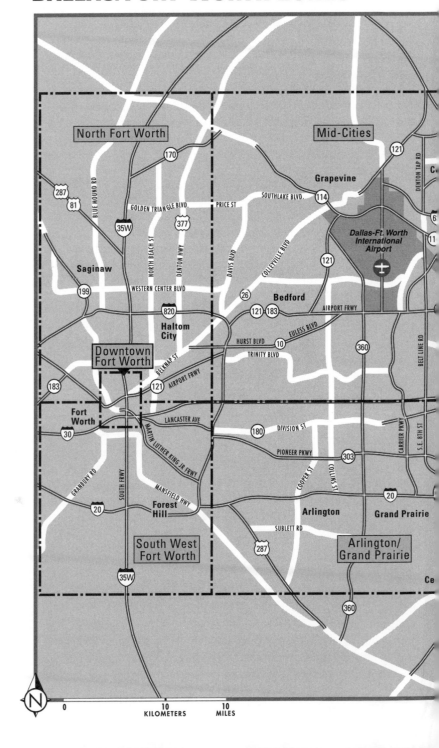

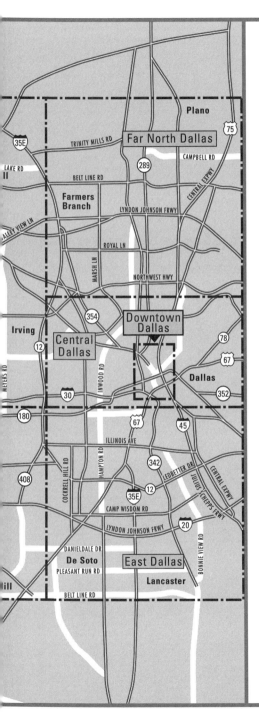

DALLAS/FORT WORTH ZONES

Downtown Dallas (DD) - Bounded by I-30 on the south, I-35E on the west, US-75 on the east, and Lemmon Ave. on the north.

Central Dallas (CD) - Bounded by the Dallas city limits on the west and LBJ Frwy (I-635) on the north and east. Includes Market Center, and University Park.

East Dallas (ED) - Bounded by I-30 on the north, and the Dallas city limits on the west. Includes Deep Ellum and Mesquite.

Far North Dallas (FND) - From LBJ Frwy (I-635) north. Includes Addison, Carrollton, Lewisville, Plano, and Richardson.

Mid-Cities (MC) - Hurst, Euless, Bedford, Colleyville, Irving, and Grapevine. Includes DFW International Airport.

Arlington/Grand Prairie (AGP) - The cities of Arlington and Grand Prairie.

Downtown Fort Worth (DFW) - Bounded by I-30 on the south, Henderson St. on the west, and I-35 on the east. Includes Sundance Square.

North Fort Worth (NFW) - Bounded on the southwest by Jacksboro Hwy and on the east by US-377. Includes the Stockyards Historic District.

Southwest Fort Worth (SFW) - Bounded on the north by State Hwy. 199 and I-30, and on the east by Loop I-820. Includes the Cultural District.

Dallas CVB

1

WELCOME TO
DALLAS AND FORT WORTH

Howdy and Welcome to "Big D" and "Cowtown"! The first thing you need to know is that even though the sprawling metropolitan area known simply as "The Metroplex" in these parts is viewed by non-Texans as one gigantic mass with two cities connected by dozens of suburbs, Dallas and Fort Worth are two distinctly separate cities—and fierce rivals at that. The once cutthroat competition is now more good-natured rivalry, but it is omnipresent nonetheless.

In 1875, the Dallas Daily Herald reported that Fort Worth was so quiet that a panther had been seen sleeping, undisturbed, in the dirt on the main street. Fort Worth never forgave that insult and the conflict began. The spirited Fort Worthians responded by accepting the "Panther City" nickname, one that some businesses still use today. Legend has it that the Fort Worth Fire Station kept two panthers as mascots. Flamboyant civic leader Amon Carter perpetuated the feud by taking his own sack lunch when he had to be in Dallas on business so he wouldn't spend a nickel in "that town." The 1974 opening of the Dallas/Fort Worth International Airport, a cooperative project jointly owned by the two cities, was supposed to end the long-standing rivalry.

The ninth-largest city in the United States, Dallas projects an upscale, cosmopolitan image with glitzy skyscrapers, luxury hotels, and more shopping centers per capita than any U.S. city. It's a culturally diverse city, a vibrant business and financial center, and a popular tourist and convention destination.

"Cowboys and Culture" is a phrase continually used to describe the staggering contrasts in Fort Worth. Fiercely proud of its Western heritage, it's also a sophisticated town of world-class museums and performing arts

A taste of the Old West at Fort Worth's Stockyards National Historic District

venues. Designated an All-American City twice in the last three decades, Fort Worth is a city where the laid-back spirit of the Old West lives side by side with the frenzied world of high-tech industry, international business, and state-of-the-art medical centers.

North Texas offers so many sights and activities and so many "firsts" and "biggests" and "bests" that some people might think the residents are bragging (as some Texans have been known to do). But it's all here, so enjoy!

Getting To Know Dallas and Fort Worth

Sprawling across an area of more than 10,000 square miles and encompassing parts of 12 counties containing approximately 5 million people, the Dallas and Fort Worth metropolitan areas and the numerous adjacent, connecting, and intertwined suburbs and small cities are known in Texas as "The Metroplex." Not all of the cities are pleased about this designation, however. Arlington, in particular, has struggled to create and maintain an identity of its own. And well it should because as home to several of the top tourist attractions in the area, it now boasts a population of more

T I P

The greater Dallas area requires 10-digit dialing; use the area code along with the seven-digit phone number.

Founding Father

To know Fort Worth is to know Amon G. Carter, Sr. His rags-to-riches story portrays the spirit of Fort Worth. Born in a log cabin in north central Texas, Carter came to Fort Worth in 1905 to work at the city's newspaper. In 1923, he bought the newspaper. He became a millionaire and an exuberant city booster, leading the business community, bringing several major oil companies, a public health hospital, and the aviation industry to Fort Worth. He was instrumental in building the Hotel Texas, The Fort Worth Club, and Harris Methodist Hospital. And of course, he put the slogan "Where the West Begins" on the front page of the Fort Worth Star-Telegram, where it remains today. A friend of such notable figures as Franklin D. Roosevelt and Will Rogers, the flamboyant Carter had a wide range of interests. The many facilities in Fort Worth that bear his name testify to his myriad accomplishments.

than 300,000. Irving is home to Texas Stadium and the Dallas Cowboys, and Grapevine has a delightfully distinct character, proud of its history and namesake vineyards.

So many smaller cities and communities, such as Addison, Coppell, Carrollton, Duncanville, Garland, Mesquite, Plano, and Richardson, surround Dallas that it's nearly impossible to tell where one stops and the next one begins. Benbrook, Colleyville, Keller, North Richland Hills, and the area known as HEB (Hurst, Euless, Bedford) surround Fort Worth. Don't let this sprawl discourage you, though, because the boundaries are invisible. Just get a map of the area and go.

Many of Dallas's attractions are centered in three major areas in and near Downtown. The West End Historic District is a 20-block area of restored warehouses and other buildings that now house trendy shops, eateries, and nightclubs. The Arts District (see Chapter 6, Museums and Art Galleries, and Chapter 11, Performing Arts) is an area just north of the central business district that was set aside in 1978 as part of a Downtown revitalization plan. Slightly southeast of Downtown, Fair Park, built for the Texas Centennial Exposition of 1936, is an attraction itself. It has been designated as a National Historic Landmark for the spectacular Art Deco buildings on the 277-acre complex. The buildings now house a variety of museums, historic sites, and entertainment and sports venues.

Two other areas of note in Dallas include McKinney Avenue/Uptown, just north of Downtown, where the refurbished McKinney Avenue trolley shuttles visitors along the street lined with galleries, antique and specialty shops, and restaurants, mostly located in converted vintage homes. Greenville Avenue, northeast of Downtown, is a "strip" lined with numerous nightclubs and funky shops selling antiques, Middle Eastern rugs, health food, and jewelry. Although this area is very popular after dark, proper safety precautions are in order.

Dallas has fashionable residential neighborhoods, past and present. In the Swiss Avenue Historic District, several architectural styles are reflected in nearly 200 preserved or restored houses. Still the most prestigious address in Dallas is Highland Park, which was laid out by William D. Cook, designer of Beverly Hills. North of Highland Park is University Park, the area surrounding Southern Methodist University (SMU) with beautiful old homes on large, landscaped lots.

Most of Fort Worth's tourist attractions are also concentrated in three areas. Downtown's Sundance Square is a 14-block historic district with red brick streets and turn-of-the-century restored buildings filled with restaurants, specialty shops, theaters, clubs, art galleries, and the majestic Nancy Lee and Perry R.Bass Performance Hall. North of Downtown, the Stockyards National Historic District has been preserved, renovated, and restored as a tribute to Fort Worth's history and to safeguard the spirit of the Old West. Today, it's a bustling enclave of shops, dining establishments, and entertainment, all with a western flavor. Just west of the central business area, several exceptional museums and theaters within easy walking distance of one another are clustered in the Cultural District (see Chapter 6, Museums and Art Galleries).

Residential neighborhoods of note in Fort Worth include historic Elizabeth Boulevard on the city's near south side. Once called "Silver Slipper Row," this street is still lined with mansions from the early 1900s. The luxurious homes in Rivercrest and Westover Hills on the city's west side, built with cattle and oil money, have hosted generations of social events.

Dallas and Fort Worth History

The frontier towns that were carved out of the dusty prairies have shorter, but probably more colorful, histories than some of our nation's older settlements. Native Americans, primarily Comanche, had occupied the land for generations when the French and Spanish explorers came in the mid-seventeenth and eighteenth centuries.

TRIVIA

Although Dallas County has never had a working oil well, the region's role as the financial and technical center for much of the state's drilling industry has been as good as gold—black gold, that is.

DALLAS TIMELINE

John Neely Bryan builds a cabin, lays claim to 640 acres, and sketches out a town.	1841
Dallas is selected as a permanent county seat.	1850
Dallas is incorporated as a town.	1856
Texas and Pacific Railroad arrives.	1873
First electric lights are installed in Dallas.	1882
The Texas State Fair opens.	1886
"Old Red," Dallas' sixth courthouse, is built.	1892
Theodore Roosevelt is the first U.S. President to visit Dallas.	1905
Neiman Marcus department store opens in downtown Dallas, redefining fashion.	1907
Federal Reserve Bank opens.	1914
Southern Methodist University is established.	1915
Highway 80 between Dallas and Fort Worth is paved.	1926
Dallas Love Field Airport opens.	1927
Oil is struck in east Texas.	1930
Texas Centennial Exposition opens in Fair Park.	1936
Ford Motor Company plant is converted to build military trucks and jeeps.	1942
President John F. Kennedy is assassinated.	1963
Dallas/Fort Worth Regional Airport opens.	1974
Republican National Convention is hosted in Dallas.	1984
100th anniversary of The State Fair of Texas is recognized.	1986
Dallas Sesquicentennial is celebrated.	1991

Dallas began slowly. John Neely Bryan, a Tennessee lawyer and adventurer, erected a single cabin in 1841. He hoped to start a trading post along the banks of the Trinity River, which he believed was navigable all the way to the Gulf of Mexico. Bryan was mistaken, and his new settlement languished until after the Civil War.

Eventually, the settlement did grow as a trading post, and in 1872, with bribes and gifts of land, the town leaders convinced the railroad to divert its tracks to the community. One year later, the Texas Pacific Railroad arrived, and the population soared to 6,000. As wagonloads of products

FORT WORTH TIMELINE

1849 Major Ripley Arnold and the U.S. Second Dragoons found Camp Worth.

1856 Fort Worth is chosen as Tarrant County seat.

1867 Chisholm Trail is established, passing through Fort Worth.

1873 Fort Worth is incorporated as a town.

1876 Texas and Pacific Railroad reaches Fort Worth.

1885 First electric lights are installed in Fort Worth.

1889 The Stockyards open north of downtown.

1894 Tarrant County Courthouse is completed on site of original fort.

1896 First Fat Stock Show is held.

1902 Armour and Swift & Co. open regional packing plants in the Stockyards.

1905 Theodore Roosevelt is the first U.S. president to visit Fort Worth.

1911 Texas Christian University opens.

1917 Oil boom begins; Camp Bowie opens to train troops for WWI.

1918 Saloons close because of prohibition.

1926 Highway 80 between Fort Worth and Dallas is paved.

1926 Meacham Field airport opens.

1936 Original Casa Mañana theater opens to salute Texas Centennial.

1941 Consolidated Vultee Aircraft opens an aircraft/bomber plant.

1942 Tarrant Field Airdrome opens as an Army training center.

1947 WBAP-TV becomes the first television station in Texas.

1962 Fort Worth hosts the first Van Cliburn International Piano Competition.

1969 Alan Bean becomes the first Fort Worthian to walk on the moon.

1974 Dallas/Fort Worth Regional Airport opens.

1981 Fort Worth Stock Yards Co. dissolves; Sundance Square opens.

1999 Fort Worth Sesquicentennial is celebrated.

Chisolm Trail Mural

arrived to be shipped by rail, Dallas became an agricultural market and trade center. By the turn of the century, Dallas was the established banking center for North Texas farmers and one of the world's largest inland cotton markets. Although Bryan's dream of a port on the Trinity River was never realized, Dallas was well on its way to becoming the largest city in the country *not* on a navigable body of water.

In 1930, C.M. "Dad" Joiner struck oil 100 miles east of Dallas, leading to the development of the East Texas Oil Field, the largest petroleum deposit on earth at the time. Dallas became the center of business for the nearby oil fields. Many citizens became millionaires, and the city reaped the benefits of this affluence. Today, Dallas is the third-largest city in Texas and exceedingly cosmopolitan; it is the banking center of the Southwest, a commercial center, home to international corporations, and a major convention city.

Fort Worth began as an Army post in 1849, shortly after the war with Mexico, as one of eight forts established on the frontier to protect the settlers from Indian attack. Major Ripley Arnold and his small detachment of U.S. Dragoons camped at the forks of the Trinity River. Arnold named it Camp Worth, in honor of his commanding officer in the Mexican war, unaware that General William Jenkins Worth had died a few days earlier. Later it was upgraded to Fort Worth, but by the mid-1850s, the frontier had

TIP

For the local time and temperature, call the hotline at 214/844-2211 or 214/844-4444.

moved westward and the forts were abandoned. The settlement became a trading post.

Post-Civil War times brought the great cattle drives to the American Southwest. From 1866 to the mid-1880s, millions of Texas cattle were driven north to market. The famed Chisholm Trail passed through Fort Worth, and as the last outpost until Abilene, Kansas, it became both a supply center and a bawdy merriment capital for cowboys, adventure-seekers, land speculators, outlaws, and settlers. Robert Leroy Parker (Butch Cassidy) and Harry Longbaugh (the Sundance Kid) frequented the legendary area of town called "Hell's Half Acre."

The future of Fort Worth was threatened in 1873 when the railroad was left stranded in nearby Dallas by a financial panic. In the midst of financial depression in 1875, the town was told that the land grant agreement with the railroad would expire at the end of the next legislative session. An early example of the pride and determination of the citizens of Fort Worth was displayed as nearly every man who could swing a pick or drive a mule worked around the clock to finish the roadbed in a desperate effort to beat the deadline. The women worked in shifts to feed them. To add to the drama, Tarrant County Representative Nicholas Henry Darnell, although extremely ill, demanded to be carried on a cot into the House chambers every day to shout "nay" when adjournment was voted on. The workers made the deadline, and on July 19, 1876, Texas and Pacific Railway Company Engine No. 20 pulled into Fort Worth.

The arrival of the railroad transformed Fort Worth into a major shipping center for livestock, and the enormous stockyards developed. In 1902, with the construction of the huge Swift and Armour meat-packing facilities, Fort Worth became the second-largest livestock market in the nation.

With the discovery of vast oil fields in West Texas in 1917, Fort Worth grew in importance as the last large commercial center before the prairie.

The State Fair of Texas

The State Fair of Texas is the largest Exposition in all of North America. The "Texas Star" Ferris wheel is the largest in the western hemisphere and second largest in the world. The State Fair of Texas wouldn't be complete without a Fletcher Corny Dog, created in Dallas in the 1940s by Neil Fletcher. Big Tex, the State Fair's official greeter, wasn't always a 52-foot-tall cowboy wearing a 75-gallon hat and size 70 boots; he started life in 1949 as a giant Santa Claus. For more information about the State Fair of Texas, call 214/565-9931 or check out the web site at www.texfair.com.

Mounted police patrol the Stockyards National Historic District in Fort Worth

Deals were made and supplies were procured. Fort Worth's population tripled in the next two decades. During the 1930s, oil surpassed cattle and remained the city's leading industry for the next 30 years.

From these freewheeling Western roots and the spirited men and women who stayed, came the Fort Worth of today, a city that has been named All-American City twice in the past three decades.

People of Dallas and Fort Worth

The Dallas/Fort Worth Consolidated Metropolitan Statistical Area (CMSA), with more than 4.8 million residents, is larger than 31 U.S. states. Statistics show an ethnic breakdown of approximately 65 percent Caucasian, 14.5 percent African American, 18 percent Hispanic, 2 percent Asian/Pacific Islander, and 0.5 percent Native American.

Statistics aside, this community consists of many assimilated peoples and cultures. African Americans have contributed since the early days of settlement, yet have suffered the same racial injustices as in the rest of the segregated South. The large Hispanic population accounts for multilingual benefits in the school system, media, and culinary realms. Recent decades have brought a medley of immigrants from Asia and the Pacific Islands. All of these peoples have found a home in this culturally diverse area.

The people of Dallas and Forth Worth are friendly and exhibit world-famous Texas hospitality. Fort Worthians consider their home an overgrown small country town and are fiercely proud of their Western heritage. You'll see businessmen in suits, Stetsons, and cowboy boots, and you'll likely receive a few "howdys" and nods. Dallasites exhibit the staidness of a cosmopolitan financial and market center, while celebrating the trends and styles of today. Many residents have come to the area from

Metroplex Weather

By David Finfrock, Chief Meteorologist at KXAS-TV, NBC, Channel 5

The Dallas/Fort Worth Metroplex has some of the most varied weather on the planet. Its geographic location explains part of the reason for that variety.

The Rocky Mountains block moisture from incoming Pacific storms and result in the dry desert regions of west Texas. The Gulf of Mexico, with its supply of warm, moist air, provides the rainfall for the dense forests of the east Texas Pineywoods region. South Texas, with its proximity to Mexico, has an almost tropical climate. The high plains of the Texas panhandle experience numbing subzero cold almost every winter.

And in between, north Texas is subject to all of those effects. A "Blue Norther" (a cold front) can shift the wind from south to north, changing the weather from tropical to Arctic overnight. And a dry west wind can shift to the east and bring torrents of rain.

There is one thing you can count on: summer in the Metroplex is going to be hot. A typical summer day is in the upper 90s. And an average summer hits 100 degrees at least 16 times.

Winter brings frequent northers. They can drop the temperature below freezing for a day or two. But it generally warms up again quickly, and even in mid-winter you can count on a lot of sunny days with temperatures in the 60s or higher.

Most of our rain comes in the spring and fall. March, April, September, and October account for the biggest portion of our annual rainfall of almost 34 inches. But even in those months, the bulk of the rain falls in brief thunderstorm, then sunny the rest of the time.

Snow is rare in this area. Every two or three years we get a couple of inches of snow. The bigger concern is the more frequent ice storm, which may make roads slick and hazardous a couple of times each winter.

All in all, north Texas weather is usually great!

other parts of the country, as well as from around the world. That global diversity may partly explain why Dallas has a much more open political climate than does Fort Worth. It's often said that Dallas is the "back door of the East" and Fort Worth is the "front door of the West."

Weather

The Metroplex has a moderate climate most of the year. Although northerners complain that Texas doesn't have four seasons, most natives enjoy not owning snow shovels and tire chains. Winters are usually mild, but the temperature can drop below freezing for several days; snow is rare, but occasional ice storms can plague the area in winter. Spring and fall are quite pleasant and show off the best of Texas weather. Summers can be beastly hot, especially with a vile thing called the temperature-humidity index (THI), which tells you that it feels hotter than it actually is, as if you didn't know that already.

For Statistics Lovers:
    The average high temperature is 76 degrees.
    The average low temperature is 51 degrees.
    Temperatures exceed 90 degrees an average of 96 days of the year and fall below freezing an average of 63 days of the year.
    The average relative humidity at noon is 57 percent.
    Winds average 11 mph and are predominantly from the south.

Metroplex Weather

	Average Temperature Range (Fahrenheit)	Average Precipitation (inches)
January	34-54	1.5
February	38-59	2.0
March	45-68	2.5
April	55-77	3.8
May	63-84	4.6
June	71-93	2.9
July	74-98	2.2
August	74-98	2.2
September	68-89	3.1
October	57-79	3.4
November	45-66	2.2
December	37-58	1.9

Fort Worth's "Thunder Road"

By Ann Arnold, author of Gamblers and Gangsters: Fort Worth's Jacksboro Highway in the 1940s and 1950s

In the 1940s and 1950s, Jacksboro Highway was the main artery to and from dry (we're not talking about lack of rainfall) west Texas. Cowboys and roughnecks came in for a bit of carousing and gambling, then returned, usually broke, to the ranch or oil rig. Slot machines were as common as pay telephones.

Ranchers and oil operators traveled the same highway, only in Cadillacs or Lincolns. They gambled at the 3939 Club or the 2222 Club. The 3939 Club was the prototype for many of the casinos later built in Las Vegas. Pat Kirkwood, who grew up at 2222 Jacksboro Highway, said that as much as $200,000 might change hands in a single night at his father's club.

Ballrooms such as the Casino, Skyliner, and Rocket Club were neighbors to honky tonks, liquor stores, and "no-tell motels." In the swanky ballrooms, nationally touring big bands such as Tommy Dorsey and Benny Goodman played for the elite of Fort Worth. Dancers swayed to the crooning of Frank Sinatra and the trumpet playing of Harry James. In one of the not-so-swanky places, Willie Nelson fronted a band that was protected by chicken wire from flying beer bottles.

With so much action, and so much money floating around, it was a natural for the gangsters to be right at home in the middle of it. Several

Dressing in Dallas and Fort Worth

Clothing styles in Dallas and Fort Worth are as varied as in any other major city. Casual dress is acceptable almost anywhere except the zillion-star restaurants, country clubs, and formal performing arts events. Don't be surprised to see men in business suits wearing cowboy boots and Stetsons. For the most part, Dallas "dresses up" more than Fort Worth.

Dress for comfort and the weather. Although heat is a major factor for much of the year, air conditioning is a way of life, so it's comfortable to chilly inside. In the winter months of January and February, a jacket comes gangsters worked at the clubs, whereas others worked the crowds. After the Skyliner lost its luster, it offered gambling as well as exotic dancers. Gangster Tincy Eggleston was indicted, but not convicted, for running a game there.

The 1950 death of gambler Nelson Harris, who reputedly worked at the 2222 Club, blew the lid off the vice and corruption that some lawmen condoned and/or profited from. After the investigation of Harris' death, the police chief was demoted, the sheriff was indicted for income tax evasion, and the district attorney was thrown out of office.

The gangsters killed each other over turf wars or fights over women. Farther out Jacksboro Highway, near Lake Worth, so many bodies were found in shallow graves that the site seemed to rival some of the local cemeteries. By the end of the 1950s, the gangsters were dead and the gamblers were in Las Vegas. So long, Thunder Road.

Arlington was not without its gamblers, too. The Top of the Hill Club on Division Street was the hot spot. It had an escape tunnel so patrons could evade Texas Ranger raids. During one such raid, a well-known Fort Worth man, who happened to have a cast on his broken leg, got stuck in the tunnel. Everyone ahead of him got away, but those behind him got arrested. Morale of thea story: stay in front of guys with broken legs. Similar to clubs in Fort Worth, the Top of the Hill Club went out of business in the 1950s and is now a Bible College.

in handy, but you won't have many opportunities to wear fur coats and wool clothing; the best way to dress in winter is by layering so you can add and subtract layers of clothing as needed.

When to Visit

The Metroplex is a marvelous place to visit at any time of the year. Summer bustles with tourists and festivities and is a good time to visit some of the amusement parks and outdoor activities that close or have limited schedules in the winter months. Shopping, museums, attractions, sports, and entertainment are available year round. Usually, Indian summer leads into an autumn that lasts only a few weeks (or days, if you believe the locals), then into a mild winter. Spring is undoubtedly the most pleasant and colorful season, when fields of spectacular Bluebonnets, Indian Paintbrush, and other wildflowers blanket the roadsides.

Calendar of Events

JANUARY
Southwestern Bell Cotton Bowl Classic at the Cotton Bowl Stadium in Dallas; Dallas Video Festival at the Dallas Museum of Art; Dallas Winter Boat Show (late January or early February) at the Dallas Market Hall; Southwestern Exposition and Livestock Show and Rodeo (mid-January through early February) at Will Rogers Memorial Complex in Fort Worth

FEBRUARY
Tri Delta Charity Antiques Show at the Dallas Convention Center

MARCH
Dallas Blooms at the Dallas Arboretum; Dallas New Car Auto Show at the Dallas Convention Center; Home and Garden Show at Dallas Market Hall; North Texas Irish Festival at Fair Park in Dallas; Texas Indian Market at the Arlington Convention Center

APRIL
USA Film Festival at AMC Glen Lake Theater in Dallas; Texas Heritage Day at Old City Park in Dallas; Texas New Vintage Wine and Food Festival at

Main Street Arts Festival tantalizes all the senses with art, music, and food

Ft Worth CVB

Tarrant County's Top Ten Employers
By Fort Worth Chamber of Commerce
(First quarter, 2000)

1. AMR Corporation (American Airlines), Fortune 500 headquarters
2. Lockheed Martin Tactical Aircraft Systems
3. Fort Worth Independent School District
4. Bell Helicopter-Textron
5. Arlington Independent School District
6. Teleservice Resources
7. United States Postal Service
8. City of Fort Worth
9. Delta Airlines
10. Sabre

the Grapevine Convention Center; Prairie Dog Chili Cookoff and World Championship of Pickled Quail Egg Eating at Traders Village in Grand Prairie; Main Street Arts Festival on Main Street in Fort Worth

MAY
Artfest at Fair Park in Dallas; Main Street Days and The Grapevine Heritage Festival in the Main Street Historic District in Grapevine; GTE Byron Nelson Golf Classic at Four Seasons Resort and Club in Irving; Canalfest (May or June) on Mandalay Canal in Irving; Mayfest at Trinity Park in Fort Worth; Mastercard Colonial Golf Tournament at Colonial Country Club in Fort Worth

JUNE
Texas Scottish Festival and Highland Games at the University of Texas at Arlington; Riverfest at River Legacy Park in Arlington; Antique Auto Swap Meet at Traders Village in Grand Prairie; Chisholm Trail Round-Up in the Stockyards National Historic District in Fort Worth; Shakespeare in the Park (June to July) at the Trinity Park Playhouse in Fort Worth; Juneteenth Heritage and Jazz Festival at various locations around the Metroplex

JULY
Fourth of July Celebrations throughout the Metroplex; Ringling Brothers, Barnum & Bailey Circus at Reunion Arena in Dallas; Taste of Dallas in the West End in Dallas; Mesquite Balloon Festival at Paschall Park in Mesquite

AUGUST
Pioneer Days in the Stockyards National Historic District in Fort Worth

SEPTEMBER
Montage in the Dallas Arts District; Grapefest in the Main Street Historic District in Grapevine; Plano Hot Air Balloon Festival in Bob Woodruff Park in Plano; Texas Heritage Crafts Festival at Six Flags Over Texas in Arlington; National Championship Indian Pow-Wow in the Traders Village in Grand Prairie; State Fair of Texas (late September to mid-October) at Fair Park in Dallas

OCTOBER
Texas-Oklahoma University football game at Cotton Bowl Stadium in Dallas; FrightFest at Six Flags Over Texas in Arlington; Oktoberfest at the Tarrant County Convention Center in Fort Worth; Fort Worth International Air Show at Alliance Airport in Fort Worth; Red Steagall Cowboy Gathering & Western Swing Festival in the Stockyards National Historic District in Fort Worth

NOVEMBER
American Indian Arts Festival and Market in Downtown Dallas; Dallas Video Festival at the Dallas Museum of Art; Christmas at the Arboretum (through end of December) at the Dallas Arboretum

DECEMBER
Candlelight Tour at Old City Park in Old City Park in Dallas; Holiday in the Park at Six Flags Over Texas in Arlington

Business and Economy

The entire Metroplex is a bustling center of business activity with 140,000 businesses and 5,000 corporate headquarters. Some of the major companies that make their homes here include aircraft/aerospace giants Lockheed Martin, Bell Helicopter-Textron, and American Airlines; retailers Pier 1 Imports, Tandy Corporation, and J.C. Penney; high-tech firms Intel, Motorola,

TRIVIA

Juneteenth is specifically June 19th, observed every year by Texas blacks to commemorate the date in 1865 when a major general of the Union Army landed in Galveston and first informed Texas slaves that they were, at last, free. The holiday's real name is Emancipation Day, although everyone in Texas, regardless of ethnicity, calls it Juneteenth. The celebration is a legal holiday only in Texas.

The sound is country and western at the White Elephant Saloon

and Texas Instruments, inventor of the microcomputer chip. Dallas has been rated one of the country's "Best Cities for Business" by *Forbes* magazine, and a 1998 Dun & Bradstreet study ranked the Fort Worth/Arlington area 15th in the nation for small businesses.

The Metroplex, with its attractive tax and financial incentive programs, is the leading business and financial center of the Southwest. Dubbed the "Silicon Prairie," the area is among the largest high-tech employment centers in the United States and accounts for 47 percent of technology revenue in Texas. The Alliance Development in North Fort Worth contains one of the nation's largest foreign trade zones, inhabited by such international firms as Mitsubishi Motor Corporation and Nokia Mobile Phones. Fort Worth is also home to the only U.S. coinage mint outside Washington, D.C.

The sales tax rate is a combination of the state rate (6.25 percent) and the local rate (maximum of 2.0 percent). Texas does not collect business or personal income tax.

Cost of Living

The cost of living in the Metroplex is moderate, considerably lower than most major cities on the east and west coasts. Based on a national average of 100, the cost of living index is 100.4 for Dallas and 92.9 for Fort Worth, according to the American Chamber of Commerce Researchers Association (ACCRA), first quarter 1999.

Typical Prices
    Five-mile taxi ride: $7.50
    Hotel double room: $101

Dinner for two:	$30
Movie admission:	$7
Daily newspaper:	50¢

Housing

Dallas/Fort Worth is one of the most affordable metropolitan areas in the country to buy or rent a home, ranking eighth out of 75 U.S. housing markets, according to the E&Y Kenneth Leventhal Real Estate Group.

According to real estate statistics, the median sale price of a home is $116,000 in Dallas and $112,000 in Fort Worth. Average monthly rent for a two-bedroom apartment is $638 in Dallas and $662 in Fort Worth. Real estate taxes are assessed locally by cities, counties, and school districts. Usually, the combined tax rate ranges from $2.75 to $3.25 per $100 of assessed value.

Schools

Both Dallas and Fort Worth schools offer programs for the talented and gifted. Fort Worth Independent School District (ISD) is a model district, recognized by numerous government entities for excellence in a variety of educational programs. Commitment to education is a citywide venture because corporations donate millions of dollars and equipment to local schools, and many companies are actively involved in programs such as Adopt-A-School and The Vital Link.

Institutes of higher education include Dallas Baptist University, Southern Methodist University, Southwestern Baptist Theological Seminary, Tarrant County College (five campuses), Texas A&M University at Dallas, Texas Christian University, Texas College of Osteopathic Medicine, Texas Wesleyan University, Texas Woman's University, University of Texas at Arlington, University of Texas at Dallas, and many community and specialty colleges.

Chad Ehlers

2

GETTING AROUND DALLAS AND FORT WORTH

The hardest thing for first-time visitors to comprehend is the sprawling vastness of the Metroplex. Statistics (depending on what they include in the term "Metroplex") indicate that the Dallas/Fort Worth metropolitan areas and the numerous adjacent, connecting, and intertwined suburbs and small cities cover an area of more than ten thousand square miles. Dallas measures 378 square miles, and Fort Worth is about 300.

The area is flat and is situated about 500 feet above sea level. Unfortunately, no mountains or seashores are available to serve as navigational aids. So, before you read the "City Layout" and "Driving in the Cities" sections that follow, get a map of the area and follow along.

The Metroplex is easy to reach. The region is home base for American Airlines and Southwest Airlines, top-notch carriers that fly in and out of DFW International Airport and Love Field, respectively. Many other domestic and international airlines serve DFW International Airport, which is one of the busiest and most efficient airports in the world. Amtrak and Greyhound also provide scheduled service into the cities, and four interstate highways and numerous U.S. and state highways provide easy routes for motorists.

Once in the area, you can zip around the cities by way of rental cars, taxis, buses, and in Dallas by light rail commuter trains. In Downtown Dallas, you can see the sights from an historic trolley or a nostalgic horse-drawn carriage. If you'll be staying entirely in the downtown areas of Dallas or Fort Worth, check on shuttle service from the airport; a few downtown hotels furnish complimentary shuttles. Both cities have public transportation in the downtown districts.

TIP

> Sightseeing tours are offered by Gray Line of Dallas and Fort Worth, 972/263-0294; and Longhorn Tours, 972/228-4571.

Dallas and Fort Worth Layout

Basically, Interstate 30 runs east-west through the center of the Metroplex, and Interstate 20 runs east-west along the southern edge. Interstate 35E goes north-south through Dallas (where it is called Stemmons Freeway north of Downtown and R. L. Thornton Freeway south of Downtown), and Interstate 35W goes north-south through Fort Worth. Interstate 35 splits into 35East and 35West at Denton to the north and reconnects at Hillsboro to the south. Interstate 45 comes into Dallas from the southeast (Houston). Dallas North Tollway runs north from Stemmons Freeway (I-35E) just north of Downtown to about four miles beyond LBJ Freeway (I-635).

Now it gets more complicated. Dallas has an "inner loop," Loop 12 (which changes names as it circles the city), and about half of an "outer loop," I-635 (LBJ Freeway), which starts north of DFW Airport and continues around the northern and eastern parts of the city until it joins I-20 on the south side. Dallas has an extensive freeway system (see sidebar, Dallas Freeways).

Fort Worth has a less complicated method of naming its freeways; there's the "east-west" freeway, the "north-south" freeway, and the "loop." The loop around Fort Worth is I-820 (Loop 820). The Airport Freeway (parts of State Highways 121 and 183) runs northeast through some of the mid-cities to DFW Airport.

Areas of the cities have some semblance of reasonable numbering systems, but just as you figure them out, you'll be in another city and everything changes. It would take far too much time to understand all the details; for example, Fort Worth has numbered streets that run east and west and numbered avenues that run north and south. Luckily, lots of maps are available, and lots of friendly Texans will gladly give you directions.

Public Transportation

Dallas Area Rapid Transit (DART) buses serve a dozen suburban cities, and DART's light rail system provides quick and efficient service to popular destinations primarily on a north-south route. Future plans include Railtran, a commuter rail system connecting Dallas and Fort Worth and DFW Airport. The McKinney Avenue Trolley (more a sightseeing/tourist attraction than a transportation system) connects the Downtown Arts District

The Neighborhoods of Dallas

- **Downtown:** *The heartbeat of the business center contains fine hotels, shops, restaurants, historical buildings and museums, and cultural facilities in the Arts District, an area at the north end of Downtown anchored by the Dallas Museum of Art and the Morton H. Meyerson Symphony Center.*

- **West End:** *This multi-block area has been transformed from a warehouse district to a lively, popular entertainment area with more than one hundred shops, eateries, and nightclubs plus street entertainers, vintage street lights, and an outdoor ice skating rink.*

- **Deep Ellum:** *Around the "deep end of Elm" street east of Downtown, this was the center of African-American life and culture at the turn of the century, home to some great blues and jazz artists and speakeasies. Today, it's an avant-garde collection of alternative clubs, galleries, shops, and restaurants.*

- **McKinney Avenue/Uptown:** *Leading north from Downtown, McKinney Avenue, with its old red-brick streets, is lined with antique shops and fine restaurants, many in renovated historic homes. The McKinney Avenue Trolley, an authentic restored trolley, connects much of the area to Downtown.*

- **Greenville Avenue:** *Lower Greenville Avenue (south of Mockingbird) is one of the city's oldest entertainment areas, popular with Southern Methodist University (SMU) students and soon-to-be-yuppies crowding the lively bars and clubs. Upper Greenville Avenue (north of Mockingbird) is more commercial, featuring newer, more trendy establishments, ranging from casual to elegant.*

- **North Dallas:** *Straddling LBJ Freeway (I-635) between North Central Expressway (Highway 75) and the North Dallas Tollway, North Dallas is an area of huge homes, huge shopping centers, and bustling streets offering some of the most fashionable and trendy stores, boutiques, restaurants, and theaters.*

DART

DALLAS AREA RAPID TRANSIT

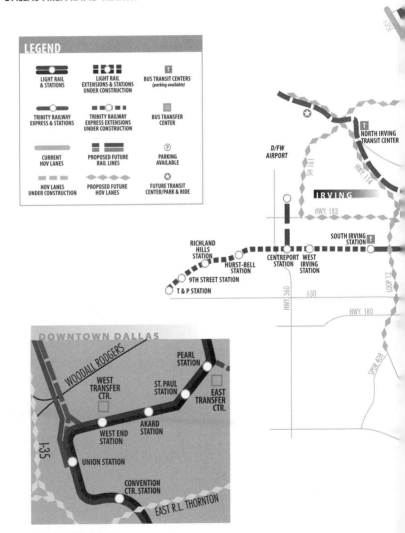

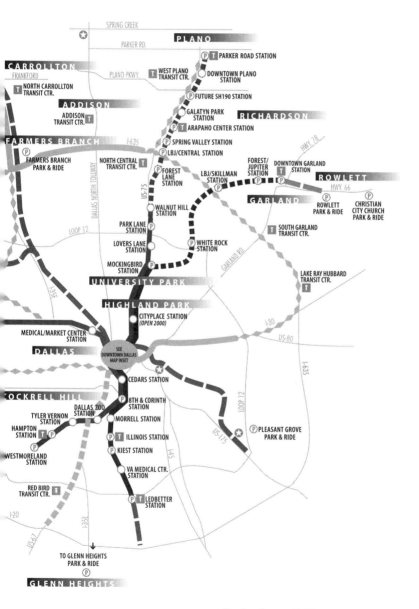

SPRING CREEK

PARKER RD.

PLANO

CARROLLTON

FRANKFORD

PLANO PKWY.

Ⓟ Ⓣ PARKER ROAD STATION

Ⓣ WEST PLANO TRANSIT CTR.

Ⓞ DOWNTOWN PLANO STATION

Ⓣ NORTH CARROLLTON TRANSIT CTR.

Ⓟ FUTURE SH190 STATION

ADDISON

ADDISON TRANSIT CTR. Ⓣ

Ⓞ GALATYN PARK STATION

Ⓟ Ⓣ ARAPAHO CENTER STATION

RICHARDSON

FARMERS BRANCH

I-635

Ⓟ FARMERS BRANCH PARK & RIDE

NORTH CENTRAL TRANSIT CTR.

Ⓞ SPRING VALLEY STATION

Ⓟ LBJ/CENTRAL STATION

HWY. 78

Ⓟ FOREST LANE STATION

FOREST/ JUPITER STATION

DOWNTOWN GARLAND STATION

LBJ/SKILLMAN STATION

Ⓣ

Ⓣ

ROWLETT

HWY. 66

Ⓟ WALNUT HILL STATION

GARLAND

Ⓟ ROWLETT PARK & RIDE

Ⓟ CHRISTIAN CITY CHURCH PARK & RIDE

DALLAS NORTH TOLLWAY

US-75

PARK LANE STATION

LOOP 12

LOVERS LANE STATION

Ⓟ WHITE ROCK STATION

Ⓟ SOUTH GARLAND TRANSIT CTR.

MOCKINGBIRD STATION

GARLAND RD.

LAKE RAY HUBBARD TRANSIT CTR. Ⓣ

UNIVERSITY PARK

HIGHLAND PARK

Ⓞ CITYPLACE STATION *(OPEN 2000)*

I-30

US-80

MEDICAL/MARKET CENTER STATION

SEE DOWNTOWN DALLAS MAP INSET

I-35E

DALLAS

Ⓟ CEDARS STATION

LOOP 12

I-635

ROCKRELL HILL

TYLER VERNON STATION

DALLAS ZOO STATION

Ⓟ 8TH & CORINTH STATION

HAMPTON STATION Ⓣ Ⓟ

Ⓞ MORRELL STATION

US-175

Ⓟ PLEASANT GROVE PARK & RIDE

WESTMORELAND STATION Ⓟ

Ⓟ Ⓣ ILLINOIS STATION

Ⓟ KIEST STATION

RED BIRD TRANSIT CTR. Ⓣ

VA MEDICAL CTR. STATION

I-45

I-35E

I-20

Ⓟ Ⓣ LEDBETTER STATION

US-67

↓
TO GLENN HEIGHTS PARK & RIDE Ⓟ

GLENN HEIGHTS

Map Compliments of DART, Dallas Area Rapid Transit

with the shops, galleries, and restaurants of the bustling "Uptown" McKinney Avenue area.

In Fort Worth, The "T" provides regular bus service throughout the city and operates free buses around Downtown. The "T" also operates the "Airporter" bus service to DFW Airport.

DART buses (214/979-1111, www.dart.org) run more than 130 routes throughout the city and serve 12 suburbs (Addison, Carrollton, Cockrell Hill, Farmers Branch, Garland, Glenn Heights, Highland Park, Irving, Richardson, Rowlett, Plano, and University Park). The entire system is fast, comfortable, and economical. Pick up a schedule at the DART Store at Akard Rail Station (or other government centers or libraries) and familiarize yourself with the color-coded routes. Similar to any other large city, public buses can be unsafe at night, so take precautionary safety measures.

Eliminate the hassle of driving and the expense of parking by using DART's Trolley-Bus circulator service, which provides inexpensive visitor-oriented trolley buses that continually circulate in Downtown and connect with the DART light rail stations. Trolleys look like turn-of-the-century streetcars for a bit of nostalgia. Available Monday through Friday only, rides are 50¢ and correct change is required.

The speedy, inexpensive DART light rail system (214/979-1111, www.dart.org) has stations every few blocks in Downtown Dallas, including the Convention Center and the West End, and is rapidly expanding to points north and south. A new addition to the public transportation scene, it operates clean, air-conditioned electric train cars for commuters and visitors alike. The neighborhood stations also display cultural artwork of the area. Route maps and ticketing instructions are posted; tickets are available from vending machine at all the stations, although the instructions are a bit confusing. Generally, fares are $1 each way ($3 all-day tickets available), and

The DART light rail system offers an alternative to driving with its electric trains

Dallas CVB

- *Allied Taxi*-Dallas 214/654-4444; Ft Worth: 817/318-0999
- *Checker Cab*-Dallas 214/426-6262; Ft Worth: 817/332-1919
- *City Cab*-Dallas 214/902-7020
- *Cowboy Cab*-Dallas: 214/428-0202
- *Republic Taxi*-Dallas: 214/902-7077
- *WestEnd Cab*-Dallas: 214/902-7000
- *Yellow Cab*-Dallas: 214/426-6262; Ft Worth: 817/534-5555

correct change is required. In the downtown area, between the Convention Center and the Pearl stations, passengers can ride for up to 90 minutes for 50¢. Plans through 2005 include extending the light rail system to Fort Worth, DFW Airport, Richardson, Garland, and Plano.

The McKinney Avenue Trolley (3153 Oak Grove, Dallas, 214/855-0006) is operated and managed by volunteers dedicated to the history and preservation of electric railways. More of a nostalgic and fun ride than a means of transportation, the trolley consists of restored streetcars dating to 1906. It runs daily along McKinney Avenue past assorted restaurants, fine antique shops, retail stores, several museums and theaters in the Arts District, the Morton Meyerson Symphony Center, and the shops and galleries of the Crescent Center. The fare is $1.50 roundtrip or $3 for a one-day unlimited ticket, correct change is required.

You can also visit and tour the Car Barn, watch the ongoing restoration of the cars, and learn about streetcars of the past that are now a part of the present. Located in the Car Barn, the gift shop sells T-shirts, postcards, caps, pins, and other souvenirs.

The Fort Worth Transportation Authority, The "T" (817/215-8600), offers regular city bus service, express bus service (from designated free park-

TIP

When you go from one suburban city to another, the color or city logo on the street signs often change.

Dallas Freeways

- **LBJ Freeway:** *I-635 beginning at the north entrance to DFW Airport, circling Dallas around the north, east, and part of the south side where it joins I-20*
- **Loop 12:** *An "inner" loop around Dallas consisting of Northwest Highway on the north, Walton Walker Boulevard on the west, Ledbetter Drive on the south, and Buckner Boulevard on the east*
- **North Central Expressway:** *US-75 from Downtown north*
- **Stemmons Freeway:** *I-35E from Downtown north*
- **Marvin D. Love Freeway:** *US-67 southwest of Downtown*
- **R.L. Thorton Freeway:** *I-35E south of Downtown continuing as I-30 east of town*
- **Airport Freeway:** *Highway 183 from Texas Stadium to the south entrance of DFW Airport and on through the Mid-Cities where it joins Highway 121 into Downtown Fort Worth*
- **John Carpenter Freeway:** *Highways 114 and 183 from I-35E to the north entrance of DFW Airport*
- **Julius Schepps Freeway:** *I-45 south of Downtown*
- **Woodall Rodgers Freeway:** *Spur 366, a short freeway on the north side of Downtown connecting I-35E, I-45, and US 75 (Central Expressway)*
- **Dallas North Tollway:** *from Stemmons Freeway (I-35E) just north of Downtown to about four miles beyond LBJ Freeway (I-635)*

and-ride lots to Downtown Fort Worth, Downtown Dallas, and the Alliance corridor), and rider request service, a personalized service within the route. More than one hundred buses are equipped with front-end bike racks, but if they are full, cyclists may bring their bikes aboard any of the T's buses. The T's Downtown Free Zone allows free travel within the district bounded by Henderson, Jones, Belknap, and Lancaster streets.

The T's Airporter Bus Service (817/215-8987) operates from major downtown hotels and the Airporter park-and-ride lot (1000 E. Weatherford St.) to DFW Airport. The T is $8 one way, and $4 for seniors or the disabled. For schedules or more information, call 817/334-0092.

The Longhorn Trolley (817-215-8600) uses old-fashioned-looking trolley cars to transport tourists (and locals) around the Stockyards Historic District, Downtown Fort Worth including Sundance Square and the Cultural District, and the zoo. They run every 20 minutes and cost $2 one way. A Day Pass is a great value at $5 because it includes unlimited trolley as well as regular bus rides.

Tandy Subway, (817/336-5248) the only privately owned subway in the world, runs between a free 14-acre parking lot along the banks of the Trinity River, northwest of the central business district, and Fort Worth Outlet Square in Downtown's Tandy Center (see Chapter 5, Sights and Attractions).

Driving in Dallas and Fort Worth

Unless you plan to stay exclusively Downtown, you will feel lost without a car. Taxis can be expensive; for example, from Downtown Dallas or Fort Worth to DFW Airport will cost $28 to $34. Yes, public transportation is available, but the city is so spread out that your explorations will be quite limited. Mass public transportation is a relatively new concept in these parts, or maybe it's just the Texans' independent spirit, but for whatever reason, most locals drive a car (or pickup). It's really the only practical way to get around.

First, the facts. Drivers and front seat passengers must wear seatbelts, and child passenger safety seats are required for children under two. Texas has a mandatory liability insurance law, and you may have to show proof of insurance if you're stopped. Making a right turn on red after a stop is legal. Consuming alcohol while driving is not. The speed limit on most freeways is 55 miles per hour unless posted differently. Traffic exiting from a freeway has the right of way on access roads.

A good city map is indispensable. The area is fairly easy to navigate if you study the maps and pick your route before you get in traffic; however, it's still possible that you'll have to take an alternate route because of the ever-present road construction throughout the Metroplex.

One of the main confusion factors is the tendency for roads to have two names or a name and a number; for example, I-635 is LBJ Freeway, and Highway 183 through the Mid-Cities is Airport Freeway. Most locals tend to call these roads by their name, whereas maps identify highway numbers.

Avoid driving (if possible) during morning and evening rush hours from 7 to 9 a.m. and from 4 to 7 p.m., respectively.

Nobody tells you to take Highway 75 because it's considered North Central Expressway. Take heart, though, this system can be confusing to locals as well.

Biking in Dallas and Fort Worth

Biking around the Metroplex is not really a practical means of transportation. But you'll see lots of folks peddling around their neighborhoods or parks for recreation and exercise. Extensive biking trails are available in some areas (see Chapter 10, Sports and Recreation). The sport is becoming more popular every day, but few people commute to work this way.

Air Travel

Chances are you'll be arriving in the area through the Dallas/Fort Worth International Airport (DFW), located halfway between Dallas and Fort Worth. It's about 18 miles and a 30-minute drive to or from either downtown areas. One of the world's busiest airports, DFW serves more than 25 commercial carriers with more than 2,300 flights daily to more than 200 destinations around the world. Covering almost 28 square miles of north Texas prairie, the airport is larger than the island of Manhattan.

In 1999, the airport began a multi-billion-dollar expansion intended to nearly double its capacity. Roads are being rerouted, and the terminals are undergoing major overhauls. New terminals, concourses, and runways are being built, as are new skywalks and people movers. The

Restored street cars are a bit of nostalgia along Dallas's bustling McKinney Avenue

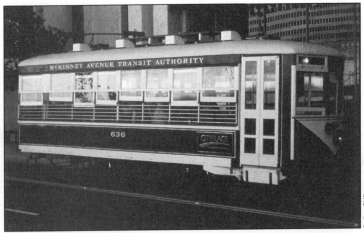

Dallas CVB

construction is being done methodically, so detours and congestion are minimal.

Terminals are designed for passenger convenience. The lower level of each terminal is for dropping off passengers and curbside baggage. The upper level is for picking up arriving passengers. Baggage claim areas are located on the arrival level. The convenient, user-friendly facilities are designed with multilingual signage and efficient customs clearance in three terminals. Food and retail concessions line the terminal buildings. Taxis, shuttle vans, and rental cars are available; some hotels near the airport have courtesy transportation. Most rental car agencies will provide a courtesy van to take you to their off-airport location. The reason for this system is that an extra 8 percent surcharge is levied to pick up rental cars at the airport.

All the terminals and facilities are located along International Parkway, the major north-south thoroughfare (toll road) through the airport. All roads off the parkway to the terminals exit to the left. You can enter the airport from the south from Highways 183 or 360. The north entrance comes in from Highways 114/121, or I-635 (LBJ Freeway).

The four classes of airport parking, in descending financial order, are terminal parking (in a covered parking garage directly in front of each terminal; $12 per day), infield parking (open parking behind the terminal garages; $9 per day), reduced-rate parking (farther removed from the terminals; $7 per day), and shuttle parking (parking off-site with shuttle bus service to the terminals; $5 per day). From the remote lots, you can ride a bus or tram to the terminal buildings.

DFW International Airport

For airport information, contact the following:
www.dfwairport.com
Visitor Information, 972/574-3694
Multi-Lingual Airport Information, 972/574-4420
Recorded Information, 972/574-8888
Airport Assistance Center, 972/574-4420
Ground Transportation, 972/574-5878

Las Colinas

Las Colinas is a commercial and residential community loosely bordered by Interstate 35E, LBJ Freeway (I-635), Highway 183, and Belt Line Road within the city of Irving. In the late 1960s, the owners of a six-thousand-acre ranch saw the westward expansion of Dallas and decided to develop their land as a residential area. Shortly thereafter, they heard the plans for DFW International Airport revealed and changed their strategy to develop a planned commercial and residential community. Housing developments, office parks, a 125-acre lake, recreational facilities, and a public transportation system were designed. A country club and shopping center were already in the area, and land nearby had been donated for the University of Dallas and a park. People and businesses came. Now Las Colinas has more than one thousand companies in its business community (including 50 Fortune 500 companies), a population of about 25,000, myriad stores and restaurants, more than a dozen hotels, and three country clubs.

Major Airlines Serving DFW Airport

Aeromexico, 800/237-6639
Air Canada, 800/776-3000
American, 800/433-7300
American Eagle, 800/433-7300
AmericaWest, 800/235-9292
Atlantic Southeast, 800/282-3424
British Airways, 800/247-9297
Continental, 800/525-0280
Delta, 800/221-1212
Japan Airlines, 800/525-3663
Korean Air, 800/438-5000
Lufthansa, 800/645-3880
Northwest, 800/225-2525
TWA, 800/221-2000
United, 800/241-6522
US Air, 800/428-4322

Love Field (8008 Cedar Springs, 214/670-6080) is about three miles northwest of Downtown Dallas. Owned and operated by the City of Dallas, the

TIP

Ask if your hotel has courtesy van service to and from DFW or Love Field.

airport serves more than 7 million passengers annually. Since DFW International Airport was built, Love Field has been home to Southwest Airlines (800/533-1222; Spanish 800/826-6667; www.iflyswa.com). Direct, nonstop service is limited to destinations within Texas and the states that border Texas because of the Wright Amendment. The Wright Amendment, enacted in 1979, prohibits commercial planes with more than 55 seats leaving Dallas Love Field from traveling nonstop beyond the states bordering Texas. Southwest Airlines offers nationwide service, but a change of plane is required. Recently, limited service from Love Field has been added by American (800/433-7300) and Continental Express (800/525-280) airlines.

Established in 1917 as a military training base, passenger service from Love Field began in 1927. Charles Lindbergh landed the Spirit of St. Louis at Love Field on September 27, 1927. Love Field is also home to the Frontiers of Flight Aviation Museum (see Chapter 6, Museums and Art Galleries).

The most economical way to get to either airport, or into town from the airport, is by DART airport bus from Dallas or the T airport bus from Fort Worth, but these services are sometimes inconvenient. A few shuttle services, such as SuperShuttle (800/BLUE-VAN) and Classic Shuttle (214/841-1900) are reasonably priced and have door-to-door pick-up service.

Many visitors arrive in the Metroplex through one of the busiest airports in the world

Ft Worth CVB

Greyhound Stations

Greyhound stations can be found at the following locations:

- ***205 S. Lamar St., Dallas**, 214/655-7082; 800/231-2222 (Spanish 800/531-5332)*
- ***901 Commerce St., Fort Worth**, 817/429-3089; 800/231-2222 (Spanish 800/531-5332)*
- ***2075 E. Division, Arlington,** 817/461-5337*
- ***1017 Elm, Carrollton,** 972/242-3133*
- ***969 E. Irving Blvd., Irving,** 972/254-8412*
- ***1331 E. Hwy. 80, Mesquite,** 972/288-1374*
- ***400 N. Greenville Ave., Richardson,** 972/231-1763*

Taxi service is probably the most expensive option. Some hotels near the airport have courtesy transportation, so be sure to ask.

Train Service

A 1914 vintage station that was once the hub of train transportation for the Southwest, Union Station (400 S. Houston St., Dallas, 214/653-1101, 800/USA-RAIL) is now home to Amtrak and a downtown DART light rail station. Amtrak service to San Antonio, Austin, and Fort Worth is provided every Wednesday, Friday, and Sunday. Going north, trains travels to Little Rock, St. Louis, and Chicago.

Located in the historic former Santa Fe Depot, Amtrak (1501 Jones, Fort Worth, 817/332-2931, 800/USA-RAIL) offers service to Dallas, Austin, and San Antonio every Wednesday, Friday, and Sunday. Northbound trains travel to Chicago, Little Rock, and St. Louis.

Ft Worth CVB

3

WHERE TO STAY

The choice of accommodations is nearly as vast as the Metroplex itself. Literally hundreds of hotels and motels crowd the area. From the opulence of a luxurious five-star mansion to rustic walls adorned with hanging hides and longhorns—the choice is yours.

Major chain hotels and motels have numerous locations and offer pretty standard quality and few surprises. Wherever premier hotels are located, the moderately priced chain establishments usually cluster nearby. The Metroplex has few artsy, quaint hostelries such as those found in San Francisco or Greenwich Village, but the flavor of the Old West is still found on Fort Worth's north side. Most campgrounds and RV parks are located on the outskirts of town or nearby lakes.

Most listed accommodations are concentrated by location for convenience: near the airport, in the Downtown areas, and near major tourist attractions, upscale shopping malls, and business districts. You'll notice there are no listings for the East Dallas zone. This area is mostly industrial and residential with few tourist accommodations.

For the most part, Downtown tends to be pricier but include some splendid historic hotels that have undergone dramatic restorations. If the heart of the city is your destination, then the price may be worth the convenience because parking can present a challenge. Both Dallas and Fort Worth have public transportation in their Downtown districts.

Some visitors are astonished at the distances in this area. Dallas/Fort Worth is not a compact city with boundaries; it sprawls for miles in every direction. Driving from the Southwest Fort Worth to Far North Dallas can take up to two hours, depending on traffic conditions. So choosing a hotel near your main interests should be a major consideration.

DOWNTOWN DALLAS

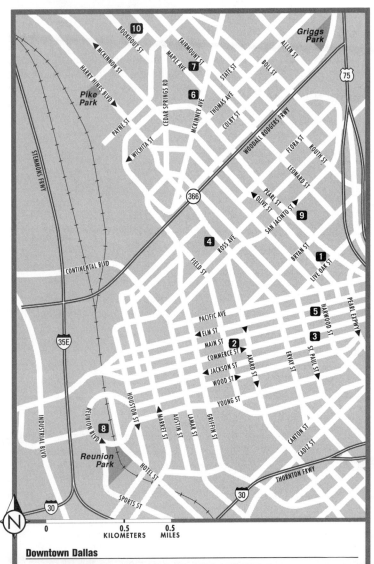

Downtown Dallas

1. Adam's Mark Hotel
2. Adolphus
3. Dallas Grand Hotel
4. Fairmont Hotel
5. Holiday Inn Aristocrat Hotel
6. Hotel Crescent Court
7. Hotel St. Germain
8. Hyatt Regency Dallas at Reunion
9. Le Meridien
10. Stoneleigh Hotel

DOWNTOWN DALLAS

Hotels

ADAM'S MARK HOTEL
400 North Olive Street
214/922-8000, 800/444-ADAM
www.adamsmark.com
$$-$$$

The largest hotel in Texas contains 1,844 rooms and suites, 23,000 square feet of meeting space, five ballrooms, five restaurants, and four lounges. After a recent extensive renovation and expansion, new additions include an indoor/outdoor swimming pool, a full-service health club, and meeting facilities for almost five thousand. The comfortable, luxurious guestrooms and amenities will please the most discerning traveler. The lobby, with its rich woodwork and fine furnishings, is dominated by an 18-foot bronze sculpture, "Slicker Shy," the largest project ever created by acclaimed artist Herb Mignery of Colorado. The 24-hour staff offers all the expected services. & (Downtown Dallas)

THE ADOLPHUS
1321 Commerce Street
214/742-8200, 800/221-9083
www.noblehousehotels.com/
adolphus
$$$$$

The grande dame of the grand hotels of yesteryear, The Adolphus was built in 1912 by beer baron Adolphus Busch and still retains its Old World opulence. Named one of the best hotels in the whole world on *Condé Nast Traveler* magazine's Reader's Choice Gold List, it also has earned AAA four-diamond and Mobil four-star ratings. Known the world over for its attentive staff, it remains the gathering place of the social elite. It retains the charming custom of serving afternoon tea (Wednesday to Saturday 3 to 5 p.m.) in the Grand Lobby, amid the Flemish tapestries, Louis XV clocks, and French antique furnishings. Furnished with Queen Anne and Chippendale, the guestrooms average 550 square feet and offer separate sitting and dining areas, down comforters, and marble baths. It has all the services you would expect, along with two restaurants, a Bistro bar, a lounge with entertainment, and meeting facilities. The award-winning French Room (see Chapter 4, Where to Eat) was recently named the "best restaurant in Dallas and Fort Worth" by *Gourmet* magazine. Valet parking is available. & (Downtown Dallas)

DALLAS GRAND HOTEL
1914 Commerce
214/747-7000
$$-$$$
www.dallasgrandhotel.com

Formerly the Statler Hilton, the Dallas Grand Hotel is conveniently located two blocks east of the original Neiman Marcus department store and two blocks north of the Majestic Theater. After its recent 7-million-dollar renovation, the 710 rooms and suites average 500 square feet, and several have two beds and two baths. Hotel conveniences include valet parking, abundant meeting space and a complete business center. The Plaza Café offers three meals a day and late night room service. Monday through Friday, Gatsby's Club lounge serves complimentary hors d'oeuvres during the cocktail hour. A fitness center is available for guests and the rooftop Jacuzzi, overlooking the Dallas skyline, is a popular place in the evenings. ♿ (Downtown Dallas)

THE FAIRMONT HOTEL
1717 North Akard Street
214/720-2020, 800/527-4727
www.fairmont.com
$$$$-$$$$$

Conveniently located in the Dallas Arts District, The Fairmont combines luxury and service with Texas hospitality. Deluxe, individually furnished guestrooms and suites include every amenity you can think of along with twice-daily maid service, goose down pillows, plush terrycloth robes, luxurious toiletries, and a telephone in the bathroom. Every service imaginable is available from a 24-hour concierge and multilingual staff to in-house shops, a pharmacy, a barber/beauty shop, and babysitting services. Complete business services are also available. The hotel has an Olympic-size outdoor pool, and the Metropolitan Fitness Center is located across the street. The Fairmont is connected to Downtown Dallas's underground pedestrian walkways. The award-winning Pyramid Restaurant is one of Dallas's finest. A not-to-miss experience is the Sunday Jazz Brunch. The Pyramid Lounge features a tremendous selection of wines and specialty beverages. ♿ (Downtown Dallas)

TRIVIA

The first hotel of the famous chain owned by entrepreneur Conrad Hilton was built in Dallas in 1925. Prior to that, he had managed his very first hotel in Cisco, Texas, a town so proud that it later renamed its main street Conrad Hilton Avenue.

HOLIDAY INN ARISTOCRAT HOTEL
1933 Main Street
214/741-7700, 800/231-4235
www.holiday-inn.com
$$$$

Built in 1925, this was the first hotel to bear the name of Conrad Hilton. Listed in the National Register of Historic Places, it has been meticulously restored to retain the wealth of architectural detail of yesteryear. The lobby is resplendent with rich wood paneling, crown molding, etched glass, and fine furnishings. Located in the central business district, it is connected to the tunnel system and skywalks that connect banks, shops, and office buildings of Downtown Dallas. You'll find the room amenities you'd expect, meeting rooms, the Aristocrat Bar & Grill, and the Club Room retreat. Valet garage parking is extra. Free airport transportation to Love Field is provided. ♿ (Downtown Dallas)

HOTEL CRESCENT COURT
400 Crescent Court
214/871-3200, reservations 800/654-6541
www.crescentcourt.com
$$$$$

On the edge of the central business district and the Arts District, the classy Hotel Crescent Court is the center of an upscale complex, including The Shops and Galleries of the Crescent and the Crescent Office Towers. A member of Preferred Hotels® and Resorts Worldwide, it's an intimate, classic European-style establishment with luxurious amenities and attentive service. Rooms are spacious and feature cable TV with on-command video, a desk, a fax machine, voice mail, individually controlled air conditioning, luxurious baths with marble and brass fixtures, a hair dryer, and Lady Primrose toiletries. The award-winning Beau Nash Restaurant offers international favorites and New American cuisine. The Crescent Club features live jazz on weekends. & (Downtown Dallas)

HOTEL ST. GERMAIN
2516 Maple Avenue
214/871-2516
$$$$$

This AAA four-diamond, four-star "boutique hotel" offers seven luxury suites, two parlors, and a New Orleans-style walled courtyard as a tranquil oasis for travelers to this busy city. The Old World ambience is a reflection of proprietor Claire Heymann's childhood in New Orleans. All suites are decorated with exquisite French antiques and feature elaborately canopied beds, fireplaces, and baths with Jacuzzis or soaking tubs and European toiletries. A sumptuous continental breakfast is included in the rate. Additionally, the conveniences of a 24-hour concierge, a butler, and room service are available. The excellent gourmet restaurant (by reservation only) serves French cuisine, a $75, fixed-price, seven-course dinner. Built in 1909, it was one of the first residences on fashionable Maple Avenue. Now its location couldn't

be more avant-garde—near the shops and restaurants of the Crescent Court, McKinney Avenue/Uptown, and the gallery district along Fairmount and Maple Avenues. & (Downtown Dallas)

HYATT REGENCY DALLAS AT REUNION
300 Reunion Boulevard
214/651-1234, reservations
800/233-1234
www.dallas.hyatt.com/dfwrd
$$$$-$$$$$

Adjoining the 50-story Reunion Tower, the Dallas landmark recognizable for miles in the Downtown skyline, this glittering hotel is located in the heart of the historic West End district. It's convenient to the business, cultural, and shopping districts of Downtown. A $65-million expansion, opened in early 2000, added enormous new meeting/ballroom facilities, additional guestrooms and parking, expanded lobby and public rooms, an upgraded phone system, and tons more. Upper floor rooms have excellent views of the city. The hotel has an outdoor heated pool, a sauna, a fitness center, lighted tennis courts, basketball courts, a jogging track, restaurants, a lounge, and meeting facilities. In the Reunion Tower, eat and revolve high above Dallas at one of the two restaurants (see Chapter 4, Where to Eat) or at the Top of the Dome lounge. Valet parking in the garage is extra. & (Downtown Dallas)

LE MERIDIEN
650 N. Pearl St.
214/979-9000, 800/225-5843
$$$$-$$$$$

Extensively remodeled in 1998, this hotel is in the Plaza of the Americas complex with two levels of offices, shops, restaurants, and an ice-skating rink around a 15-story atrium. Conveniently located two blocks from the Morton H. Meyerson Symphony Center in the arts district on the northern edge of the business district, it's close to all the Downtown attractions as well as a light rail station. The nearly 400 rooms and suites are large with fresh new appointments and elegant décor. All rooms overlook the atrium or the Dallas skyline. Amenities include tennis courts, a jogging track, an exercise room, a sauna, business services, free newspapers, and a multilingual staff. Meeting rooms can accommodate groups as large as 1,000. ♿ (Downtown Dallas)

STONELEIGH HOTEL
2927 Maple Avenue
214/871-7111, reservations
800/255-9299
$$$-$$$$$
When built in 1924, the Stoneleigh was the tallest hotel west of the Mississippi, with 11 floors. Quite a showplace of the time, it was the first hotel in Dallas to get air conditioning in 1945. Past guests include Bob Hope, Judy Garland, and Elvis Presley. Located in the prestigious area of Turtle Creek, it's still a posh, small hotel offering classic European-style hospitality and personal service. Furnishings in the rooms and suites are beautifully designed, yet with a feel for comfort. Rich woods, traditional stuffed sofas and chairs, and high ceilings create an ambience of luxury. Pampered guests find a special treat on fluffy pillows at day's end. Ewald's, Stoneleigh's landmark restaurant (see Chapter 4, Where to Eat), serves ex-quisite continental cuisine in an elegant setting. The Lion's Den lounge is reminiscent of an intimate English pub. ♿ (Downtown Dallas)

CENTRAL DALLAS

Hotels

DOUBLETREE HOTEL
AT LINCOLN CENTRE
5410 LBJ Freeway (I-635)
972/934-8400, reservations
800/222-TREE
www.dallaslc.doubletreehotels.com
$$$
This 20-story Doubletree Hotel is across LBJ Freeway from the Galleria shopping mall and just minutes from DFW airport and Texas Stadium. Located in Lincoln Centre, a 32-acre business complex on an artificial lake, the hotel has nonsmoking floors and floors designed for the handicapped. The recipient of AAA's prestigious four-diamond rating, it features all the expected amenities and services. The 502 guestrooms include 18 luxury executive suites with spacious work areas. There's an outdoor pool, a jogging track, a sauna, an exercise room, and a children's pool. Guest memberships in a nearby health club are available, as well as free transportation to the Galleria. On-site restaurants include Crockett's for fine dining, the Center Café for casual meals, Cricketers sports bar, and Basie's Lounge, a scotch and cigar bar. ♿ (Central Dallas)

EMBASSY SUITES-
MARKET CENTER
2727 Stemmons Freeway (I-35E)
214/630-5332, reservations
800/EMBASSY

www.embassy-suites.com
$$$
Embassy Suites has several Metroplex locations, all very similar and very nice. Spacious two-room suites consist of a living room with comfortable seating, a table and chairs, a remote-control cable TV, dual-line phones with voice mail, and a dataport. A kitchen area contains a coffeemaker, a microwave, a refrigerator, and a wet bar. The bedroom contains a king or two double beds, an additional TV, and a phone. A complimentary cooked-to-order breakfast, evening reception with beverages, and *USA Today* newspaper (weekdays) are nice amenities. This location has an indoor heated pool, a sauna, and an exercise room. Complimentary shuttle service is available to and from Love Field. & (Central Dallas)

HOLIDAY INN MARKET CENTER
1955 Market Center Boulevard
214/747-9551
$$$-$$$$
Located in the southern part of Market Center, this 245-room Holiday Inn was completely remodeled in 1994. It has the usual amenities for business travelers, cable TV and movies, an outdoor swimming pool, a restaurant, and free parking. & (Central Dallas)

THE MANSION ON TURTLE CREEK
2821 Turtle Creek Boulevard
214/559-2100, reservations
800/527-5432
www.mansiononturtlecreek.com
$$$$$
Visualize country charm and elegance a palatial mansion on a beautifully landscaped hilltop. Originally the home of a Texas cotton magnate, The Mansion on Turtle Creek

is the only hotel in Texas to earn the prestigious five-diamond AAA and five-star Mobil ratings. This property is the epitome of luxury, style, and service. Reflecting the intimate ambience of a private residence, the spacious, comfortable rooms have fresh flowers, plush carpets, fine furnishings, cable TV, modem links, large closets, marble baths, deluxe terry bathrobes, and customized toiletries. All the expected services and amenities, including foreign currency exchange and multilingual staff, are available. Former guests include Presidents Clinton, Bush, Carter, and Ford, as well as European royalty. There's a small outdoor pool, fitness studio, sauna, and steam bath. The award-winning dining room is in a five-star class of its own (see Chapter 4, Where To Eat). & (Central Dallas)

MELROSE HOTEL
3015 Oak Lawn Avenue
214/521-5151, 800/635-7673
$$$-$$$$$
Similar to most of the older hotels, the Melrose (circa 1924) has undergone extensive renovation and now receives impressive ratings for accommodations and service. Located in the Oak Lawn district, this Dallas Historical Landmark combines old-world comfort, elegant dining, and gracious service. The rooms in this European-style luxury hotel feature antique-style mahogany furnishings, rich crown moldings, and 10-foot ceilings, and contain every amenity imaginable. Several rooms (including the 1,500-square-foot Presidential Suite) have a wonderful panoramic view of Downtown. A concierge, multilingual staff, and bellmen attend to every need. The classic Landmark

GREATER DALLAS

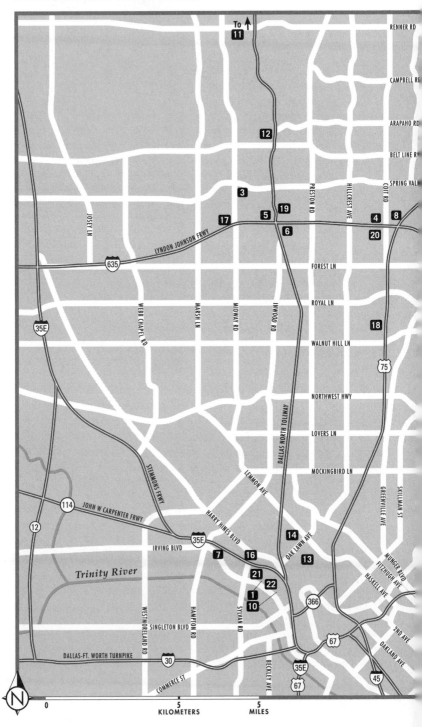

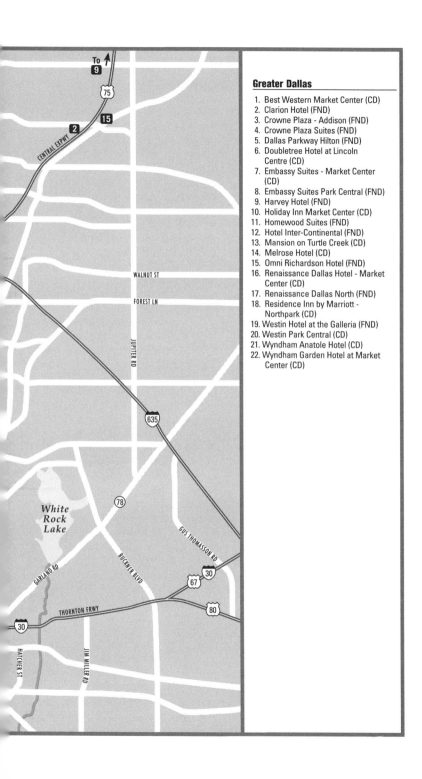

Greater Dallas

1. Best Western Market Center (CD)
2. Clarion Hotel (FND)
3. Crowne Plaza - Addison (FND)
4. Crowne Plaza Suites (FND)
5. Dallas Parkway Hilton (FND)
6. Doubletree Hotel at Lincoln Centre (CD)
7. Embassy Suites - Market Center (CD)
8. Embassy Suites Park Central (FND)
9. Harvey Hotel (FND)
10. Holiday Inn Market Center (CD)
11. Homewood Suites (FND)
12. Hotel Inter-Continental (FND)
13. Mansion on Turtle Creek (CD)
14. Melrose Hotel (CD)
15. Omni Richardson Hotel (FND)
16. Renaissance Dallas Hotel - Market Center (CD)
17. Renaissance Dallas North (FND)
18. Residence Inn by Marriott - Northpark (CD)
19. Westin Hotel at the Galleria (FND)
20. Westin Park Central (CD)
21. Wyndham Anatole Hotel (CD)
22. Wyndham Garden Hotel at Market Center (CD)

restaurant features cuisine and wines from around the world. The Library lounge resembles an English pub. ♿ (Central Dallas)

RENAISSANCE DALLAS HOTEL-MARKET CENTER
2222 Stemmons Freeway (I-35E)
214/631-2222, 800/892-2233 (in Texas), 800/468-3571 (outside Texas)
www.renaissancehotels.com
$$$-$$$$
It's hard to miss this elliptical, 30-story hotel made of pink granite towering above one of the largest wholesale markets in the world. Located in the heart of the district, it's within walking distance of Market Hall, the Apparel Mart, the Info-Mart, and the World Trade Center. With a four-diamond AAA rating, it offers two restaurants, a bar, and live entertainment. Two floors offer club accommodations with butler service. The rooftop health club has an outdoor heated pool, a whirlpool spa, a sauna, a steam room, and Nautilus equipment. If you don't stay here, visit the lobby to view what is billed as the "world's longest chandelier," with 7,500 Italian crystals winding four floors up the marble and brass staircase. ♿ (Central Dallas)

THE WESTIN PARK CENTRAL
12720 Merit Drive
972/851-2021
www.westin.com
$$$$
Combining four-diamond AAA luxury with convenient access to Downtown and North Dallas, this hotel has it all. The large guestrooms provide abundant upscale personal amenities as well as business necessities such as dual-line

phones with dataports and voice mail. Executive Club-level accommodations have exceptional features. The hotel offers every service imaginable, as well as extensive meeting and recreational facilities. The Landmark Club, a state-of-the-art fitness center, welcomes the public. Danielle Custer is the acclaimed, award-winning chef at Laurel's, the rooftop restaurant featuring fine dining and an exceptional view (see Chapter 4, Where to Eat). ♿ (Central Dallas)

WYNDHAM ANATOLE HOTEL
2201 Stemmons Freeway (I-35E)
214/748-1200, reservations 800/WYNDHAM
www.wyndham.com
$$$-$$$$$
Quite literally, the Anatole is a village within the city, spread over 45 acres in the heart of the Market District, just minutes from the Arts District and the West End. The complex of wings and towers has 1,620 rooms and suites, a seven-acre park with a pond, and an 82,000-square-foot fitness center. The Verandah Club has world-class health and fitness facilities, including indoor and outdoor pools, whirlpools, steam rooms, massage rooms, lighted tennis courts, a basketball gymnasium, a boxing gym, racquetball courts, and indoor and outdoor jogging tracks. Two stadium-sized atriums are filled with trees, flowers, and sculptures. Dining is an international experience with six restaurants offering everything from gourmet Tex-Mex to a breathtaking view of the city from the Nana Grill. Bars and lounges fit every taste-lobby bar, sports bar, dancing/rock-and-roll bar, Mexican cantina, and swim-up bar at the

pool. A museum-quality art collection is scattered throughout the hotel, including the world's-largest piece of Wedgewood china and one of the largest private jade collections in the country. ♿ (Central Dallas)

WYNDHAM GARDEN HOTEL AT MARKET CENTER
2015 Market Center Boulevard
214/741-7481, reservations
800/WYNDHAM
www.wyndham.com
$$
In the heart of the Market Center district, this Wyndam property is surrounded by a Holiday Inn and Best Western, and is convenient to both Downtown and North Dallas. The guestrooms are designed for business travelers with large, well-lighted work areas, dataports, in-room coffee, and free *USA Today* newspapers delivered to the rooms. Personal amenities include a hairdryer, an iron and ironing board, a shower massage, and cable TV with in-room movies. ♿ (Central Dallas)

Motels

BEST WESTERN MARKET CENTER
2023 Market Center Boulevard
214/741-9000, reservations
800/275-7419
www.bestwestern.com
$$
This Best Western is a moderately priced alternative to the more expensive hotels in the Market Center area, yet offers many of the same amenities and services. It features contemporary Southwestern décor and comfortable rooms with cable TV, coffeemakers, and dataports. A free continental breakfast is in-

cluded in the room rate. ♿ (Central Dallas)

RESIDENCE INN BY MARRIOTT-NORTHPARK
10333 North Central Expressway (U.S. 75)
214/750-8220, reservations
800/331-3131
www.marriott.com
$$$
Similar to the other Residence Inns, this one is attractive to both business and leisure travelers. Each apartment-like suite has a full kitchen, a remote-controlled cable TV, in-room movies, a work desk, and a dataport. Some rooms have a fireplace. A complimentary buffet breakfast has something for everyone, and complimentary weekday newspapers are available in the lobby. There's also an outdoor heated pool and sauna. ♿ (Central Dallas)

FAR NORTH DALLAS

Hotels

CLARION HOTEL
1981 North Central Expressway (U.S. 75)
Richardson
972/644-4000, 800/CLARION
www.choicehotels.com
$$$
All the guestrooms in this hotel have been recently remodeled and upgraded with amenities for the business traveler. A large work desk is stocked with office supplies, phones have dataports and speaker features, new remote-controlled TVs have sports and movie channels, and several of the rooms have a microwave and a refrigerator.

With 9.2 million square feet of showroom space in eight buildings sprawling over 175 acres, the Dallas Market Center is the world's largest wholesale merchandise mart.

A business center is also available. Complimentary services include morning coffee and muffins, weekday newspapers, shoeshines, and shuttle service to nearby businesses. A restaurant serves all three meals, and a lounge offers cocktails and hors d'oeuvres. An indoor/outdoor heated pool and a sauna are on site, and guests enjoy complimentary use of an adjacent fitness center. ♿ (Far North Dallas)

CROWNE PLAZA
14315 Midway Road
Addison
972/980-8877, reservations
800/2CROWNE
www.crowneplaza.com
$$$-$$$$
Conveniently located just off I-635 (LBJ Freeway) near the Galleria, this luxury hotel is near dozens of restaurants as well as shopping and entertainment. A recent $12-million renovation resulted in tastefully appointed guestrooms with work desks, dataports, two phones, coffeemakers, hair dryers, and irons and ironing boards. The comfortable lobby features a bar and two restaurants, American and Delta ticket counters, a gift shop, and a guest services desk. There's also a pool, a whirlpool, and a fitness center. Complimentary garage parking is provided, as is complimentary shuttle service to the Galleria. ♿ (Far North Dallas)

CROWNE PLAZA SUITES
7800 Alpha Road
Dallas
972/233-7600, reservations
800/2CROWNE
www.crowneplaza.com
$$$-$$$$
Located near the intersection of I-635 (LBJ Freeway) and U.S. 75 (North Central Expressway) between Downtown and the Richardson/Plano business corridor, this hotel offers easy access to several areas of Dallas and is a good choice for business travelers. Each of the tastefully furnished suites contains two 25-inch remote-controlled TVs, an executive work desk with phone and dataport, a coffeemaker, a microwave, a stocked refrigerator, a hairdryer, and an iron and ironing board. For after-work relaxation, enjoy the large indoor/outdoor heated pool, a hot tub, a fully equipped fitness room, and the Atrium bar located in the spacious atrium lobby. A café serves all meals and has a late-night menu. Nice meeting facilities are also available. ♿ (Far North Dallas)

DALLAS PARKWAY HILTON
4801 LBJ Freeway (I-635)
Dallas
972/661-3600, 800/356-3924
Just north of the LBJ Freeway and west of the North Dallas Tollway, this is a businessman's hotel with 310 oversized rooms, each with three telephones. It provides all the

expected amenities, including cable TV and movies, a free weekday newspaper, free parking, indoor and outdoor swimming pools, and Cottonwood's lobby restaurant. Its proximity to the Galleria Mall makes it a fine choice for mall visitors also, and complimentary shuttle service is available. & (Far North Dallas)

EMBASSY SUITES
13131 North Central Expressway at LBJ Freeway (I-635)
Dallas
972/234-3300, 800/EMBASSY
Similar to all Embassy Suites, this one offers luxury room suites with separate living areas and bedrooms. Suites also have cable TV and movies, and a wet bar with a refrigerator and a microwave. The hotel has an indoor swimming pool, racquetball courts, and a restaurant and lounge. & (Far North Dallas)

HARVEY HOTEL-PLANO
1600 North Central Expressway
Plano
972/578-8555
www.bristolhotels.com
$-$$$
Here you'll find comfortably furnished, spacious guestrooms with sitting areas, work desks with dataports, and a cable TV. The full-service hotel offers complimentary coffee and *USA Today* newspapers in the lobby. Recreational facilities include a pool, a spa, and a fitness room. The location is convenient to the businesses and attractions of the Plano/Richardson corridor. & (Far North Dallas)

HOTEL INTER-CONTINENTAL
15201 Dallas Parkway
Addison
972/386-6000, 800/327-0200
www.interconti.com
$$$$
Formerly the Grand Kempinski, this four-diamond AAA, European-style luxury hotel is a landmark in Addison. The oversized guestrooms are beautifully decorated and include sitting areas, desks, and dataports. On-premise conveniences include a travel agency, a car rental agency, a florist and gift shop, a hair salon, and other retail stores. Recreational facilities offer a full-service health club with state-of-the-art equipment, indoor and outdoor pools with spas, indoor racquetball courts, and lighted rooftop tennis courts. Choose from three restaurants offering excellent dining from casual to elegant, a lobby bar with live entertainment, and Kempi's, a high-energy nightclub (see Chapter 12, Nightlife). & (Far North Dallas)

OMNI RICHARDSON HOTEL
701 East Campbell Road
Richardson
972/231-9600, reservations
800/THE-OMNI
www.omnihotels.com
$$$
Luxury and convenience are combined in this classic hotel featuring spacious rooms, excellent meeting facilities and catering, a multilingual staff, and complete concierge services. The tastefully appointed rooms feature all expected amenities, and recreational facilities include a fitness center, a heated pool, a whirlpool, and a sauna. The Pheasant Room offers fine dining, the Prime Bird offers casual dining and a lovely Sunday brunch, and the Pheasant Room lounge has live jazz on weekends. The Chase Oaks Golf Club, under the same ownership, is

only a few minutes away and has 27 holes, a lighted driving range, putting greens, and a full pro shop and club facilities. ♿ (Far North Dallas)

RENAISSANCE DALLAS NORTH
4099 Valley View Lane
Dallas
972/385-9000, 800/808-1011
www.renaissancehotels.com
$$$-$$$$
Located in the North Dallas business corridor along the LBJ Freeway, this hotel is an excellent choice for discriminating business travelers. In addition to 25,000 square feet of meeting space and excellent facilities, it offers an American Airlines office, and 90 concierge-level rooms with first-rate services. Following your wake-up call, complimentary coffee and a *USA Today* newspaper is delivered to your room. At day's end, enjoy the outdoor pool and fitness center, or relax in the ten-story atrium lobby listening to the sounds of a waterfall and a garden fountain. Then visit the Palm Terrace lobby lounge, or the award-winning restaurant, Seasons, for a steak or fine regional cuisine. ♿ (Far North Dallas)

THE WESTIN HOTEL
AT THE GALLERIA
13340 Dallas Parkway
Dallas
972/934-9494, 800/228-3000
www.westin.com
$$$$$
This premier hotel is located within the upscale glass-domed Galleria shopping mall, offering more than 200 exclusive shops, two dozen restaurants, and entertainment options including an indoor ice-skating rink and multiscreen movie theater. Awarded a four-diamond

rating by AAA, this hotel offers every luxurious amenity and service you would expect and more. The Guest Office® rooms are designed especially for traveling executives. Two restaurants and two lounges provide a choice of casual or fine dining and beverages. ♿ (Far North Dallas)

Motels

HOMEWOOD SUITES PLANO
4705 Old Shepard Place
Plano
972/758-8800, 800/CALL-HOME
(225-5466)
www.homewood-suites.com
$$-$$$$
One of Plano's newest all-suites hotels is designed for both business and leisure travelers. Promoting "all the comforts of home," it definitely has the feeling of being in a residential apartment. Each location has a socializing "lodge," where guests begin each day with a complimentary breakfast buffet and relax at the end of the day with an evening reception (Monday through Thursday) featuring complimentary beverages and hors d'oeuvres. There's also a mini-convenience store, an executive business center, a fitness/workout room, and an outdoor pool. Each suite contains a fully equipped kitchen with a microwave, a refrigerator with icemaker, a coffeemaker, and a twin-burner stove—plus pots, pans, and utensils. ♿ (Far North Dallas)

MID-CITIES

Hotels

DFW AIRPORT MARRIOTT
8440 Freeport Parkway

Irving
972/929-8800, 800/228-9290
www.marriott.com
$$-$$$
Located only one mile from DFW Airport, this hotel is specifically designed for the business traveler. Each room has a work desk, dataport, remote-controlled cable TV, in-room coffee, and a complimentary newspaper each weekday. A full business center contains all the necessities of the office. When work is finished, relax and exercise at the fully equipped health club with indoor and outdoor pool, sauna, and whirlpool. Then, there's a choice of three restaurants—a steakhouse, a café, and a sports bar. And finally, there's free transportation to the airport. ♿ (Mid-Cities)

DFW LAKES HILTON EXECUTIVE CONFERENCE CENTER
1800 Highway 26 East
Grapevine
817/481-8444, 800/445-8667
www.hilton.com/hotels
$$$-$$$$
This hotel provides a second home to business travelers. For those who can't leave the office behind, it offers a business resource center and a VIP floor. For those who can, it offers heated indoor and outdoor pools, tennis courts, racquetball courts, a complete fitness center,

and a game room. Its scenic lakeside setting on 40 acres, four-diamond AAA rating, special amenities, and recreational facilities give it the feel of a vacation resort. And the lake is stocked if your fishing pole lives in your suitcase. There are three restaurants—the Vineyard serves all meals and a Sunday brunch buffet; the Meritage Grille features steak, seafood, and Southwestern cuisine; and the Boardroom lounge, with large TV and games, has a casual dining menu. ♿ (Mid-Cities)

EMBASSY SUITES-OUTDOOR WORLD
2401 Bass Pro Drive
Grapevine
972/724-2600, 800/EMBASSY
www.embassy-suites.com
$$-$$$
Embassy Suites' brand-new facility has a spacious, plant-filled atrium entrance. The accommodations are similar to most other suite hotels, with spacious one- and two-bedroom suites. The living room has a sofa bed, comfortable seating, table and chairs, TV, phone, and modem link. A kitchen area contains a coffeemaker, refrigerator, and wet bar. The bedroom contains a king or two double beds, an additional TV, and a phone. A complimentary cooked-to-order breakfast, evening reception with beverages, and *USA*

Most luxury hotels have special rates/discounts and package deals, especially on weekends.

ARLINGTON, GRAND PRAIRIE, & MID-CITIES

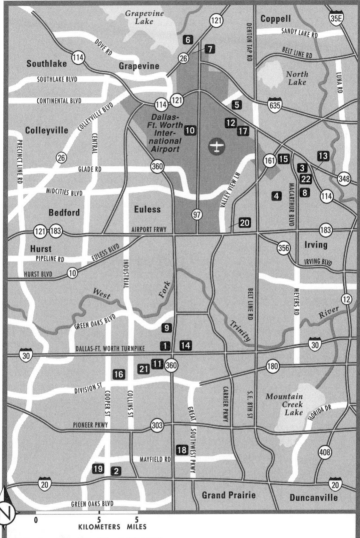

Arlington, Grand Prairie, & Mid-Cities

1. Arlington Hilton (AGP)
2. Best Western Cooper Inn & Suites (AGP)
3. Candlewood Suites - Las Colinas (MC)
4. Courtyard by Marriott - Las Colinas (MC)
5. DFW Airport Marriott (MC)
6. DFW Lakes Hilton Executive Conf. Ctr (MC)
7. Embassy Suites - Outdoor World (MC)
8. Four Seasons Resort (MC)
9. Holiday Inn Arlington (AGP)
10. Hyatt Regency DFW (MC)
11. La Quinta Inn Arlington (AGP)
12. La Quinta Inn- DFW Airport North (MC)
13. Omni Mandalay Hotel at Las Colinas (MC)
14. Radisson Suite (AGP)
15. Residence Inn by Marriott at Las Colinas (MC)
16. Sanford House (AGP)
17. Sheraton Grand Hotel at DFW Airport (MC)
18. Trader's Village RV Park (AGP)
19. Treetops RV Village (AGP)
20. Wilson World (MC)
21. Wyndham Arlington (AGP)
22. Wyndham Garden Hotel - Las Colinas (MC)

Today newspaper (weekdays) are nice amenities. It's located adjacent to the Bass Pro Shop Outdoor World and Grapevine Mills Mall. A complimentary shuttle is available to the mall and the airport. "Family Fun Paks" are summer specials. ⅊ (Mid-Cities)

FOUR SEASONS RESORT AND CLUB
4150 North MacArthur Boulevard
Irving
972/717-0700, 800/332-3442
www.fourseasons.com
$$$$$

A world-class luxury resort offering every imaginable amenity. It's a showplace located on 400 acres of lushly landscaped grounds resplendent with colorful flowers year-round. In addition to the main building with 300 rooms and suites, there are 50 villa-style rooms situated around the golf course. There's an indoor pool, three outdoor pools, a 176,000-square-foot indoor sports complex, a championship golf course, tennis, racquetball, and squash courts, and a European-style full-service spa. Two top-notch restaurants and a conference center make this resort a favorite destination for conventions from around the country. There's even a child care center with children's programs, and children under 18 stay free in the room with parents. Consistently rated one of the best hotels in the United States in the *Condé Nast Travelers* magazine "Readers Choice Awards," it also boasts a four-diamond AAA and four-star Mobil rating. ⅊ (Mid-Cities)

HYATT REGENCY DFW
International Parkway in DFW Airport
DFW Airport
972/453-1234, reservations
800/233-1234
www.dallas.hyatt.com/dfwap
$$$$-$$$$$

For those who want to stay close to the airport, you can't get any closer than this hotel. The Hyatt Regency, with 1,367 rooms and 35 suites, is located within the DFW Airport. The two tower buildings, one on each side of International Parkway, are connected by covered walkways. Business-oriented, it's not the place for a romantic weekend with noisy planes constantly taking off from one of the busiest airports in the world. It has exceptional meeting, banquet, and exhibit space, a business communications center, and an executive conference level. Memberships are available in the Hyatt Bear Creek Golf and Racquet Club located at the south entrance to the airport and include free shuttle service to the recreation area. ⅊ (Mid-Cities)

OMNI MANDALAY HOTEL AT LAS COLINAS
221 East Las Colinas Boulevard
Irving
972/556-0800, reservations
800/THE-OMNI
www.omnihotels.com
$$-$$$$

This 27-floor luxury hotel sits on five acres of landscaped lakefront in the heart of Las Colinas. Named on *Condé Nast Traveler* magazine's Gold List of top five hundred hotels in the world, and rated four-diamond by AAA and four-star by Mobil, all the expected amenities are here. There's a very good restaurant, a lounge with entertainment, meeting facilities, and an exercise room. In addition, there's a playground and programs for children, babysitting available, bicycles for rent, and a heated lakeside pool. Guest memberships are available in local golf and health clubs. ♿ (Mid-Cities)

SHERATON GRAND HOTEL AT DFW AIRPORT
4440 West John Carpenter Freeway (Highway 114)
Irving
972/929-8400, 800/325-3535
www.sheraton.com
$$$
Near the DFW Airport, it offers free airport transportation, concierge and business-class floors, meeting facilities, a health club, an indoor/outdoor heated pool, a sauna, a hot tub, a restaurant, a lobby bar, and a sports bar. The rooms are tastefully decorated and contain dataports, coffeemakers, and cable TV. ♿ (Mid-Cities)

WILSON WORLD HOTEL & SUITES
4600 West Airport Freeway (Highway 183)
Irving
972/513-0800, 800/945-7667
$$
Located one mile south of the airport at Highway 183 and Valley View, a convenient location is the major attribute of this hotel. Choose from rooms, suites, and deluxe suites, all nicely appointed and furnished with work desks and dataports. Suites have microwaves and refrigerators and balconies overlooking the five-story atrium lobby. The Garden Terrace restaurant serves a breakfast and lunch buffet Monday through Friday and dinner specials during the week. There's also an atrium bar with fresh popcorn, an indoor pool, a whirlpool, a

video game room, and an exercise room. A complimentary shuttle to DFW airport is available 24 hours a day. ♿ (Mid-Cities)

WYNDHAM GARDEN HOTEL-LAS COLINAS
110 West John Carpenter Freeway (Highway 114)
Irving
972/650-1600, reservations 800/ WYNDHAM
www.wyndham.com
$-$$$
Similar to most of the Wyndham hotels, this one is business-oriented. Each room has a large work area with good lighting, long phone cords, voice mail, and a dataport; iron and ironing board, cable TV, and coffeemaker; and a free *USA Today* newspaper delivered on weekdays. There's an indoor heated pool, sauna, and exercise room; guest memberships are available to a nearby athletic club. A restaurant serves all meals, and several popular dining establishments are within walking distance. ♿ (Mid-Cities)

Motels

CANDLEWOOD SUITES-LAS COLINAS
5300 Green Park Drive
Irving
972/714-9990, 888-Candlewood
www.candlewoodsuites.com
$-$$
All-suites motels are popping up like mushrooms. This chain offers lower prices and fewer services, which is an acceptable combination for many people. The studio and one-bedroom suites are spacious and contain 25-inch TVs with VCRs and CD players, hairdryers, irons and ironing boards, large work desks, refrigerators, and

dishwashers. There's no restaurant, but a Candlewood Cupboard offers a wide variety of snacks and meal fixins 24 hours a day. A 24-hour fitness center is equipped with a treadmill, a bike, a stepper, and a TV. This facility offers a nice alternative for the budget-conscious traveler. & (Mid-Cities)

COURTYARD BY MARRIOTT-LAS COLINAS
1151 West Walnut Hill Lane
Irving
972/550-8100, reservations
800/321-2211
www.marriott.com
$$-$$$
No surprises here, the Courtyard is much like the rest of the chain—business-oriented and comfortable. Complimentary *USA Today* newspapers are delivered weekdays, and rooms contain work desks, dataports, remote-control cable TVs, irons and ironing boards, and in-room coffee. A café is open for breakfast, and several restaurants are located in the area. There's an exercise room, an indoor and outdoor pool, a whirlpool, and several nearby golf courses. & (Mid-Cities)

LA QUINTA INN & SUITES-DFW AIRPORT NORTH
4850 John Carpenter Freeway
Irving
972/915-4022, reservations
800/687-6667
www.laquinta.com
$-$$
Another of the new "Inn & Suites" of the La Quinta chain, this one was built with guest comfort in mind. A spacious atrium-style lobby contains a fountain surrounded by comfortable sofas and chairs, big TVs, and views of the landscaped court-

yard. Outside is a sundeck, a heated pool, a spa, and a gazebo. The new rooms feature an entertainment center with, not only a 25-inch TV, but also an expanded cable selection, movies, and video games. Business travelers will find a large work desk and dataport, as well as the usual amenities. King Plus rooms and two-room suites offer even more luxuries. A complimentary breakfast is served in the lobby each morning. & (Mid-Cities)

RESIDENCE INN BY MARRIOTT AT LAS COLINAS
950 Walnut Hill Lane
Irving
972/580-7773, reservations
800/331-3131
www.marriott.com
$$-$$$
This all-suites inn offers comfortable one- and two-bedroom suites with kitchens (coffeemaker, microwave, and refrigerator). Attractive to business travelers, rooms have work desks with lamps, dataports, cable TV, and free newspapers in the lobby. It's also attractive to families because children under 12 stay free in rooms with parents. There's an exercise room and an outdoor pool, and rooms have a patio or balcony; most rooms also have a fireplace. A continental breakfast is complimentary, as is airport transportation. & (Mid-Cities)

ARLINGTON/ GRAND PRAIRIE

Hotels

ARLINGTON HILTON
2401 East Lamar Boulevard
817/640-3322, 800/527-9332 (direct)

www.hilton.com/hotels
$$-$$$
Located smack-dab in the middle of Arlington's attractions Six Flags Over Texas, Hurricane Harbor, and the Ballpark in Arlington this hotel offers free trolley service to those sites as well as to the Convention Center. Both Dallas and Fort Worth are easily accessible on I-30. The Hilton Arlington caters to both business and leisure travelers with facilities such as an indoor/outdoor pool, sauna, Jacuzzi, and health club. There's a nice restaurant, a trendy club with weekend live entertainment, and a piano bar in the lobby. ᕕ (Arlington/Grand Prairie)

RADISSON SUITE HOTEL (ARLINGTON)
700 Avenue H East
817/640-0440, reservations
800/333-3333
www.radisson.com
$$-$$$
Arlington is centrally located for exploring the entire Metroplex. Easy freeway access gets you to Dallas, Fort Worth, the airport, and the many attractions in the Mid-Cities areas. This all-suites hotel provides coffee service, refrigerators, cable TV, and dataports in the rooms, a heated indoor pool and sauna, and a free weekday newspaper. Enjoy a complimentary full breakfast each morning and beverages in the evening in the plant-filled atrium. A restaurant serves all meals and a lounge has a dance floor. ᕕ (Arlington/Grand Prairie)

WYNDHAM ARLINGTON
1500 Convention Center Drive
817/261-8200, 800/442-7275 (direct)
www.wyndham.com
$$-$$$

Directly across from The Ballpark in Arlington, Six Flags Over Texas, and the Convention Center, the Wyndham Arlington is also equidistant from Downtown Dallas and Fort Worth. In addition to attractive guestrooms with coffeemakers, hairdryers, and remote-control TVs, the rooms appeal to business travelers as well with large work areas, excellent lighting, modem links, and a free daily newspaper. There's a nice restaurant, meeting and banquet facilities, a poolside lounge, and a full-service indoor fitness center. ᕕ (Arlington/Grand Prairie)

Motels

BEST WESTERN COOPER INN & SUITES (ARLINGTON)
4024 Melear Road
817/784-9490
www.bestwestern.com
$-$$
Near from the gigantic Parks Mall, this modern motel combines a reasonable price with a convenient location. It offers some of the amenities usually associated with higher priced places, such as a complimentary "expanded" continental breakfast, *USA Today* newspaper, and free local phone calls. Children under 12 stay free in the room with parents, and of course, there's color TV and an outdoor pool. ᕕ (Arlington/Grand Prairie)

HOLIDAY INN ARLINGTON
1507 North Watson Road
817/640-7712, reservations
877-622-5395
www.holiday-inn.com
$-$$
A reasonably priced motel with a heated indoor/outdoor pool and whirlpool as well as nicely land-

scaped grounds with a gazebo. Rooms have been recently remodeled and contain cable TV, dataports, coffeemakers, hairdryers, and irons and ironing boards. There's a fitness center, lounge, and restaurant, although there are dozens of other restaurants in the area. Combining value and location, it's a good choice for the budget-conscious traveler. ᴋ (Arlington/Grand Prairie)

LA QUINTA INN ARLINGTON
825 North Watson Road
817/640-4142, reservations
800/687-6667
www.laquinta.com
$$-$$$

Even though this is not one of the new "inn & suites" properties, it was extensively renovated in 1997 into a nice hotel and conference center with a meeting planner on staff. You'll find not only business services and amenities, but also some nice treats for leisure travelers. Children under 18 stay free in the room with parents, rollaway beds and cribs are available, and rooms feature 25-inch TVs with movies and video games. The outdoor pool has a wading pool as well as a swim-up bar. Rates include a complimentary continental breakfast. ᴋ (Arlington/Grand Prairie)

Bed-and-Breakfasts

THE SANFORD HOUSE
506 North Center Street
Arlington
817/861-2129, 877-205-4914
www.thesanfordhouse.com
$$-$$$$

Centrally located near major attractions and restaurants in Arlington, The Sanford House is a tranquil al-

ternative to "hotel row." A luxury inn, it offers eight appealing rooms, each with a sitting area and private bath. Four individual cottages feature king-size beds, Jacuzzis, and fireplaces. The parlor, dining room, and library are elegantly decorated and furnished for guests' comfort. But don't stay inside for long because the beautifully landscaped grounds invite relaxation. Stroll through the French country gardens or take a cup of coffee or a good book to one of the seating areas that beckon near fountains, gazebos, or the outdoor pool with its glassed-in pavilion. For the ultimate in luxury, ask for a package that includes a visit to the new Day Spa and Salon across the street. Indeed, a visit here is a return to the era of gracious service and attention to detail. ᴋ (Arlington/Grand Prairie)

Campgrounds/RV Parks

TRADER'S VILLAGE RV PARK
2602 Mayfield Road
Grand Prairie
214/647-8205, reservations
800/323-8899
$

Adjacent to Trader's Village (see Chapter 5, Sights and Attractions), this RV park is rated one of the best in the state. It has 210 tree-shaded sites, an area for tents, and a heated indoor pool and Jacuzzi. For recreation, facilities include a lake (fishing permitted), stream, pond, boats, canoes, a playground, mini golf, horseshoes, tennis, and a game room. For convenience, there's a store, laundry, restrooms and showers, grills, and a restaurant. (Arlington/Grand Prairie)

TREETOPS RV VILLAGE
1901 West Arbrook
Arlington
817/467-7943, 800/747-0787
$
Claiming more than two thousand oak trees, this park offers large, shady lots with big patios in a quiet, residential setting. There are long, wide pull-throughs with full hook-ups, a pool, laundry, baths, and phone service. Just off I-20 on the south side of Arlington, it's convenient to the Parks Mall, dozens of shops and restaurants, and within a mile of banks, grocery stores, a post office, and medical facilities. (Arlington/Grand Prairie)

DOWNTOWN FORT WORTH

Hotels

BLACKSTONE COURTYARD BY MARRIOTT
601 Main Street
817/885-8303, 800/321-2211
www.marriott.com
$$-$$$
Far from an ordinary Courtyard motel, this was the celebrated Blackstone Hotel, a Recorded Texas Historic Landmark property originally opened in 1929 during the Art Deco era. It was Fort Worth's first skyscraper and home of Fort Worth's first radio station, WBAP, which broadcast from the 22nd floor. Through the years, notables such as Herbert Hoover, Gene Autry, Clark Gable, Bob Hope, and Elvis Presley slept here. Marriott saved this piece of history from possible demolition and transformed it into a distinctive hotel once again. Deluxe guestrooms contain an array of modern conveniences for the business or leisure traveler, and the upper floor suites have open-air terraces. The hotel also has a pool/whirlpool, an exercise room, meeting facilities, and the Corner Bakery restaurant. & (Downtown Fort Worth)

RADISSON PLAZA
815 Main Street
817/870-2100, reservations
800/333-3333
www.radisson.com
$$$
Formerly the swanky Hotel Texas, built in 1921 after the oil boom, it's listed in the National Register of Historic Places. Quite a showplace in its day, this Fort Worth landmark has hosted such famous guests as Jack Dempsey and Rudolph Valentino. President John F. Kennedy spent his last night here on November 21, 1963, before his fateful trip to Dallas. Now the Radisson group has magnificently renovated the 517 rooms and added a heated rooftop swimming pool and a fitness center. Other on-site facilities include a beauty/barber shop, gift shop, florist, dry cleaner/laundry, and an American Airlines ticket office. The Radisson Plaza offers exceptional meeting facilities, and the Grand Crystal Ballroom is the largest in Fort Worth at 14,000 square feet. The Café Texas serves traditional fare, and the Cactus Bar & Grille serves Tex-Mex cuisine with a flair. It's conveniently located near the Convention Center. & (Downtown Fort Worth)

THE WORTHINGTON RENAISSANCE
200 Main Street
817/870-1000, 800/433-5677
$$$$$
www.theworthington.com

Elegance, luxury, and superior service are hallmarks of this splendid hotel, which spans three city blocks in Downtown Fort Worth's Sundance Square. Fort Worth's only four-diamond, four-star hotel, it has 460 rooms and 44 suites, with outstanding views of the city from the upper floor rooms. Spacious guestrooms have far-above-average amenities, and the hotel offers all imaginable services for the tourist or business traveler. Guests enjoy a heated indoor pool, a sauna, an exercise room, and for a nominal fee, an athletic club and tennis courts. Convention planners find exceptional meeting and banquet facilities. The award-winning restaurant, Reflections (see Chapter 4, Where to Eat), serves consistently exquisite meals with efficient service and offers a scrumptious buffet brunch feast on Sundays and holidays. The Star Grill coffee shop offers casual dining. ♿ (Downtown Fort Worth)

Bed-and-Breakfasts

ETTA'S PLACE
200 West Third at Houston
817/654-0267
www.caravanofdreams.com/ Ettashom.htm
$$$
Named for Etta Place (according to legend, the girlfriend of the Sundance Kid), this distinctive lodging is conveniently located in Sundance Square, just around the corner from the Caravan of Dreams. This property is not what most travelers would envision as a "typical" bed-and-breakfast, probably because it's in the middle of bustling Downtown, although a delicious full, home-cooked breakfast is included in the rate. Seven rooms and three suites, named for members of the infamous Hole in the Wall Gang, are tastefully decorated and furnished with modern amenities and oversized beds. The library filled with books and overstuffed leather chairs and the music room with its Steinway grand piano are perfect places for relaxing after a busy day. Two outdoor patios offer fresh air and a nice view. ♿ (Downtown Fort Worth)

NORTH FORT WORTH

Hotels

STOCKYARDS HOTEL
109 East Exchange Avenue
817/625-6427
$$$
You can't get much more authentic than this hotel. In the heart of the Historic District, the Stockyards Hotel, established in 1907, has always offered incomparable hospitality to those who journeyed

Even if you aren't staying in a luxury hotel, wander through the lobby or visit a restaurant or bar in one of them.

across Texas. Totally restored, it offers 48 rooms and 4 suites tastefully decorated in one of four themes: Cowboy, Indian, Mountain Man, and Victorian. The Old West décor features hand-rubbed oak furniture, 12-foot pressed tin ceilings, classic brass hardware, and even saddle-topped barstools in Booger Red's Saloon. Although modern conveniences provide world-class comfort, most are not obvious—for example, televisions cleverly hidden inside turn-of-the-century armoires—and include modem links and coffeemakers in each room. The H-3 Ranch, a full service restaurant (see Chapter 4, Where to Eat) serves good vittles, too. (North Fort Worth)

MOTELS

COUNTRY INNS & SUITES BY CARLSON
2200 Mercado Drive
817/831-9200, reservations
800/849-7270
www.countryinns.com
$$-$$$

This new motel is located just minutes from the Stockyards Historic District and next door to a popular Mexican restaurant. It offers amenities associated with modern hotels and motels (data ports in the rooms, a complimentary continental break-

fast, a weekday newspaper, and 24-hour coffee and snacks in the lobby) with a country inn flavor. The king suites include a king-sized bed, a sofa sleeper, a microwave, a refrigerator, two TVs, and two phones. The comfortable lobby has a fireplace, and there's an exercise room and an outdoor pool/whirlpool. ⅍ (North Fort Worth)

LA QUINTA INN & SUITES
4700 North Freeway
817/222-2888, reservations
800/687-6667
www.laquinta.com
$$

One of La Quinta's newest additions, this moderately priced motel has a Spanish tile roof, balconies, and an attractive landscaped courtyard and grounds with a heated pool, a Jacuzzi, and a fitness center. Bright, clean rooms have dataports and 25-inch TVs with movies and video games. A free continental breakfast is included in the rate, and local phone calls are free. It's situated alongside a busy highway but has inside corridors to the rooms. ⅍ (North Fort Worth)

BED-AND-BREAKFASTS

AZALEA PLANTATION
1400 Robinwood Drive
817/838-5882, 800/687-3529
www.texassleepaways.com/
azalea
$$

Enjoy Texas hospitality at its best in this inviting, antique-filled mansion. The stately Plantation-style home is nestled among two acres of majestic oaks, magnolia, and azaleas. You'll also find a fountain, a yard swing, and a gazebo for relaxing under the trees. Choose from two lavishly furnished guestrooms in the main house and two cottages behind. Individual rooms and cottages may feature a king-size canopy bed, a Texas-size whirlpool tub, or a veranda. All rooms have full, modern baths, terrycloth robes, and fine toiletries, and the cottages have mini-kitchens. The gracious hosts serve a gourmet breakfast on weekends and a continental "plus" breakfast weekdays in the ornate Victorian dining room. No smoking, please. (North Fort Worth)

BED & BREAKFAST AT THE RANCH
8275 Wagley Roberson Road
817/232-5522
www.fortworthians.com/bbranch
$$-$$$
Originally built in the early 1900s, this house was ranch headquarters for a several-thousand-acre cattle ranch. Now it sits on 20 acres a few minutes north of the Stockyards Historic District and minutes south of the Texas Motor Speedway. The décor is thoroughly western, but that doesn't mean without modern conveniences. The patio room contains a hot tub, a wet bar, a jukebox, and doors that open onto the tennis court. Guests enjoy the comfortable living room with its leather sofas and stone fireplace, TV, board games, and books. A full, Southwestern-style breakfast is served in the elegant dining room appointed with 1840s period furniture. Accommodations include three downstairs rooms, one upstairs room, and a separate cozy cottage, the "Smokehouse." Smoking is not allowed in the house. (North Fort Worth)

MISS MOLLY'S HOTEL
109 West Exchange Avenue
817/628-1522, 800/99-MOLLY
www.missmollys.com
$$
Once a prim and proper boarding house, later a popular bordello, this historic hotel (circa 1910) now operates in the true bed-and-breakfast tradition. Eight authentic turn-of-the-century rooms surround a central parlor, lighted predominantly by a stained glass skylight. Seven rooms share three antique-appointed full hall bathrooms. Robes are provided during your stay. The largest room, with a private bath, features fancy Victorian décor and is named for the Madame, Miss Josie. The other rooms are reminiscent of hotel rooms in old western movies. The B&B is on the second floor (above the Star Café) and is nonsmoking. Its location in the heart of the Stockyards National Historic District makes it convenient, but be aware that it can be noisy until the wee hours. (North Fort Worth)

SOUTHWEST FORT WORTH

Hotels

GREEN OAKS HOTEL
6901 West Freeway
817/738-7311, 800/772-2341 (in Texas), 800/433-2174 (outside Texas)
$$-$$$
A long-time fixture on Fort Worth's west side, this two-story hotel has undergone several renovations. The most recent was at the end of 1999, so rooms have new wallpaper, carpet, and furnishings, along with up-to-date amenities. Because it's the only full-service hotel in the area, a meeting or function is almost always underway. Facilities include two

GREATER FORT WORTH

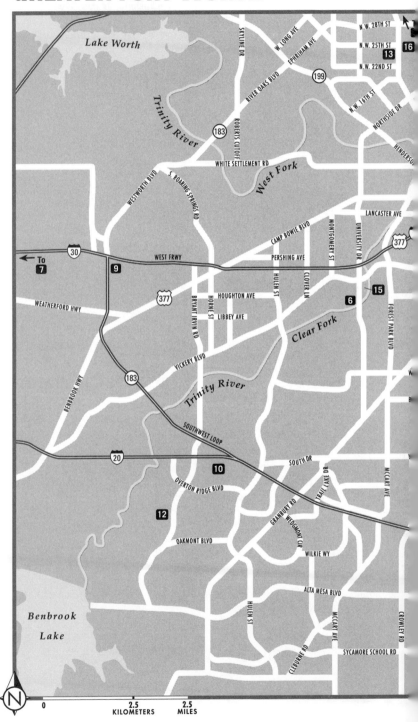

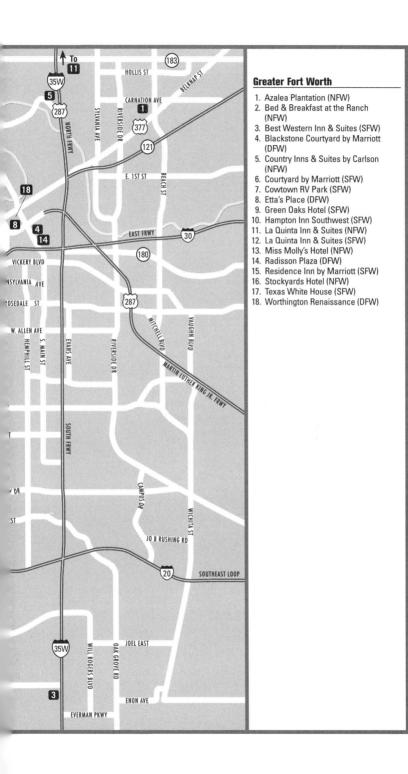

Greater Fort Worth

1. Azalea Plantation (NFW)
2. Bed & Breakfast at the Ranch (NFW)
3. Best Western Inn & Suites (SFW)
4. Blackstone Courtyard by Marriott (DFW)
5. Country Inns & Suites by Carlson (NFW)
6. Courtyard by Marriott (SFW)
7. Cowtown RV Park (SFW)
8. Etta's Place (DFW)
9. Green Oaks Hotel (SFW)
10. Hampton Inn Southwest (SFW)
11. La Quinta Inn & Suites (NFW)
12. La Quinta Inn & Suites (SFW)
13. Miss Molly's Hotel (NFW)
14. Radisson Plaza (DFW)
15. Residence Inn by Marriott (SFW)
16. Stockyards Hotel (NFW)
17. Texas White House (SFW)
18. Worthington Renaissance (DFW)

pools, two lighted tennis courts, an exercise room, a restaurant, and a lounge. The hotel is adjacent to the Z. Boaz public golf course. ♿ (Southwest Fort Worth)

Motels

BEST WESTERN INN & SUITES
6500 South Freeway (I-35W)
817/551-6700
www.bestwestern.com
$$
The Best Western chain has come a long way in the past few years. This facility offers their new "inn & suites" concept and has many features of higher priced hotels, such as dataports in the rooms, a pool, a hot tub, and a fitness center. There are also coffeemakers, refrigerators, and 25-inch color TVs in each room. Local phone calls are free, as is a nice continental breakfast. It's located on the far south side along a busy freeway, but the rooms seem amazingly soundproof. ♿ (Southwest Fort Worth)

COURTYARD BY MARRIOTT
3150 Riverfront Drive
817/335-1300, reservations
800/321-2211
www.marriott.com
$$-$$$
The location of this Courtyard is its strong point. Just off University Drive, it's convenient to Texas Christian University, the zoo, the botanical gardens, the cultural district, shopping, and restaurants, and only a few minutes from Downtown and the medical district. Most of these comfortable, business-oriented establishments are quite similar, with room amenities including modem links, coffeemakers, and refrigerators. Here, there's a heated

pool, fitness center, and restaurant. ♿ (Southwest Fort Worth)

HAMPTON INN SOUTHWEST
4799 Southwest Loop 820
817/346-7845, reservations
800/426-7866
www.hampton-inn.com
$
This recent addition to the familiar motel chain is located near a new shopping and dining area of Southwest Fort Worth. The rooms have dataports, cable TV, and coffeemakers; the king rooms also have mini-refrigerators and microwaves. There's an indoor pool and whirlpool. Local phone calls are free, and so is a continental breakfast bar and a copy of *USA Today* (weekdays). The motel has no restaurant on the premises, but several are located nearby. ♿ (Southwest Fort Worth)

LA QUINTA INN & SUITES
4900 Bryant Irvin Road
817/370-2700, reservations
800/687-6667
www.laquinta.com
$$
A sunlit lobby and fountain welcomes guests. A sitting area of comfy sofas and chairs, facing a courtyard, soothe the weary. Beyond the landscaped grounds, a sundeck, outdoor pool, spa, and gazebo beckons. This is definitely not the La Quinta of old.

Rooms feature an entertainment center with a 25-inch TV and expanded cable selection, movies, and video games. Business travelers will find a large work desk and dataport, as well as a coffeemaker, a hairdryer, and an iron and ironing board. King Plus rooms and two-room suites have even more amenities. A complimentary breakfast is served in the lobby each morning. ♿ (Southwest Fort Worth)

RESIDENCE INN BY MARRIOTT
1701 South University Drive
817/870-1011, reservations
800/321-2211
www.marriott.com
$$-$$$

This all-suites inn offers one- and two-bedroom suites with kitchens (coffeemaker, microwave, refrigerator). Designed to be a "home away from home," the suites are attractive to business travelers and families as well because children stay free in rooms with parents. The suites have cable TV with HBO, modem links, a patio or balcony, and most have a fireplace. There's a pool for the kids, free weekday newspapers for the parents, and a free continental breakfast for all. ♿ (Southwest Fort Worth)

Bed-and-Breakfasts

THE TEXAS WHITE HOUSE
1417 Eighth Avenue
817/923-3597, 800/279-6491
www.texaswhitehouse.com
$$

Recipient of the Historic Preservation Council Pedestal Award for restoration to its original 1910 grandeur, this traditional bed-and-breakfast home is furnished with simple, yet elegant décor. Three upstairs guestrooms each have a queen-size bed (featherbed upon request), comfortable sitting area, and private bath. Guests are welcome to enjoy the living room with fireplace, parlor, dining room, and large wraparound porch. A full breakfast may be served in the dining room or to the guestrooms and features treats homemade by the hosts. The nonsmoking home is located on the edge of the medical district, convenient to Downtown, Texas Christian University, and the Cultural District. (Southwest Fort Worth)

Campgrounds/RV Parks

COWTOWN RV PARK
7000 I-20
Aldeo
817/441-7878, reservations
800/781-4678
www.cowtownrv.com

About 20 to 30 minutes west of Downtown, this park has paved pull-throughs with 50-amp service, restrooms and showers, a laundry, swimming pool, playground, meeting room, and a store with groceries and RV supplies. Instant phone service and cable TV is available at every site. Pets are welcome. (Southwest Fort Worth)

Ft Worth CVB

4

Dallas boasts ten thousand restaurants, four times more per capita than New York City. Add the thousands more eating establishments in the Mid-Cities, Arlington, and Fort Worth, and if you go hungry here, it's your own fault. The Metroplex is a melting pot, and its growth has brought ethnic dining from virtually around the world, so the choices are truly unlimited. Select fine dining at The Mansion on Turtle Creek or The French Room in the Adolphus Hotel, both displaying the prestigious AAA five-diamond award. Or sample trendy Southwestern cuisine prepared by award-winning chefs such as Grady Spears of Reata or Stephen Pyles of Star Canyon. But also try the local favorites: chicken-fried steak, Mexican/Tex-Mex, barbecue, and steak.

Listed on many Texas menus as CFS, chicken-fried steak is a tradition, a staple of the Old West food group. Originally, it was a way to prepare a tough cut of beef, beaten until it was tender, coated with batter, fried like chicken, then served drenched in cream gravy made from the pan drippings. Usually made with round steak, some high-class chefs make it with sirloin; everyone has his own special secret and boasts to be "the best." Unfortunately, many restaurants are surrendering to the convenience of the frozen cardboard-tasting patties, so ask the locals for recommendations.

Tex-Mex (Mexican with a Texas flair) restaurants abound, although restaurants serving genuine dishes from the interior of Mexico are rare. You'll find lots of Tex-Mex chain restaurants, but you'll also find many family-owned, unique neighborhood places. Ask twenty locals about their favorite and you'll get twenty different recommendations.

The same is true about barbecue: locals flock to Sonny Bryan's or Dickey's (see sidebars on pages 68 and 75), but most people have a neighborhood hole-in-the-wall favorite, too.

In an area famous for thick, juicy steaks, you'll find some excellent, individually owned steakhouses listed. Chain establishments such as Del Frisco's Double Eagle Steak House, Ruth's Chris Steakhouse, Outback Steakhouse, Morton's of Chicago, and Saltgrass Steakhouse, all of which have multiple locations throughout the Metroplex, are also good choices.

Unfortunately, space permits describing only a sampling of the best eateries, or local favorites, or those of special interest. Chain restaurants are not listed, but if you have a favorite restaurant, chances are you'll find it in the Metroplex. This chapter begins with a list of restaurants organized by cuisine type. Restaurant names are followed by zone abbreviations (see page v) and the page numbers where you can find descriptions. The descriptions are organized alphabetically within each zone. The dollar symbols indicate the price of a typical entrée only.

Price rating symbols:
$ **$10 and under**
$$ **$11 to $20**
$$$ **$21 and over**

American/New American
Angeluna (DFW), p. 90
Antares (DD), p. 65
Beau Nash (DD), p. 65
Café Aspen (SFW), p. 98
Café on the Green (MC), p. 83
City Café (CD), p. 71
Dakota's (DD), p. 67
Dorris House Café (MC), p. 84
Plano Café (FND), p. 82
Raven's Grill (MC), p. 85
Wilhoite's (MC), p. 87
Zodiac Room (DD), p. 69

Barbecue
Angelo's Bar-B-Que (SFW), p. 95
Cousin's Pit Barbecue (SFW), p. 99
North Main BBQ (MC), p. 85
Peggy Sue Barbecue (CD), p. 78
Railhead Smokehouse (SFW), p. 101

Breakfast
Bayley's (MC), p. 83

British
Barclay's (CD), p. 70

Chinese
Liberty (CD), p. 76
May Dragon (FND), p. 82
Szechuan Chinese Restaurant (SFW), p. 102

Continental
The Balcony of Ridglea (SFW), p. 95
Bistro Louise (SFW), p. 95
Ewald's at the Stoneleigh (DD), p. 67
Old Warsaw (CD), p. 78

Deli/Sandwiches
Back Porch (SFW), p. 95
Carshon's Deli (SFW), p. 98
Kuby's Sausage House (CD), p. 74

Eclectic
8.0 Restaurant (DFW), p. 90
Baby Doe's Matchless Mine (CD), p. 70
Chaparral Club (DD), p. 65
The Grape (CD), p. 74
Landmark (CD), p. 74
Monica's Aca y Alla (ED), p. 79
Rainforest Café (MC), p. 85
Sambuca (ED), p. 79

Fine Dining
The French Room (DD), p. 69
Laurel's (CD), p. 76
The Mansion on Turtle Creek (CD), p. 76
Nana Grill (CD), p. 77

The Pyramid Room (DD), p. 69
Reflections at the Worthington
  (DFW), p. 93

French
Cacharel (AGP), p. 88
Chez Gerard (CD), p. 71
Marsala Restaurant (AGP), p. 88
Saint Emilion (SFW), p. 102

German
Edelweiss (SFW), p. 99

Greek
Veranda Greek Café (MC), p. 87
Ziziki's (CD), p. 79

Hamburgers
Al's (AGP), p. 87
Billy Miner's Saloon (DFW), p. 90
Charley's Old-Fashioned Hamburgers
  (SFW), p. 99
Kincaid Grocery & Market (SFW),
  p. 100
Mike's Famous Hamburgers (MC),
  p. 85
Prince of Hamburgers (CD), p. 78

Home Cooking
Celebration (SFW), p. 98
Marquez Bakery (AGP), p. 88
Ol' South Pancake House (SFW),
  p. 100
Paris Café (SFW), p. 101
The String Bean (FND), p. 83
Texas Grill (SFW), p.102

Indian
Kebab-N-Kurry (FND), p. 82
Mayuri (MC), p. 84

Italian
Italian Inn Ridglea (SFW), p. 100
La Bistro (MC), p.84
La Trattoria Lombardi (CD), p. 74
Picolo Mondo (AGP), p.90
Ravioli Ristorante (MC), p.87

Sardine's Ristorante Italiano (SFW),
  p. 102
Tarantino's (ED), p. 80

Japanese
Anzu (CD), p. 70
Shogun (AGP), p. 90

Mediterranean/Middle Eastern
Bistro A (CD), p. 71
Hedary's Lebanese Restaurant
  (SFW), p. 100

Mexican
El Rancho Grande (NFW), p. 93
Joe T. Garcia's Mexican Dishes
  (NFW), p. 94
Los Vaqueros (NFW), p. 94
Mercado Juarez (NFW), p. 91
Mi Cocina (DFW), p. 91
Mia's Tex-Mex (CD), p. 77
Miguelito's (MC), p. 84
Nuevo Leon (CD), p. 77
Tolbert's Texas Chili Parlor (DD), p. 69
Via Real (MC), p. 87

Seafood
AquaKnox (CD), p. 70
Catfish Sam's (AGP), p. 88
Daddy Jack's (CD), p. 71
Fish (DD), p. 67
Lefty's Lobster & Chowder House
  (FND), p. 82
Sea Grille (FND), p. 82

Steaks
Arlington Steakhouse (AGP), p. 88
Cattleman's Steakhouse (NFW), p. 93
Chamberlain's Steak and Chop
  House (FND), p.81
Cool River (MC), p. 84
H-3 Ranch (NFW), p. 94
Rodeo Steakhouse (DFW), p. 93
Star Café (NFW), p. 95

Texan
Reata (DFW), p. 91
Star Canyon (CD), p. 78

Smoking is prohibited in Arlington's public buildings (including restaurants).

Vegetarian
Dream Café (DD), p. 67

DOWNTOWN DALLAS

ANTARES
300 Reunion Boulevard
(in Reunion Tower)
Dallas
214/712-7145
$$-$$$
Named for the brightest star in the Scorpio constellation, Antares offers diners a spectacular 360-degree panoramic view from 50 stories above the street atop Reunion Tower. Considered by some locals to be a "tourist trap," it's really an excellent restaurant—perhaps a bit overpriced, but consider the view. As you slowly revolve (one revolution every 55 minutes) above the city, you can enjoy acclaimed New American cuisine. The menu offers a wide choice of creatively prepared seafood entrées as well as beef and chicken dishes; if you can't decide, try the Antares Platter with rock lobster tail, red snapper, clams, scallops, mussels, and blackened chicken. Cocktails and wine are available. Children's portions are half price. Reservations are suggested, and people tend to dress up at night. Lunch Mon-Sat, dinner nightly, Sunday brunch. ⑆ (Downtown Dallas)

BEAU NASH
400 Crescent Court (in Hotel Crescent Court)
2215 Cedar Springs
Dallas
214/871-3240
$$-$$$
This hotel dining room offers dining in an elegant setting overlooking the idyllic gardens of the Crescent Court. Watch the chefs working in the open kitchen, preparing dishes that creatively blend New American cuisine with a touch of Northern Italian. The menu changes regularly to offer a variety of seafood and steak entrées. The high level of unobtrusive service is part of the first-class aura of the Hotel Crescent Court. Executive chef James Rowland puts his best foot forward for Beau Nash's celebrated Sunday brunch with such dishes as Marsala duck and veal pâté in roasted shallot vinaigrette. The adjacent lounge attracts a singles crowd looking for "beautiful people" and features live jazz on weekends. Breakfast, lunch, and dinner daily; Sun brunch. ⑆ (Downtown Dallas)

CHAPARRAL CLUB
400 North Olive Street (in Adam's Mark Hotel)
Dallas
214/777-6539
$$-$$$
From the 38th floor of the Adam's Mark Hotel in the Dallas Arts

DOWNTOWN DALLAS

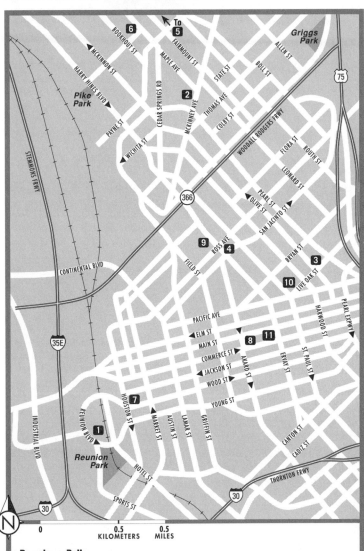

Downtown Dallas

1. Antares
2. Beau Nash
3. Chaparral Club
4. Dakota's
5. Dream Café
6. Ewald's at the Stoneleigh
7. Fish
8. French Room
9. Pyramid Room
10. Tolbert's
11. Zodiac Room

District, the Chaparral Club offers a stunning panoramic view of the Dallas skyline. The Art Deco furnishings capture the elegance of yesteryear, and vast expanses of glass provide a clean, open feeling. The menu has South American and Asian influences and features world-class dining with artfully prepared, creative cuisine. Reservations are requested. Lunch Mon-Fri, dinner nightly. ♿ (Downtown Dallas)

DAKOTA'S
600 North Akard Street
Dallas
214/740-4001
$$-$$$

Since it opened in 1985, Dakota's has been consistently mentioned not only as one of the best restaurants but also as one of the best values. The downstairs restaurant is cozy and elegant with rich wood paneling and marble. In nice weather, ask if a table is available on the tiny patio in a courtyard setting by a cascading waterfall. Enjoy entrées grilled on Dakota's wood-burning grill over native Texas woods. The classic American cuisine has a touch of the Southwest and can include choices such as ostrich, pheasant, or buffalo. Specialties include roast duck and lobster tail on the extraordinarily varied, innovative menu. They also make their own pasta and breads. The best bargain is the three-course prix fixe "twilight menu," which is served from 5 to 6:30 p.m. Diners are entertained with live piano music on Friday and Saturday evenings. Valet parking is provided at no extra charge. Lunch Mon-Fri, dinner nightly. ♿ (Downtown Dallas)

DREAM CAFÉ
2880 Routh Street

Dallas
214/954-0486
$-$$

This café was one of the first organic, vegetarian restaurants in Dallas. More than just a trend, its crowds prove that Dallasites have adopted the healthier menu as a mantra. The grilled, marinated tempeh burger is one of the most popular dishes. Breakfast, lunch, and dinner daily. ♿ (Downtown Dallas)

EWALD'S AT THE STONELEIGH
2927 Maple Avenue
(in Stoneleigh Hotel)
Dallas
214/871-2523
$$

Ewald's offers classic European, old-world charm in the elegant 1923-era Stoneleigh Hotel. Favored by the older crowd who enjoys the attentive tableside service of a gentler era, the fine restaurant serves Continental cuisine and signature dishes such as Chateaubriand, tenderloin beef medallions, veal piccata, and Dover sole. With the addition of a new chef in 1997, Ewald's has added some New American creations with Asian and Italian touches such as grilled duck breast marinated in star anise served with orzo and kalamata fig relish. A classical guitarist plays on weekend evenings. Breakfast, lunch, and dinner daily; Sun brunch. ♿ (Downtown Dallas)

FISH
302 South Houston Street
Dallas
214/747-FISH
$$$

This internationally acclaimed, award-winning restaurant was selected one of the ten best new restaurants in Dallas in 1997 by the

Sonny Bryan's

Barbecue is sacred in Texas. And Sonny Bryan's is the best of the best, known as "legendary" by many. That's quite a reputation to live up to. The tiny, original (for more than 40 years) location on Inwood Road still stands, although Sonny Bryan's has now expanded with a dozen locations throughout the Metroplex. The quality is consistently excellent, from the melt-in-your-mouth meat to the enormous onion rings. Devotees of Sonny's barbecue range from former president George Bush to Tom Hanks, Steven Spielberg to Julia Child, and Roger Staubach to The Oak Ridge Boys.

Sonny's locations include the following:

- ***2202 Inwood Road, Dallas*** *(original location), 214/357-7120*
- ***302 North Market, Dallas*** *(West End), 214/744-1610*
- ***325 North St. Paul, Dallas****, 214/979-0103*
- ***Macy's in the Galleria, Dallas****, 972/851-5131*
- ***4701 Frankfort, Dallas****, 972/447-0102*
- ***4030 North MacArthur Boulevard, Irving*** *(Las Colinas), 972/650-9564*
- ***100 Throckmorton, Fort Worth*** *(Outlet Square), 817/878-2424*
- ***2621 North Main Street, Fort Worth*** *(Stockyards), 817/626-7191*
- ***2421 Westport Parkway, Fort Worth****, 817/224-9191*
- ***322 South Park Boulevard, Grapevine****, 817/424-5978*

Dallas Morning News. The setting is elegant and spacious, with white tablecloths and understated Art Deco touches. Rave reviews have praised the exquisitely prepared and served fresh fish and seafood—from succulent rainbow trout to a New England-style shellfish bake. Reports say the restaurant has survived a recent change of chefs with minimum transition. New chef George Grieser comes with superb credentials. A graduate of the New England Culinary Institute, he has cooked in several New York restaurants and is most recently from Jake's American in Austin. The menu may see subtle changes such as the addition of steak, pork, and lamb. The house special "green soup" is still a favorite; described as a Mexican bouillabaisse, it contains lobster tails, shrimp, clams, mussels, scallops, and other fish. Attentive service and stunning presentation complement the fine food. A pianist plays jazz and/or classics nightly. Lunch Mon-Fri, dinner nightly; Sunday brunch. ⅃ (Downtown Dallas)

THE FRENCH ROOM
1321 Commerce Street (in Hotel Adolphus)
Dallas
214/742-8200
$$$

According to some long-time Dallasites, The French Room is simply the most beautiful and most romantic restaurant in Dallas. Adjectives seem inadequate—even those such as opulent, posh, and elegant. With its baroque painted ceiling, layered tablecloths, Versailles-length drapes, and hand-blown crystal chandeliers, the Fairytale room would be quite comfortable for King Louis XV. The service is impeccable and unobtrusive. The cuisine is classic French, creatively adapted to contemporary American taste. The wine list is exceptional. Rated five diamonds by AAA, *Gourmet*, *Zagat*, *Bon Appétit*, *Travel & Leisure*, and *Condé Nast Traveler* all rate this posh dining room the best French restaurant in Dallas. It draws a discerning clientele and reservations are required. Dress accordingly for the atmosphere. Dinner Mon-Sat; closed Sun and major holidays. ⅃ (Downtown Dallas)

THE PYRAMID ROOM
1717 North Akard (Fairmont Hotel)
Dallas
214/720-5249
$$$

This award-winning restaurant offers an eclectic menu featuring French/Continental/New American cuisine—beautifully prepared and presented beef, seafood, poultry, veal, and lamb. Once one of the most elegant restaurants in town, its position has been challenged by several new places. The cosmopolitan ambience, excellent service, and elegant setting combine to ensure a memorable dining experience. Enjoy music on weekends and cocktails or wine from an exceptionally well-stocked bar. Sunday Jazz Brunch combines the entertainment of the Arthur Riddles Jazz Trio and the sumptuous specialties created by Chef Jean La Font. Dressy attire is appropriate. Dinner nightly; Sunday brunch. ⅃ (Downtown Dallas)

TOLBERT'S TEXAS CHILI PARLOR
350 North St. Paul
Dallas
214/953-1353
$

In the One Dallas Centre office building, this is the last remaining Tolbert's Chili Parlor made famous by *Dallas Morning News* columnist Frank X. Tolbert. The original "five-alarm" chili is still on the menu, and it has been joined by several Tex-Mex items. Lunch and early dinner (closes at 7 p.m.) Mon-Fri. (Downtown Dallas)

THE ZODIAC ROOM
1618 Main Street (in Neiman Marcus)
Dallas
214/573-5800
$$

Inside the original Neiman Marcus store, this is the place to see-and-be-seen and have lunch in style. Open since 1953, it still serves some traditional fare such as Helen Corbitt's legendary chicken salad, but the menu has been upscaled periodically through the years and now offers some delicious New American entrée choices as well as substantial salads and sandwiches. The Zodiac Room offers consistently good food and gracious service. If possible, try to go when a lunch-time fashion show is being held. Lunch Mon-Sat. ♿ (Downtown Dallas)

CENTRAL DALLAS

ANZU
4620 McKinney Avenue at Knox
Dallas
214/526-7398
$$-$$$
Chef Larry Doyle creates Pacific Rim and Nouvelle Japanese cuisine in this upscale, yet casual, spot just a few blocks from Highland Park. Intimate booths, separated by translucent screens, are a romantic setting for dinner of sake-marinated broiled black cod, calamari "fries," and spring rolls stuffed with crawfish étouffée. The sushi is excellent, as are traditional dishes of tempura, teriyaki, and stir-fry. The innovative menu keeps getting better and better. The owner, Phina Nakamoto, and her mother made the brightly colored origami birds that flutter across the ceiling. The restaurant is popular with young professionals and the Park Cities crowd. Lunch Mon-Fri, dinner Thu-Sat; closed Sun and major holidays. ♿ (Central Dallas)

AQUAKNOX
3214 Knox Street
Dallas
214/219-2782
$$$
AquaKnox is the second endeavor of Star Canyon chef Stephen Pyles and a different fish altogether. It's cooler, more reserved, and seems

out of place in the jumpin' nightlife area. But the food is outstanding; new chef Jason Gorman has created quite a following with his imaginative style and innovative combinations. Although much of the menu is devoted to seafood, grilled steaks and a few other non-swimming entrées are available. Dinner nightly. ♿ (Central Dallas)

BABY DOE'S MATCHLESS MINE
3305 Harry Hines Boulevard
Dallas
214/871-7310
$$-$$$
This re-creation of an old mine is funky with ambience and good food. Located on a hillside overlooking Interstate 35, the restaurant offers a nice variety of entrées. If possible, go for the Sunday brunch, advertised as featuring more than one hundred items, including eggs Benedict, an oyster bar, and champagne, so save up your appetite. Lunch Mon-Fri, dinner nightly; Sunday brunch. ♿ (Central Dallas)

BARCLAY'S
2917 Fairmont Street at Cedar
Springs
Dallas
214/855-0700
www.barclays4dinner.com
$$$
British-born chef/owner Nick Barclay calls his restaurant "Euro-British." The charming 1930s-era house looks like a transplanted English cottage; inside it's comfortable, chic, and romantic with hardwood floors and crisp table linens. The service is gracious and Nick Barclay is delightful. The offering is all British, and defies all the tales of boring, tasteless pub food. The lamb is always superb. Seasonal desserts

are homemade and excellent. Dinner Tue-Sat. & (Central Dallas)

BISTRO A
6815 Snider Plaza
Dallas
214/373-9911
$$$

Word has it that this latest venture by culinary expert Avner Samuel may be his best yet. The Mediterranean restaurant offers an upscale atmosphere in a relaxed setting that is quite appropriate for a romantic night out. If you're hesitant to try the unfamiliar Mediterranean-Middle Eastern dishes, ordinary American fare is superbly prepared with interesting touches as well. Just save room for the indescribably delicious triple crème brûlée. Lunch and dinner Mon-Sat; closed Sun. & (Central Dallas)

CHEZ GERARD
4444 McKinney Avenue
Dallas
214/522-6865
$$-$$$

This small, romantic, country-French restaurant with a covered patio is similar to one that you'd expect to find in the French countryside. The décor consists of lace curtains and flowery wallpaper. The menu promotes the same ambience with classics such as escargot and onion soup topped with melted cheese. Traditional entrées of seafood, veal, lamb, and beef are elegantly presented, as are nouveau creations such as pheasant and sweetbread mousseline. *Gourmet* magazine praised the restaurant for such dishes as halibut tartare with salmon caviar and sautéed rabbit with spicy green peppercorn mustard. Lunch Mon-Fri, dinner Mon-Sat; closed Sun and major holidays. & (Central Dallas)

CITY CAFÉ
5757 West Lovers Lane
Dallas
214/351-2233
$$-$$$

What started out as a casual neighborhood restaurant has been around for more than a dozen years now, and it's popularity has spread far beyond the local borderlines. High praise has been lavished on the dimly lit bistro, which is furnished with cottage antiques. The handwritten menu changes every two weeks, rotating California-inspired dishes of seafood, veal, beef, pasta, chicken, pork, and lamb. The popular fresh tomato basil soup never leaves the menu (thank goodness). The menu offers simple and sophisticated choices of New American fare, and the wine list offers an extensive selection of all-American wines. Lunch and dinner daily; closed major holidays. & (Central Dallas)

DADDY JACK'S
1916 Lower Greenville Avenue
Dallas
214/826-4910
$$

The attraction of Daddy Jack's is

TRIVIA

What do indigestion, arteriosclerosis, cancer, colds, shingles, and migraine headaches have in common? They've all been treated with capsaicin, the chemical that makes chiles hot.

GREATER DALLAS

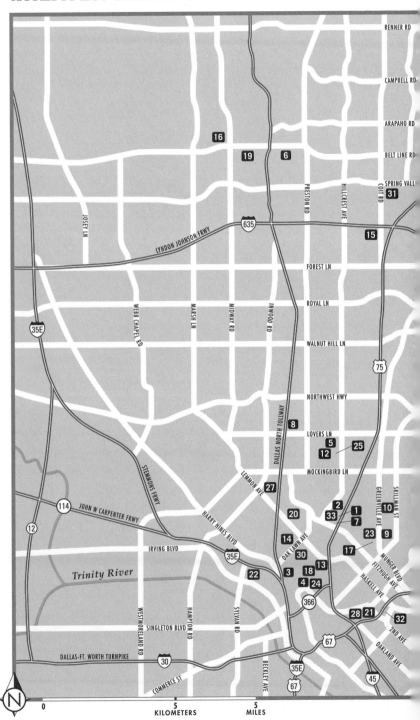

RENNER RD

CAMPBELL RD

ARAPAHO RD

BELT LINE RD

SPRING VALL

16

19   6

PRESTON RD

HILLCREST AVE

COIT RD

31

635

LYNDON JOHNSON FRWY

15

FOREST LN

JOSEY LN

35E

WEBB CHAPEL RD

MARSH LN

MIDWAY RD

INWOOD RD

ROYAL LN

WALNUT HILL LN

75

NORTHWEST HWY

DALLAS NORTH TOLLWAY

8

LOVERS LN

5

12   25

MOCKINGBIRD LN

STEMMONS FRWY

LEMMON AVE

27

114

JOHN W CARPENTER FRWY

HARRY HINES BLVD

20

OAK LAWN AVE

GREENVILLE AVE

SKILLMAN ST

2   1   10

33   7

12

IRVING BLVD

14

23   9

35E

30

17

MUNGER BLVD

Trinity River

22

3   18   13

FITZHUGH AVE

HASKELL AVE

4   24

366

WESTMORELAND RD

HAMPTON RD

SYLVAN RD

28   21

32

2ND AVE

SINGLETON BLVD

67

OAKLAND AVE

DALLAS-FT. WORTH TURNPIKE

30

BECKLEY AVE

35E

67

45

COMMERCE ST

N

0   5   5
     KILOMETERS   MILES

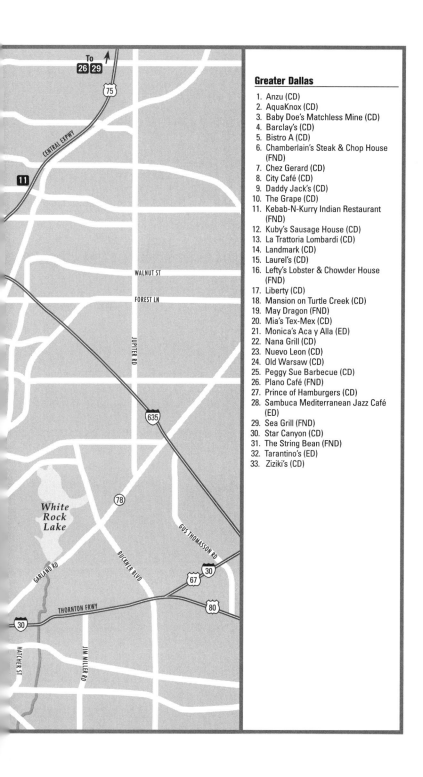

Greater Dallas

1. Anzu (CD)
2. AquaKnox (CD)
3. Baby Doe's Matchless Mine (CD)
4. Barclay's (CD)
5. Bistro A (CD)
6. Chamberlain's Steak & Chop House (FND)
7. Chez Gerard (CD)
8. City Café (CD)
9. Daddy Jack's (CD)
10. The Grape (CD)
11. Kebab-N-Kurry Indian Restaurant (FND)
12. Kuby's Sausage House (CD)
13. La Trattoria Lombardi (CD)
14. Landmark (CD)
15. Laurel's (CD)
16. Lefty's Lobster & Chowder House (FND)
17. Liberty (CD)
18. Mansion on Turtle Creek (CD)
19. May Dragon (FND)
20. Mia's Tex-Mex (CD)
21. Monica's Aca y Alla (ED)
22. Nana Grill (CD)
23. Nuevo Leon (CD)
24. Old Warsaw (CD)
25. Peggy Sue Barbecue (CD)
26. Plano Café (FND)
27. Prince of Hamburgers (CD)
28. Sambuca Mediterranean Jazz Café (ED)
29. Sea Grill (FND)
30. Star Canyon (CD)
31. The String Bean (FND)
32. Tarantino's (ED)
33. Ziziki's (CD)

great seafood and affordable prices. The casual eatery has red-and-white-checkered tablecloths and a simple menu, including steamed clams, crab cakes, shrimp scampi, salmon, soft-shell crab, Maine lobster, and Alaskan king crab. All dishes are fresh and well prepared. Dinner nightly. & (Central Dallas)

THE GRAPE
2808 Greenville Avenue
Dallas
214/828-1981
$$$
Founded in 1972 when wine bars were an unknown concept in Dallas, The Grape is still the best one around. It has a large following among the city's intellectual crowd and yuppies. Go to the intimate, dark bistro for the romance, but stay for the food. The dishes on the daily blackboard menu always seem to be innovative and well prepared, and accompanying wines are suggested. A long-time favorite is the acclaimed mushroom soup, although the new cilantro-avocado soup is becoming quite popular. Lunch Mon-Fri, dinner nightly. & (Central Dallas)

KUBY'S SAUSAGE HOUSE
6601 Snider Plaza
Dallas
214/363-2231
$
This unpretentious family-owned business has been serving home-made sausages and authentic German cuisine since 1961. Waitresses are dressed in German costume and serve hearty portions of wurst, schnitzels, and sausages, with German potato salad, kraut, and breads. The Kuby family has been in the meat business in Germany since

1728, and the recipes have been handed down for 14 generations. Live oom-pah music is usually featured on Fridays and Saturdays. Breakfast, lunch, and dinner Mon-Sat; lunch Sun. (Central Dallas)

LA TRATTORIA LOMBARDI
2915 North Hall Street at
McKinney Avenue
Dallas
214/954-0803
$$-$$$
Luciano Cola was serving heavenly traditional Italian food in this quiet, dark restaurant long before McKinney Avenue/Uptown became the trendy, hip hangout for yuppies. All the dishes are well prepared with the freshest ingredients, from the crusty focaccia flatbread to the exquisitely light tiramisú. Several entrées are in the to-die-for category; the linguine del pescatore is packed with shrimp, scallops, and mussels in a garlic and herb sauce. Although variations of traditional Italian dishes, they are superbly prepared with an innovative, creative twist. A delightful bonus is the professionalism of the well-trained, old-style staff. Lunch Mon-Fri, dinner nightly. & (Central Dallas)

LANDMARK
3015 Oak Lawn Avenue (in
Melrose Hotel)
Dallas
214/521-5151
$$$
Located in the heart of the artsy Oak Lawn district, this attractive, bright, and airy dining room is decorated with mirrors and marble. The Landmark's eclectic (and expensive) menu features an innovative and creative blending of American cuisine with Southwestern and

Riscky's World

The Riscky family has a long history in Cowtown. Joe Riscky was a Polish immigrant when he started a lone barbecue place in 1927. Joe's son Pete took over the business in 1952, and today Pete's son Jim runs the company, which has grown to include nine restaurants. The original location on Azle Avenue has giant smokepits and rotis- series where the meat for all the restaurants is smoked, around the clock. The secret homemade "Riscky Dust" is hand-rubbed on all the meat before it's cooked.

Riscky's Bar-B-Q (www.risckys.com) locations throughout the Metroplex include:

- ***300 Main Street, Sundance Square*** *(Downtown Fort Worth), 817/877-3306*
- ***2314 Azle Avenue*** *(North Fort Worth), 817/624-8662*
- ***140 East Exchange Avenue, Stockyards Historic District*** *(North Fort Worth), 817/626-7777*
- ***9000 U.S. 377, Benbrook*** *(Southwest Fort Worth), 817/249-3320*
- ***8100 Grapevine Highway, North Richland Hills*** *(Mid-Cities), 817/581-7696*

Folks jokingly call the Stockyards Historic District "Riscky's World" because the Riscky family has acquired a stronghold with the following restaurants:

- ***Riscky's Bar-B-Q***, *140 East Exchange Avenue, 817/626-7777*
- ***Riscky Rita's*** *(Mexican), 140 East Exchange Avenue, 817/ 626-8700*
- ***Riscky's Catch*** *(seafood), 140 East Exchange Avenue, 817/ 625-1070*
- ***Riscky's Steakhouse***, *120 East Exchange Avenue, 817/624- 4800*
- ***Buckaroo's Soda Shoppe***, *140 East Exchange Avenue, 817/ 624-6631*

Cajun influences. Specialties include superb seafood dishes such as pasta-crusted salmon, sizzling shrimp, and Louisiana crab cakes. Beef, lamb, and fowl offerings are also delicious and well prepared. The Sunday brunch is especially popular. The inviting, wood-paneled Library Bar, stuffed with books and comfortable armchairs, adjoins. Breakfast daily, lunch Mon-Fri, dinner Mon-Sat, Sun brunch. ♿ (Central Dallas)

LAUREL'S
12720 Merit Drive (in Westin Park Central Hotel)
Dallas
214/851-2021
$$$

From the 20th floor of the Westin Park Central Hotel, the view of Downtown Dallas through the floor-to-ceiling windows is dazzling. But the star of this restaurant is executive chef Danielle Custer and her brilliant cutting-edge cuisine, creativity, and enthusiasm. She blends North and South American recipes using beef, seafood, lamb, veal, and game into palate-pleasing fare extraordinaire. Laurel's signature soufflés remain a perfect ending to a perfect meal. A health-conscious menu lists calories and fat grams. The setting is elegant and the service is impeccable. A pianist or harpist entertains nightly. Dinner Mon-Sat; closed Sun. ♿ (Far North Dallas)

LIBERTY
5631 Alta Avenue at Greenville
Dallas
214/887-8795
$-$$

A lot has happened since Annie Wong left her world behind in 1986 and sailed alone for a new world.

She has made Thai food an art form at her three widely successful restaurants in Dallas, but Liberty is her new stage. She performs with creativity and imagination, creating such dishes as spicy coconut shrimp soup and crispy spring rolls. Liberty is a softly lit stage with twinkling Christmas lights and a friendly atmosphere. Lunch Tue-Sat, dinner Tue-Sun; closed Mon. ♿ (Central Dallas)

THE MANSION ON TURTLE CREEK
2821 Turtle Creek Boulevard
Dallas
214/559-2100
www.mansiononturtlecreek.com
$$$

This restaurant is the only one in Texas to consistently earn a rating of five diamonds from AAA and five stars from Mobil. Living up to its legend, the Grand Dame of Dallas Dining continues to provide a most glamorous dining experience for body, mind, and soul. It's located in the posh, five-diamond hotel of the same name, which is a converted 1920s-era cattle baron's Italian Renaissance style mansion. The rooms create a warm ambience because they occupy what was originally the home's living room with a fireplace at each end, and the library with its original oak paneling. Additional seating is situated on the glass-walled veranda with a view of the landscaped courtyard. Long-time, award-winning executive chef Dean Fearing creates Southwestern cuisine with a Texas flair. The menu is varied and imaginative, using fresh seasonal ingredients. Offerings might include creative dishes featuring ostrich, elk, or antelope. Everything is superbly prepared and presented and very expensive. Live musical entertainment adds to the ambience. Jackets are required for dinner and Sunday brunch. Lunch and dinner nightly; Sun brunch. ☕ (Central Dallas)

MIA'S TEX-MEX
4322 Lemmon Avenue
Dallas
214/526-1020
$$

Mia's is a small, family-owned neighborhood restaurant that has elevated Tex-Mex to new heights. It's an extremely popular place that serves gigantic portions of high-quality food and the best chiles rellenos in town. Expect long lines at peak hours. The service is typically Texas-friendly, and a children's menu is offered. Rumor has it that this place is where the Dallas Cowboys fatten up. Lunch and dinner Mon-Sat; closed Sun. ☕ (Central Dallas)

NANA GRILL
2201 Stemmons Freeway (in Wyndham Anatole Hotel)
Dallas
214/761-7479
$$-$$$

The opulent dining room located on the 27th floor of the Wyndham Anatole has a magnificent view of Downtown. But the view isn't the only attraction of Nana's; fine cuisine is served in this casually elegant setting. The menu changes daily, depending on what chef Doug Brown finds fresh and appealing. He describes the cuisine as "Progressive American." The selection is mindboggling and all sounds exquisite. If you can't decide, yield to temptation and try the seven-course chef's tasting menu ($65) and spend the evening in dining ecstasy. The extensive, decadent Sunday brunch buffet offers more than 75 items, including champagne. Nana's features live jazz Wednesday through Saturday. Lunch Mon-Fri, dinner Mon-Sat; Sun brunch. ☕ (Central Dallas)

NUEVO LEON
2013 Greenville Avenue
Dallas

Mexican Inn

One of the original restaurants on Fort Worth's Tex-Mex scene makes signature small, puffy, homemade chips to serve with its tasty salsa. But be careful not to fill up on baskets of those delicious, habit-forming chips before your platter of food comes. Now at several locations around Fort Worth:

- *516 Commerce Street (Downtown), 817/332-2772*
- *1625 Eighth Avenue, 817/927-8541*
- *612 North Henderson, 817/336-2164*
- *2700 East Lancaster, 817/534-2512*

214/887-8148
$-$$

Serving a wide range of authentic Mexican fare from the Monterrey and Guanajuato regions, the three Nuevo Leon restaurants have already developed a reputation for excellent food and good service. For the brave, they offer such dishes as *cabrito al horno* (goat wrapped in banana leaves), but tasty enchiladas and more recognizable fare are also on the menu. The rich, chocolatey mole sauce is exceptional. This is a superb choice for affordable, classy Mexican food. The other locations are at 3211 Oak Lawn at Cedar Springs Road in Dallas (214/522-3331), and the original at 12895 Josey Lane in Farmers Branch. Lunch and dinner daily. ⅙ (Central Dallas)

OLD WARSAW
2610 Maple Avenue
Dallas
214/528-0032
www.gtesupersite.com/
warsawmanor
$$$

The "Old" in the name Old Warsaw signifies it as one of the oldest Continental restaurants in Dallas (since 1948) and describes the old-world elegance and classic service. The dark, rich décor makes a romantic setting for strolling violinists and waiters preparing Caesar salad at your table. Despite the name, the cuisine is French/Continental, and the menu features traditional fare such as Chateaubriand, pheasant, and rack of lamb. Seafood is fresh and prepared to perfection. The crepes are delectable and the soufflés are awesome. An excellent wine list is available and a fitting accompaniment to the old-style, high-end, classic dining experience.

Dress up and don't be in a hurry. Dinner nightly. ⅙ (Central Dallas)

PEGGY SUE BARBECUE
6600 Snider Plaza
Dallas
214/987-9188
$

Smoked chicken quesadillas and brisket fajitas at a barbecue joint? Yup. And they're fabulous! But Peggy Sue's made its name with outstanding ribs and brisket, and that's still why crowds flock to the place. The side dishes and sauces are also scrumptious. In Snider Plaza near Southern Methodist University, it's packed at lunchtime. Lunch and dinner daily. ⅙ (Central Dallas)

PRINCE OF HAMBURGERS
5200 Lemmon Avenue
Dallas
214/526-9081
$

A locally famous, pre-McDonald's drive-in (with curb service no less), Prince of Hamburgers has been serving tasty burgers on toasty buns, fabulous fries and onion rings, thick shakes, and frosty root beer since 1927. Park under the orange-and-white awning and enjoy a superb chili-bacon cheeseburger and homemade root beer. Lunch and dinner daily. (Central Dallas)

STAR CANYON
3102 Oak Lawn
Dallas
214/520-STAR
$$$

Acclaimed celebrity chef/owner Stephen Pyles has created a destination and carved out a new niche with his imaginative New Texas Cuisine. Star Canyon has won every award and accolades from every reviewer imaginable in all categories: food, service, and atmosphere. According to *D Magazine,* the signature "bone-in cowboy ribeye on a bed of pinto beans, covered with a mound of shoestring onion rings dusted with red chili should be listed in *Fodor's* under Dallas's top attraction." Pyles creates his dishes from several regional cultures of Texas: Mexican, South American, Southern, and Creole. One example is grilled coriander-cured venison with sweet potato-creamed corn tostada and chipotle barbecue. The vegetarian platter features wild mushrooms, wood-roasted corn, green olive llapingachos, maple-glazed sweet potato, and ratatouille tamale. If possible, save room for Star Canyon's Heaven and Hell™ cake. The 7,000-square-foot restaurant's décor is all Texan, blending natural Texas colors and artistic cowboy murals. Reservations are still hard to come by because they are booked up several months ahead for weekends. Lunch Mon-Fri, dinner nightly. & (Central Dallas)

ZIZIKI'S
4512 Travis Street
Dallas
214/521-2233
$$
This contemporary Greek café on the edge of Highland Park is usually packed, but the wait is worth it. The Greek/Mediterranean menu offers a great choice of lamb entrées such as grilled rack of lamb, sliced leg of lamb, herbed lamb souvlaki, and moussaka. The lighter lunch menu focuses on gyros, pasta, and sandwiches. The Greek salad is especially wonderful. Traditional Greek dishes are fabulous, usually with a surprise, gourmet touch. For example, the *hummus* (a mixture of chickpeas, garlic, and olive oil) contains bits of artichoke as a tasty addition. In addition to lamb, several chicken dishes, grilled shrimp souvlaki, and filet mignon are all well prepared and attractively served. Save room for the Baklava ice cream cake. Service is attentive and helpful. A new location opened in December 1999 in the Spanish Village shopping center on the northwest corner of Coit and Arapaho (15707 Coit Road, Suite A, 972/991-4433). Lunch and dinner Mon-Sat; Sun brunch. & (Central Dallas)

EAST DALLAS

MONICA'S ACA Y ALLA
2914 Main Street (Deep Ellum)
Dallas
214/748-7140
$$
Mexico meets nouvelle-chic in the heart of Deep Ellum, with a touch of Italian, French, and Asian thrown in. Specialties such as lime-drenched ceviche, spinach-jalapeño fetticine with grilled marinated chicken, and pumpkin-stuffed chile ravioli are excellent. The popular Sunday brunch offers eggs Benedict, migas, huevos rancheros, and traditional brunch choices. Monica's margaritas are awesome! Lunch Tue-Fri, dinner Tue-Sun, brunch Sat-Sun. & (East Dallas)

SAMBUCA MEDITERRANEAN JAZZ CAFÉ
2618 Elm Street (Deep Ellum)
Dallas
214/744-0820
$$
Sambuca has been one of the most popular jazz clubs in the city since

Top Ten Romantic Places to Dine in Dallas

by Ginnie Siena Bivona, food columnist and author of *Dirty Dining*

1. **The French Room,** 1321 Commerce Street (in the Adolphus Hotel), 214/742-8200; The most elegant and beautifully romantic place in all of Dallas. Fabulous cuisine, candlelit old-world atmosphere with incredible food. Lovers will fall in love all over again.

2. **The Mansion on Turtle Creek,** 2821 Turtle Creek Boulevard, 214/559-2100, www.mansiononturtlecreek.com; This restaurant in a B&B is the top glamour spot in Dallas. See and be seen in love or not. Internationally famous chef Dean Fearing dazzles diners night after night. Service is perfection; everyone is a Duke and Duchess here. For the ultimate in romance, plan a private rendezvous in the wine cellar.

3. **St. Martins,** 3020 Greenville Avenue, 214/826-0940; This place is a long-time fave of the young and the beautiful. Champagne Brie soup to get "nekkid" and swim in is a must for romantics.

4. **The Grape,** 2808 Greenville Avenue, 214/828-7666; This establishment has been around forever. It's dark and romantic, and the blackboard menu is delightful. Everybody in love should dine here at least once.

it opened in 1991 (see Chapter 12, Nightlife). The jazz may be a major attraction, but the food is also superb. One of the reasons is executive chef Pete Nolasco, a young, energetic guy with myriad talents-including being an ice sculpture artist. He creates an innovative menu enhanced with fresh ingredients and delicious sauces. The offerings are numerous and well prepared, including pasta dishes, chicken, beef, and seafood. The Aegean Pasta Salad makes a great lunch. The music menu features local traditional and contemporary jazz every night. A second location at 15207 Addison Road in Addison (972/385-8455) is larger and has the same menu and live jazz nightly. Lunch Mon-Fri, dinner nightly. &. (East Dallas)

TARANTINO'S
3611 Parry Avenue (Deep Ellum/Fair Park)
Dallas
214/821-2224
$$
Directly across from the State Fair Music Hall, this dim, intimate café has a menu with Italian and Spanish cuisine featuring dishes of lamb, seafood, pasta, and salads in small portions to be eaten in family-style spirit. A nice wine list is available.

TOP
TOP
TOP
TOP
TOP
TOP
TOP
TOP
TOP
TOP
TOP
TOP

5. **Javier's Gourmet Mexicano,** 4912 Cole Avenue, 214/941-4304; Fabulous Mexico City-style food is served in a sophisticated atmosphere that is good for hand-holding across the table.

6. **Barclay's,** 2917 Fairmount Street, 214/855-0700; *D Magazine* says this restaurant is one of the best places to pop the question. (You know which one!) It is a beautiful place with fabulous food.

7. **Rugerri's Ristorante,** 2911 Routh Street, 214/871-7377; Romantic piano music to woo by accompanies your meal here. The atmosphere is dark and elegant, and excellent service and a great menu of classic Italian favorites round out the experience.

8. **Toscana,** 4900 McKinney Avenue, 214/521-2244; What could be more romantic than a divine Italian meal, a glass (or two) of wine, and thee? All of the above at Toscana.

9. **Jennivine,** 3605 McKinney Avenue, 214/528-6010; This charming English-style restaurant is dimly-lit and cozy. Interesting art shows from time to time, and wonderful food is always freshly prepared.

10. **Sambuca,** 1520 Addison Road, 972/385-8455; This lively spot for lovers offers great jazz and great food to put you in a happy mood. Chef Pete Nolasco's creative eclectic menu always delights.

Dinner Mon-Sat; closed Sun. &
(East Dallas)

FAR NORTH DALLAS

**CHAMBERLAIN'S STEAK
& CHOP HOUSE
5330 Belt Line Road
Addison
972/934-2467
$$-$$$
www.Chamberlains.com**
Namesake chef/owner Richard Chamberlain's passion for cooking has led him from positions as executive sous chef at the acclaimed Mansion on Turtle Creek in Dallas and the world-famous Hotel Bel-Air in Los Angeles to executive chef at San Simeon Restaurant, and now to prestigious awards of his own. Chamberlain's has received rave reviews from *Zagat, Gourmet* magazine, and many others. He serves outstanding steaks, prime rib, lamb, and a mixed grill that includes game. The menu has several steak options, but the pork, veal, chicken, and seafood entrées are also skillfully prepared by the innovative chef. The décor of warm woods provides the ambience of a classic chop house. A recent addition is the Havana Cigar Room, a perfect spot to relax before or after dinner.

Cocktails and wine are available. Dinner nightly. & (Far North Dallas)

KEBAB-N-KURRY INDIAN RESTAURANT
401 North Central Expressway, #300
Richardson
972/231-5556
$

They use clay-oven cooking to enhance the low-fat element of the North Indian cuisine. The popular tandoori entrées on the menu include chicken, lamb, and shrimp, or sample all three in the tandoori mixed grill. Other entrées feature a variety of authentic Indian techniques for cooking chicken, beef, lamb, seafood, and vegetarian dishes. Lunch and dinner daily. & (Far North Dallas)

LEFTY'S LOBSTER & CHOWDER HOUSE
4021 Belt Line, #101
Addison
972/774-9518
$-$$

The menu is small, but you can get lobster whole, stuffed, baked, boiled, or broiled. Boston clam chowder, lobster bisque, and steamed clams are on the appetizer menu. Specialties include Cajun dishes and the fish of the day, which is prepared sautéed or stuffed. Dinner nightly. & (Far North Dallas)

MAY DRAGON
4848 Belt Line
Addison
972/392-9998
$$

This upscale Chinese restaurant is consistently named one of the best in the Metroplex. The extensive menu offers Chinese, Cantonese,

Hunan, Mandarin, and Szechuan-style entrées and Pacific Rim cuisine from Indonesia, Malaysia, and Polynesia, all presented in a tradition of fine dining. Specialties include dishes such as Peking duck, sesame chicken, and orange beef. A pianist entertains on Friday and Saturday evenings. Lunch and dinner daily. & (Far North Dallas)

PLANO CAFÉ
1915 North Central Expressway, Suite 500
Plano
972/516-0865
$$

It may be touted as a European-style bistro, but the menu offers a lot of American favorites like ribeye steaks. Everything is grilled or sautéed, not fried. Delectable vegetables accompany each dinner, and tasty vegetarian entrées are available. A children's menu and a yummy dessert list are also offered. Lunch Mon-Sat, dinner daily. & (Far North Dallas)

SEA GRILL
2205 North Central Expressway, Suite 180
Plano
972/509-5542
$$-$$$

The chef/owner here prepares the fresh seafood New York style, medium-rare so as not to overcook it and spoil the natural flavor. He also prepares it with a flair to produce entrées such as lobster and shrimp rigatoni with vodka cream sauce, grilled jumbo sea scallops with teriyaki-lime butter glaze, and seared lemon-pepper salmon with braised leeks and whole-grain mustard-dill sauce. Overall, the menu features seafood dishes that

"Chili" is the correct spelling for the combination of meat, peppers, and spices. "Chile" means pepper (the vegetable, not the spice) and usually a hot pepper to boot. Chile con carne originally meant peppers stewed with meat, although it is now widely considered the same thing as chili.

range from New American to French to Asian cuisine. Beef and chicken entrées are included on the menu, too, but just barely. A full bar is available. Lunch Mon-Fri, dinner nightly. ♿ (Far North Dallas)

THE STRING BEAN
7879 West Spring Valley Road
Dallas
972/385-EATS
www.thestringbean.com
$-$$
A local favorite began in 1977 with a menu shaped like a string bean, offering a modest choice of four entrées and four vegetables and homemade pies, ice cream, and cobbler. Regular customers requested additional selections, and the tiny restaurant thrived. Now catering to a larger crowd at Spring Valley Road and Coit, it still features "grandma's" recipes, plus a large variety of others offering quality food at reasonable prices. Lunch, dinner daily; Sun brunch. ♿ (Far North Dallas)

MID-CITIES

BAYLEY'S
109 Harwood Road
Hurst
817/268-5779
$
It may be located in a generic shop-ping mall in a residential area, but it seems as if everyone in the area is at Bayley's for breakfast. Treats include scrumptious pancakes, muffins, croissants, and cinnamon rolls, as well as superb omelets and frittatas served with brunch potatoes or fresh fruit. Diners also flock here at lunchtime to enjoy excellent salads and sandwiches. Go early or late on Sunday to avoid the church crowd. Breakfast and lunch daily. ♿ (Mid-Cities)

CAFÉ ON THE GREEN
4150 North MacArthur Boulevard
(in the Four Seasons Resort)
Irving
972/717-0700
$$-$$$
Innovative New American cuisine with an emphasis on lighter, healthier fare is the specialty at this pleasant restaurant. The floor-to-ceiling windows give diners a restful view of the pool and landscaped grounds of the Four Seasons Resort. Order from the menu or partake of the buffet, which is available for all meals. The dinner buffet offers a wide selection of items from appetizers to desserts. The Sunday brunch buffet features a lavish selection of appetizers, salad offerings, cold seafood, carved meats, vegetables, a pasta station, and a dessert station. Breakfast, lunch, and dinner daily. ♿ (Mid-Cities)

COOL RIVER
1045 Hidden Ridge
Irving
972/871-8881
$$-$$$
This upscale steakhouse and south-western grill reflects the creativity of executive chef Robert Stephenson. He elevates "southern cooking" to an art form with such dishes as pork chops stuffed with cheese, ham, and mushrooms; encrusted trout with salsa fresca; and pepper-cheese cornbread. Located in a residential neighborhood, the huge restaurant (23,000 square feet) was designed with a river running through it for ambience. The dining area is deco-rated with dark, rich woods and river rock, and the bar/game room resembles an English pub and con-tains a trendy new Cigar and Co-gnac Room. Lunch Mon-Fri, dinner daily; Sun brunch. The bar keeps later hours. & (Mid-Cities)

DORRIS HOUSE CAFÉ
224 East College Street
Grapevine
817/421-1181
$$
Located in a restored house, the site of Dorris House Café is considered one of the finest examples of Queen Anne architecture remaining in Grapevine. Built in 1896, it features a hand-carved staircase and six fire-places. In this lovely setting, enjoy one of the house specialties, a prix fixe three-course dinner, or selec-tions of steak, chicken, or fresh seafood. Save room for the home-made strawberry cheesecake ice cream. Lunch Tue-Fri, dinner Tue-Sat; closed Sun-Mon. & (Mid-Cities)

LA BISTRO
722 Grapevine Hwy.

Hurst
817/281-9333
$$-$$$
Don't let the modest location in a strip shopping center fool you. This place is classy, with crisp white tablecloths and an excellent wine selection. Efficient, attentive service combines with superbly prepared pastas, veal, chicken, and seafood dishes. Lunch Sun-Fri, dinner daily. & (Mid-Cities)

MAYURI
397 East Las Colinas Boulevard,
Suite 180
Irving
972/910-8788
$-$$
If you're not familiar with Indian food, then this is a good place to try it. A large lunch buffet offers sev-eral different North and South In-dian specialties for $6.95. Entrees include exotic-sounding items that are served with numerous side dishes—a soup, bread, vegetables, potato, and dessert. Beer and wine are available. Lunch and dinner daily. & (Mid-Cities)

MIGUELITO'S
209 Bedford Euless Road
Hurst
817/268-0404
$
It just keeps growing and growing. This family-owned restaurant has expanded three times since it opened in 1997. Why? It's the food, folks! Standing-room-only crowds wait patiently on weekends for the *carne asada*—tender grilled steak covered with cheese—with or without ranchera sauce. Or they crave the fajitas, the six delicious shrimp specialties, or the traditional enchiladas, chimichangas, and

tacos. Lunch and dinner daily. ♿ (Mid-Cities)

MIKE'S FAMOUS HAMBURGERS
2816 Brown Trail
Bedford
817/285-8646
$

Honest-to-goodness, old-fashioned hamburgers draw huge lunchtime crowds to this neighborhood favorite. Look for the former Taco Bell building painted black and white just south of the intersection of Harwood and Brown Trail in Bedford. Mike is usually in the kitchen cooking up the burgers, which are juicy enough to rate two thick napkins. His wife takes orders and answers the phone. The decadent chili-cheese fries are a popular favorite with the kids from L.D. Bell High School just down the street. Lunch and dinner (until 7 p.m.) Mon-Sat; closed Sun. ♿ (Mid-Cities)

NORTH MAIN BBQ
406 North Main Street
Euless
817/267-9101
$

Long lines are commonplace at this popular barbecue joint, which is open only on weekends. Nobody would ever suspect that world-famous, internationally recognized barbecue is hiding next to a trucking garage in the small but friendly town of Euless. What started out as some folks inviting their friends and neighbors for barbecue and tall cold ones just kind of turned into a barbecue restaurant. It's still owned by the same family, and you're "one of 'em" when you walk in the door. Pay your $10 (cash only) and eat all you want; the menu is brisket, ribs, sausage, pork, chicken, beans, potato salad,

coleslaw, bread, relishes, and tea. Lunch Fri-Sun, dinner Fri-Sat; closed Mon-Thu. ♿ (Mid-Cities)

RAINFOREST CAFÉ®
Grapevine Mills Mall
3000 Grapevine Mills Parkway
Grapevine
972/539-5001
$-$$

Dining here is an adventure with a meal on the side. It's a Disneylike encounter with talking trees, animatronic animals and birds, recorded jungle noises amid cascading waterfalls, and giant saltwater aquariums. Dine in a simulated rainforest under a star-filled night sky created by a fiber optic "starscape." Watch (or talk to) live tropical parrots, with trainers on hand to answer questions. A spacious gift shop offers a wild array of unusual gifts and souvenirs. Oh yes, the food is actually quite good, too. The menu offers international dishes of Mexican, Italian, American, and Cajun fare and an amazing selection of exotic drinks. Open for lunch and dinner daily. ♿ (Mid-Cities)

RAVEN'S GRILLE
1400 Texas Star Parkway
Euless
817/685-1843
www.texasstargolf.com
$-$$

Okay, so most people don't go to golf courses to eat. Well, Raven's Grille is worth a trip if you don't know a seven-iron from a basketball. The grille is located at the championship Texas Star Golf Course; the pro shop is at the end of the building. The décor is Texan, the ambience is relaxing and informal, and the food is outstanding. Try Texas-shaped waffles for breakfast before hitting the

Basic Tex-Mex Definitions

Al carbon: *charcoal grilled*
Burrito: *rice, beans, and/or meat rolled in a flour tortilla*
Cabrito: *kid goat, usually grilled on a spit*
Camarones: *shrimp*
Carne: *meat*
Chalupa: *flat, deep-fried corn tortilla with anything piled on top*
Chile: *peppers, from mild to fire-out-the-ears*
Chili: *stew-like concoction of meat, herbs, and spices*
Chorizo: *spicy pork sausage*
Enchilada: *rolled soft corn tortilla filled with cheese or meat and covered with sauce*
Fajitas: *marinated, grilled strips of meat served with flour tortillas and a variety of accompaniments*
Guacamole: *mashed avocados, usually with tomatoes, garlic, and onions*
Guisada: *stew*
Huevos: *eggs*
Jalapeño: *a HOT, green chile*
Picante: *spicy*
Pollo: *chicken*
Queso: *cheese*
Taco: *a corn tortilla, deep-fried, folded, and stuffed with meat and almost anything else*
Tamale: *meat stuffed corn dough steamed in the husk*
Tortilla: *round flat bread made of corn or flour*

links. Monster burgers and sandwiches are good for lunch fare. If you go for dinner, look for the special on the blackboard as you enter; it will probably be good. A popular favorite, the catfish filets are coated with Japanese breadcrumbs and lightly fried, resulting in a crispy, crunchy crust and moist, flaky inside. The hand-breaded chicken-fried steak, served with homemade cream gravy, overlaps the plate! Breakfast, lunch, and dinner daily. &c (Mid-Cities)

RAVIOLI RISTORANTE
120 East Worth
Grapevine
817/488-1181
$$-$$$

Ravioli's extensive menu includes a varied selection of pasta entrées as well as chicken, veal, and seafood. Most dishes are Northern Italian, with more cream sauces than tomato sauces. If you choose only pasta, you have a choice of six types of pasta and six sauces for around $10. More innovative entrées include chicken and veal dishes prepared with sherry cream sauces, wines, and sautéed mushrooms. & (Mid-Cities)

VERANDA GREEK CAFÉ
5433 MacArthur Boulevard
Irving
972/550-0055
$$

This is a great place to try something you've never eaten and can't pronounce. It's a buffet! Choose from numerous well-prepared Greek and Middle Eastern dishes and vegetarian selections, including perfect hummus, outstanding gyros, and crispy Greek salad. All the food is fresh and appealing. The service is excellent. Lunch Mon-Fri, dinner Mon-Sat; closed Sun. & (Mid-Cities)

VIA REAL
4020 North MacArthur Boulevard, #122
Irving
972/650-9001
$$-$$$

Touting Mexican Cuisine with Santa Fe style, this upscale restaurant offers some imaginative entrées with a Southwestern flair. Grilled seafood, beef, and chicken dishes are well prepared and attractively served. The daily specials are a mouthful, such as seafood tamale grilled salmon, scallops, shrimp, and crab claw on top of *poblano*—tortilla rice and tequila rancho sauce roasted asparagus. Whew! Most daily specials are approximately $22. It's a Mexican restaurant, so all the favorite Tex-Mex dishes are here, too, prepared with a touch of class. Lunch and dinner daily; Sun brunch. & (Mid-Cities)

WILHOITE'S
432 South Main Street
Grapevine
817/481-2511
$-$$

In a building dating from 1914, this restaurant pays tribute to its former life as a gas station with an early vintage Model T Ford hanging over the "Texas buffet." The buffet features not only a humongous salad bar but also meats, vegetables, and a dessert bar, and it draws a major crowd at lunchtime. In the evenings, the focus shifts (see Chapter 12, Nightlife). Lunch and dinner Mon-Sat, Sun brunch. & (Mid-Cities)

ARLINGTON/ GRAND PRAIRIE

AL'S HAMBURGERS
1001 N.E. Green Oaks Boulevard
Arlington
817/275-8918
$

The atmosphere isn't like the original 1957-vintage drive-in, but Al has kept the griddle going, and the burgers still bring back memories. The place is usually packed, attesting to the lure of a great double cheeseburger and fries. Lunch and dinner Mon-Sat; closed Sun. & (Arlington/Grand Prairie)

ARLINGTON STEAK HOUSE
1724 West Division
Arlington
817/275-7881
$-$$
A fixture in Arlington since 1931, this unpretentious restaurant specializes in home-cooking and chicken-fried steak. Imagine that. But it also serves steak, chicken, barbecue, seafood, and a kid's menu. The homemade hot yeast rolls are melt-in-your-mouth good. Lunch and dinner daily. (Arlington/Grand Prairie)

CACHAREL
2221 East Lamar
Arlington
817/640-9981 (metro)
$$$
Consistently rated one of the best restaurants in the Metroplex, this Country French restaurant offers elegant penthouse dining. The selections on the innovative Country-French/American menu change daily; the salads are superb. For dinner, you may order à la carte or have a prix fixe three-course meal. Save room for a sumptuous dessert. Wine and cocktails are available. Lunch Mon-Fri, dinner Mon-Sat; closed Sun. & (Arlington/Grand Prairie)

CATFISH SAM'S
2735 West Division
Arlington
817/275-9631
$
Always crowded on weekends, this place has been around a long time and has changed little over the years. The service is still friendly and

the catfish is still plentiful. Dinners come with beans, coleslaw, hush puppies, and yummy green tomato pickles. Other items are on the menu, too, but this is the place for catfish. It was voted "Best Catfish" three years in a row by the Texas Restaurant Association. Lunch Mon-Fri, dinner Mon-Sat; closed Sun. & (Arlington/Grand Prairie)

MARQUEZ BAKERY
1730 East Division
Arlington
817/265-8858
$
This is not a trendy, loud restaurant with fancy, upscale menu items with funny names. It's an old-fashioned Mom 'n' Pop place with family recipes for comfort food served in plentiful portions. Lunch and dinner (until 8 p.m.) daily. & (Arlington/Grand Prairie)

MARSALA RESTAURANT
1618 Highway 360
North at Avenue K
Grand Prairie
972/988-1101 (metro)
$$-$$$
Conveniently located in the heart of Arlington's hotel district, Marsala offers quiet, elegant dining. The French and Italian menu features well-prepared fresh seafood, veal, beef, poultry, and wild game, in addition to excellent pasta dishes. Meals are elegantly served on china on tables set with crystal and white linen tablecloths. Master chefs prepare tableside dishes and flaming desserts. Choose from an extensive wine list, and enjoy the music of a classical guitarist Wednesday through Saturday evenings. Lunch

ARLINGTON, GRAND PRAIRIE, & MID-CITIES

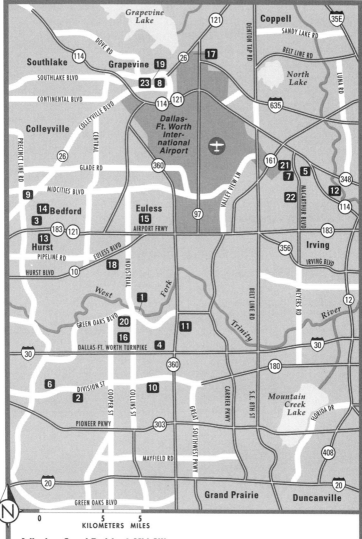

Arlington, Grand Prairie, & Mid-Cities

1. Al's Hamburgers (AGP)
2. Arlington Steakhouse (AGP)
3. Bayley's (MC)
4. Cacharel (AGP)
5. Café on the Green (MC)
6. Catfish Sam's (AGP)
7. Cool River (MC)
8. Dorris House Café (MC)
9. La Bistro (MC)
10. Marquez Bakery (AGP)
11. Marsala Restaurant (AGP)
12. Mayuri (MC)
13. Miguelito's Mexican Restaurant (MC)
14. Mike's Famous Hamburgers (MC)
15. North Main BBQ (MC)
16. Piccolo Mondo (AGP)
17. Rainforest Café (MC)
18. Raven's Grille (MC)
19. Ravioli Ristorante (MC)
20. Shogun Japanese Restaurant (AGP)
21. Veranda Greek Café (MC)
22. Via Real (MC)
23. Wilhoite's (MC)

Mon-Fri only, dinner served daily.& (Arlington/Grand Prairie)

PICCOLO MONDO
829 East Lamar
Arlington
817/265-9174 (metro)
$$
Tucked away in a strip shopping center, this upscale restaurant features mostly Northern Italian cuisine, with more cream sauces and fewer tomato sauces. The menu offers well-prepared pasta, veal, beef, seafood, chicken, and vegetarian dishes. Cocktails and wine are available, and a pianist entertains on Saturday nights. Lunch Mon-Fri, dinner daily. & (Arlington/Grand Prairie)

SHOGUN JAPANESE RESTAURANT
851 NE Green Oaks Boulevard
Arlington
817/261-1636
$$
This small, authentic Japanese restaurant resides in a little shopping center at the corner of Green Oaks Boulevard and Highway 157. Choose from yakitori, tempura, sushi, sashimi, or try a sample plate. The atmosphere is cozy and quiet. Lunch Mon-Fri, dinner Mon-Sat; closed Sun. & (Arlington/Grand Prairie)

DOWNTOWN FORT WORTH

8.0 RESTAURANT AND BAR
111 East Third Street
(in Sundance Square)
Fort Worth
817/336-0880
$-$$
Murals by local artists decorate this funky, eclectic restaurant fea-

turing steaks, seafood, pasta, and Tex-Mex items. Each category has its own unique specialties with interesting accompaniments. Then there's the appetizer called Fried Purple Worms (don't ask, just try it). Everything is made as healthy as possible using fresh ingredients with no preservatives and meat with no hormones or antibiotics. Serving martinis voted the "best martinis in Tarrant County" in a 1997 poll, the bar is the place to-be-seen-in at night, so it can be rather noisy. Enjoy listening to good jazz and blues on the patio. Lunch and dinner daily. & (Downtown Fort Worth)

ANGELUNA
215 East Fourth Street (in Sundance Square)
Fort Worth
817/334-0080
$$-$$$
Across the street from the Bass Performance Hall with its angel sculptures, Angeluna surrounds diners with cloud-painted ceilings and angels on the walls. Dine on creative New American fare and designer pizzas in this celestial setting. Sip cocktails or wine and watch the social set. The place swarms with the artsy crowd before and after events at the Bass Performance Hall. Lunch and dinner daily. & (Downtown Fort Worth)

BILLY MINER'S SALOON
150 West Third Street (in Sundance Square)
Fort Worth
817/877-3301
$
You can almost lose yourself in daydreams of the frontier era

Chicken-Fried Steak

Nothing makes a Texan salivate faster than a tender, juicy slab of chicken-fried steak swimming in cream gravy. But originally steak was chicken-fried—that is, dipped in batter and prepared like fried chicken—because it wasn't tender or juicy enough. Range cattle usually yielded tough, even stringy, beef, and ranch cooks and farm wives took to frying the bejesus out of it to soften it up. The cream gravy helped return some of the flavor that the prolonged cooking removed. But it was still a tasty dish, and today's chicken-fried steak, prepared with grain-fed beef, is better yet. Not necessarily good FOR you—but good, nonetheless.

amidst the saloon's rustic setting. This popular hamburger hangout and bar attracts a casual young crowd. The bill of fare includes the Billy Steak, an open-faced sandwich served with grilled onions and fries, nachos, hamburgers and hot dogs, and a visit to the huge fix-your-own sandwich/condiment bar. Beer and wine by the glass add to the jovial ambience. People-watch through a tier of large picture windows overlooking the Sundance Square. Lunch and dinner daily. &. (Downtown Fort Worth)

MI COCINA
509 Main Street (in Sundance Square)
Fort Worth
817/877-3600
$-$$
This stylish Tex-Mex place serves great enchiladas, tacos, and burritos, but it also puts together some fine specialties such as scrumptious shrimp dishes. Popular with the local lunch crowd, it's filled with

tourists and the young set after dark. Lunch and dinner daily. &. (Downtown Fort Worth)

REATA
500 Throckmorton, 35th floor
Fort Worth
817/336-1009
$$-$$$
Should you go to Reata for the food or the view? It's a tie. No, definitely the food. But go for both. The panoramic view is from the 35th floor of the Bank One building in Downtown Fort Worth. The food is upscale "Cowboy Cuisine"—Southwestern with a Texas twist. Movie buffs may remember Reata as the ranch in the classic 1950s movie, *Giant.* The original Reata restaurant is in Alpine, Texas, near where the movie was filmed. This one, owned by the same folks, may be even better because Chef Grady Spears makes this his home base. The menu appropriately features thick, juicy steaks, prepared to perfection. Seafood entrées and a good selection of creative Tex-Mex

DOWNTOWN FORT WORTH

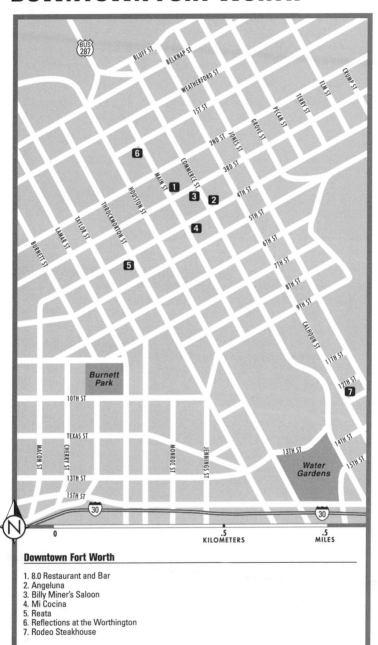

Downtown Fort Worth

1. 8.0 Restaurant and Bar
2. Angeluna
3. Billy Miner's Saloon
4. Mi Cocina
5. Reata
6. Reflections at the Worthington
7. Rodeo Steakhouse

dishes are also excellent. Try the popular Cream of Jalapeño soup. And for heaven's sake, be sure to save room for the dessert sampler. Actually, that's impossible to do, but at least order one for the table and share the five to six scrumptious treats. Cocktails and wine are available from the bar. Lunch and dinner Mon-Sat; closed Sun. & (Downtown Fort Worth)

**REFLECTIONS AT THE
WORTHINGTON
200 Main Street (in the
Worthington Hotel)
Fort Worth
817/882-1660
$$$**
Named for the reflecting pools that are its centerpiece, this dining room is located on the mezzanine of the opulent Worthington Hotel. The serene atmosphere, consistently creative chef, artistic presentation of exquisite dishes, and efficient service combine to make dining here a special occasion. The menu offers American and regional cuisine with a delicate French influence. A prix fixe menu features an exceptional three-course gourmet meal. Representative of the culinary creations are an appetizer of wild mushroom with pheasant sausage, an entree of grilled whiskey-sauced ostrich medallions with red lentil risotto, and a slice of Jack Daniels pecan pie for dessert. Sunday brunch is nothing short of breathtaking. Although a jacket is no longer required, dress up to dine in the romantic setting of this four-diamond AAA restaurant. Diners receive complimentary validated valet parking in the hotel. Dinner Tue-Sat; Sun brunch. & (Downtown Fort Worth)

**RODEO STEAKHOUSE
1309 Calhoun Street
Fort Worth
817/332-1288
www.CyberRodeo.com
$-$$**
Just east of the Convention Center and right in the midst of the downtown hotels, this restaurant is a Fort Worth steakhouse tradition. Old-timers remember it as The Keg. Booths offer privacy in a rustic, comfortable atmosphere. The menu includes numerous choices in western lingo such as Out of the Chute (appetizers), Rodeo Specials (fish and seafood), and Cattleman Traditionals (steaks, of course) and all dinners include a trip to the Trail Ride Salad Bar. The prime rib is consistently good, as are the steaks, red snapper, and salmon. Modernized with computers and a spacious meeting room, Rodeo has become a favorite hangout for local and visiting businesspeople. Dinner Tue-Sat; closed Sun-Mon. & (Downtown Fort Worth)

NORTH FORT WORTH

**CATTLEMAN'S STEAKHOUSE
2458 North Main Street
Fort Worth
817/624-3945
www.cattlemanssteakhouse.com
$-$$**
Established in 1947, this rustic restaurant is an institution in the Stockyards Historic District. The menu is heavy on, what else but, thick, juicy charbroiled steaks in all sizes from an 8-ounce filet to an 18-ounce sirloin. Other good choices include barbecued ribs and seafood. Accompany your meal with a beverage from the bar. Lunch and dinner daily. & (North Fort Worth)

EL RANCHO GRANDE
1400 North Main Street
Fort Worth
817/624-9206
$

From its beginnings in a tiny house with only a few tables, this restaurant grew into a beautifully restored building with high ceilings to handle the bustling crowds that flocked after the word got out that they served great Mexican food. The chef has worked there for more than 20 years, as have several of the waiters, which is quite a tribute to the family that owns and operates the business. Corn is freshly ground each day for the exceptionally good tortilla chips and taco and chalupa shells that are light, yet firm enough to hold that taco until you finish eating it without spilling the contents all over your plate. The "Nachos Grande" appetizer is a meal in itself, the queso is superb, and the fajita meat is so tender it melts in your mouth. Lunch and dinner Mon-Sat; closed Sun. & (North Fort Worth)

H-3 RANCH
105 East Exchange Avenue
(in the Stockyards Hotel)
Fort Worth
817/624-1246
$$

Look for the H-3 behind Booger Red's Saloon in the Stockyards Hotel. Steaks, ribs, burgers, and chicken-fried steak dominate the menu, although other offerings are featured as well. Service can be slow, but lean back and enjoy the rustic Western atmosphere. Breakfast Sat-Sun; lunch and dinner daily. & (North Fort Worth)

JOE T. GARCIA'S
MEXICAN DISHES

2201 North Commerce Street
817/626-4356
$-$$

When Joe T. opened his little restaurant in part of his home in 1935, he could seat 16 customers. Today his children and grandchildren run the sprawling establishment that extends for most of the block. The most popular seating is poolside on the beautiful flower-laden outdoor patio. Still prepared and served by family members, the Mexican dishes such as enchiladas and fajitas are served family-style on big platters. Strolling mariachis entertain on weekends. The legendary eatery does not accept credit cards. Lunch and dinner daily. (North Fort Worth)

LOS VAQUEROS
2629 North Main Street
Fort Worth
817/624-1511
$-$$

Once a tiny café serving recipes from the Cisneros family, Los Vaqueros became so popular that it had to move to larger quarters. Now housed in a restored 1915 red brick packinghouse at the north end of the Stockyards Historic District, it offers traditional and upscale Mexican and Tex-Mex entrées. Weeknight specials are popular, and be sure to save room for the dessert sopapillas. Margaritas and Mexican beer, as well as other cocktails, wine, and domestic beer, are available. Lunch and dinner daily. & (North Fort Worth)

MERCADO JUAREZ
1651 East Northside Drive
Fort Worth
817/838-8285
$-$$

This long-time local favorite serves giant portions of standard Tex-Mex fare in a festive atmosphere. Cabrito is well-prepared, and fajitas are a good choice. A second location is in a newly remodeled warehouse-turned-hacienda at 2222 Miller Road. Lunch and dinner daily. & (North Fort Worth)

STAR CAFÉ
111 West Exchange Avenue
Fort Worth
817/624-8701
$-$$
The Star is a tradition in the Stock-yards Historic District, serving "Cowboy Fare" of steaks and chicken-fried steak and potatoes. Lunch and dinner daily. & (North Fort Worth)

SOUTHWEST FORT WORTH

ANGELO'S BAR-B-QUE
2533 White Settlement Road
Fort Worth
817/332-0357
$
Angelo's began serving hickory-smoked beef brisket and pork ribs on St. Patrick's Day in 1958. Since then it has earned a reputation that not only keeps customers coming back but has also turned it into a mecca for barbecue lovers. In addition to beef and pork, the chicken (half or quarter) is quite popular and is served "while it lasts." All meats are served as sandwiches or plate dinners with your choice of beans, potato salad, or slaw and the tradi-tional sauce, pickle, onion, and bread. Go through the buffet line for your food, grab your drinks from the cooler and your chips off the rack, and eat under wildlife heads mounted on the wall. Because of health regulations, the sawdust on

the floor is gone, but the jovial at-mosphere remains and customers can enjoy wine and ice-cold beer. Credit cards are not accepted. Lunch and dinner Mon-Sat; closed Sun. & (Southwest Fort Worth)

THE BACK PORCH
3400-B Camp Bowie Boulevard
Fort Worth
817/332-1422
$
A knockout salad bar is the attrac-tion here. Priced by the ounce, it offers a tremendous variety of selections. They also make great sandwiches, pizzas, and soups, es-pecially the French Onion, served in a crockery pot with loads of melted cheese. Adjacent to the café is the Back Porch Ice Cream Parlor (the line extends out the door on hot summer evenings), with more than 40 flavors of tempting homemade ice creams to choose from. Ever have banana pudding ice cream? Or cin-namon? Try the cinnamon ice cream on homemade apple pie. Lunch and dinner daily. (Southwest Fort Worth)

THE BALCONY OF RIDGLEA
6100 Camp Bowie Boulevard
Fort Worth
817/731-3719
$$
This elegant upstairs restaurant offers seating in its elegant dining room or on the glass-enclosed namesake balcony. The chef/owner offers a traditional continental menu that features specialties such as Chateaubriand for two, rack of lamb, and a variety of seafood. Service is attentive, yet unobtrusive. Enjoy your favorite bar drink or wine and the soft music of a pianist on Friday and Saturday evenings. Lunch Mon-Fri;

GREATER FORT WORTH

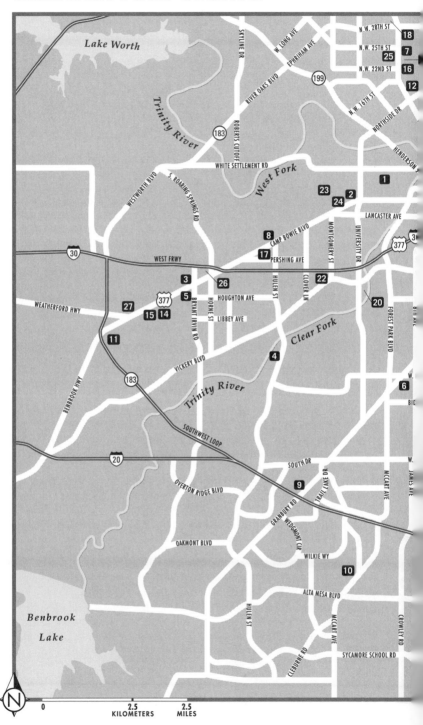

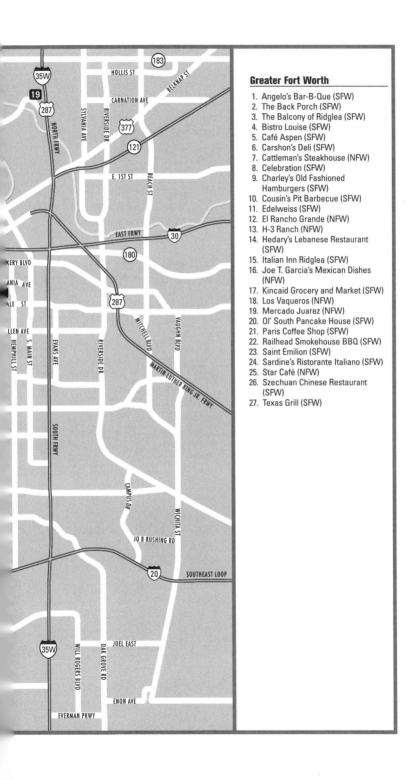

Greater Fort Worth

1. Angelo's Bar-B-Que (SFW)
2. The Back Porch (SFW)
3. The Balcony of Ridglea (SFW)
4. Bistro Louise (SFW)
5. Café Aspen (SFW)
6. Carshon's Deli (SFW)
7. Cattleman's Steakhouse (NFW)
8. Celebration (SFW)
9. Charley's Old Fashioned Hamburgers (SFW)
10. Cousin's Pit Barbecue (SFW)
11. Edelweiss (SFW)
12. El Rancho Grande (NFW)
13. H-3 Ranch (NFW)
14. Hedary's Lebanese Restaurant (SFW)
15. Italian Inn Ridglea (SFW)
16. Joe T. Garcia's Mexican Dishes (NFW)
17. Kincaid Grocery and Market (SFW)
18. Los Vaqueros (NFW)
19. Mercado Juarez (NFW)
20. Ol' South Pancake House (SFW)
21. Paris Coffee Shop (SFW)
22. Railhead Smokehouse BBQ (SFW)
23. Saint Emilion (SFW)
24. Sardine's Ristorante Italiano (SFW)
25. Star Café (NFW)
26. Szechuan Chinese Restaurant (SFW)
27. Texas Grill (SFW)

dinner Mon-Sat; closed Sun. & (Southwest Fort Worth)

BISTRO LOUISE
2900 Hulen, Suite 40
Fort Worth
817/922-9244
$$
The ambience at Bistro Louis hints of Provence. Offering "Mediterranean" cuisine, this trendy restaurant serves excellent meat, seafood, and fowl with Spanish/French/Italian influences. Louise Lamensdorf brings years of culinary experience to the eclectic bistro after studying in fine European restaurants as well as the Cordon Bleu in New York. Ever popular choices include crab cakes made with lump crab meat and chopped herbs, stuffed lamb loin, smoked duck, and potato-crusted salmon. Whatever you choose from the menu, it will be expertly prepared and delicious. The soups and salads are exceptional, as are the desserts. Lunch and dinner Mon-Sat; closed Sun. & (Southwest Fort Worth)

CAFÉ ASPEN
6103 Camp Bowie Boulevard
Fort Worth
817/738-0838
$$
This locally owned, upscale, quietly

elegant restaurant offers a creative menu featuring New American cuisine with a special flair. Imaginative salads, innovative sandwiches, and homemade soups draw crowds at lunch time. Dinner selections such as herb-crusted rack of lamb, chili-crusted tuna, and rainbow trout amandine attract evening diners. The homemade desserts are irresistible. Local artwork and photography exhibited on the walls adds to the eclectic décor. The bar in back is cozy and intimate, occasionally offering music or poetry readings. Lunch and dinner Mon-Sat; closed Sun. & (Southwest Fort Worth)

CARSHON'S DELI
3133 Cleburne Road
Fort Worth
817/923-1907
$
More than seven decades after it started as a kosher meat market in 1928, Carshon's is a fixture in Fort Worth. No fancy, newfangled place, it's a traditional kosher-style deli that offers everything you'd expect from old-fashioned two-handed sandwiches to plate lunches to chicken soup. Beer and wine are available. Carshon's does not accept credit cards. Breakfast and lunch Tue-

Sun; closed Mon. ♿ (Southwest Fort Worth)

CELEBRATION
4800 Dexter Avenue
Fort Worth
817/731-6272
$-$$

Folks say you can't beat the "home cooking" here. Fried chicken, pot roast, meatloaf, and fried catfish are all simply prepared and served family-style with salad, fresh vegetables (such as mashed potatoes, pinto beans, steamed broccoli, or squash), cornbread and rolls, and real homemade cobbler and other desserts. A children's menu offers kid-friendly fare. Lunch and dinner daily. ♿ (Southwest Fort Worth)

CHARLEY'S OLD-FASHIONED HAMBURGERS
4616 Granbury Road
Fort Worth
817/924-8611
$

This tiny burger joint looks like a hole in the wall, but it's a Fort Worth mecca for hamburger fans. Open wide to chow down on an old-fashioned burger with grilled onions while sippin' on a real lemonade and sittin' at a picnic table. Lunch and dinner Mon-Sat; closed Sun. Credit cards are not accepted. (Southwest Fort Worth)

COUSIN'S PIT BARBECUE
6262 McCart Avenue
Fort Worth
817/346-2511
$

A family-owned landmark since 1983, this local favorite is tucked away in a strip shopping center on Fort Worth's south side. It's more of a family restaurant and less of a

beer joint than many barbecue places. As you enter the line, read the wall, which displays letters of appreciation from fans and autographed pictures of the rich and famous: notable Dallas Cowboys and other football heroes, golfing greats, several Miss Texas contestants and winners, Tanya Tucker, LeAnn Rimes, and on and on. The décor consists of John Wayne posters and Coca-Cola memorabilia. The counter help is always friendly, and the meat is always succulent and delicious. Diners help themselves from a "fixin's bar" with assorted pickles, peppers, relishes, and onions. Owner Calvin "Bootsie" Payne attracted national attention when former President George Bush ordered his brisket for the White House. A bustling take-out area adjoins the restaurant. A second location opened in late 1999 at 5125 Bryant Irvin Road in the City View area. Lunch and dinner Mon-Sat; closed Sun. ♿ (Southwest Fort Worth)

EDELWEISS
3801-A Southwest Boulevard
Fort Worth
817/738-5934
$$

A Bavarian-style *bierhalle,* this 350-seat restaurant has various seating options so you can choose between a cozy candlelit corner and a raucous gathering that is only one step away from an Oktoberfest party. Owner/chef Bernd hails from Germany and serves true German traditional dishes such as sauerbraten, sausages, and a variety of schnitzels. A great sampler plate is available for those who can't make up their minds. Steaks and seafood are also on the menu, and of course, so is Black Forest cake. A Fort Worth institution for more than 30 years, Edelweiss offers entertainment nightly with a live German band and a dance floor. Fun and family-oriented, it also offers a children's menu. Unsurprisingly, the full bar has a good selection of German beers. Dinner Tue-Sat; closed Sun-Mon. &. (Southwest Fort Worth)

HEDARY'S LEBANESE RESTAURANT
3308 Fairfield
Fort Worth
817/731-6961
$$

The Hedary family has been serving fresh, prepared-from-scratch Lebanese cuisine forever. If you're a "first-timer," don't worry; Hedary's menu explains every dish in detail, and the friendly staff will answer your questions. Try the Maza, a sampler with 10 to 12 different appetizers and salads that vary daily. The menu is large for the adventurous but lists a good selection of recognizable dishes such as shish kebabs, chicken, and lamb. The lamb is always fresh because the Hedarys raise their own. Lebanese music usually plays in the background. Lunch Tue-Fri, dinner Tue-Sun; closed Mon. &. (Southwest Fort Worth)

ITALIAN INN RIDGLEA
6323 Camp Bowie Boulevard
Fort Worth
817/737-0123
$-$$

A tradition for decades on Fort Worth's west side, this upscale yet classic Italian restaurant serves well-prepared dishes of veal, chicken, seafood, and pasta. The setting is "vintage underground nightclub" because the dining room is situated downstairs and is dimly lit. Intimate booths are enclosed with swinging doors that have generations of initials carved in them. Singing waiters and waitresses complete the experience. Dinner daily. (Southwest Fort Worth)

KINCAID GROCERY & MARKET
4901 Camp Bowie Boulevard
Fort Worth
817/732-2881
$

Once a grocery store and meat market that served burgers at a stand-up counter, this Fort Worth institution has been consistently voted by food critics around the country as serving the best burgers in America. The signature burgers are fresh, juicy, and messy. Today Kincaid is more a café than a meat market, and local characters enjoy more than just burgers, including chicken and dumplings, plate lunches with fresh vegetables, and chicken-fried steak—all served in an old-fashioned corner grocery. The stand-up counter is still there, but picnic tables provide a sit-down option now. Be sure to get banana pudding or one of the huge home-made cookies for dessert; if you don't have room left, get one to go. Credit cards are not accepted. Lunch and early dinner (closes at 6 p.m.) Mon-Sat; closed Sun. &. (Southwest Fort Worth)

OL' SOUTH PANCAKE HOUSE
1507 South University
Fort Worth
817/336-0309
$

A Fort Worth landmark for more than 30 years, this pancake house was one of the first places in town to stay open 24 hours a day. Breakfast after midnight was a treat! The original

Dickey's Barbecue

Established here in 1941, Dickey's has grown to more than 35 locations throughout Texas because of their unequivocally yummy, finger-lickin'-good barbecue with all the trimmin's. Dinners are in the inexpensive range and come with heaping portions of meat (brisket, sausage, ham, turkey, chicken breast, hot links) and two sides.

A few Dickey's locations include the following:

- **4714 Colleyville Boulevard,** *817/514-6767*
- **2324 McKinney Boulevard,** *214/978-2501*
- **1150 North Plano Road at Arapaho,** *972/907-8494*
- **4610 North Central Expressway,** *214/823-0240*
- **14999 Preston Road at Belt Line Road,** *972/661-2006*
- **5390 North MacArthur (Las Colinas),** *972/580-1917*
- **17721 North Dallas Parkway,** *972/713-8909*
- **Grapevine Mills Mall,** *972/724-6701*
- **Vista Ridge Mall,** *972/316-1406*

menu selection of 39 pancakes and waffles has been extended to a full menu of breakfast, lunch, and dinner selections. The most popular menu item is the oven-baked German pancake, served with whipped butter, powdered sugar, and fresh lemon. The restaurant is still in the family and still offers unpretentious quality food served with Southern charm and hospitality. Open 24 hours a day, seven days a week. ♿ (Southwest Fort Worth)

PARIS COFFEE SHOP
704 West Magnolia
Fort Worth
$
817/335-2041
If you want to try a really local-color

place, this is it. It's one of the oldest breakfast and lunch spots in the city, serving fresh, homemade chicken-fried steak, biscuits and gravy, and pies to die for. Breakfast and lunch Mon-Fri; closed Sat-Sun. ♿ (Southwest Fort Worth)

RAILHEAD SMOKEHOUSE BBQ
2900 Montgomery
Fort Worth
$
817/738-9808
This long-time favorite serves great barbecue in a rustic setting. The servings are generous and the prices are reasonable. Choose from the usual brisket, ribs, sausage, and chicken, with or without side dishes of beans, slaw, or potato

salad. Whatever you choose, add a small order of fries. It's very crowded during happy hour. A second location opened in 1999 at 5220 Highway 121 in Colleyville. Lunch and dinner Mon-Sat; closed Sun. ⅄ (Southwest Fort Worth)

SAINT EMILION
3617 West Seventh Street
Fort Worth
817/737-2781
$$-$$$
Stepping into this brick-home restaurant is like stepping into a country-French cottage transplanted directly from a French village. The country-inn décor features hanging copper pots, candlelight, and fresh flowers on each table. Not surprisingly, the wine list features several vintages from the Saint Emilion region. The cuisine gets consistently high ratings for well-crafted entrées that include such culinary creations as seafood in puff pastry, jumbo sea scallops in anchovy butter sauce, veal medallions, duck, Australian rack of lamb, and fresh fish flown in daily. Save room for a delectable dessert like rum-laced crème brûlée. Dinner Tue-Sat. ⅄ (Southwest Fort Worth)

SARDINE'S RISTORANTE ITALIANO
3410 Camp Bowie Boulevard
Fort Worth
817/332-9937
$-$$
It may seem a hole-in-the-wall, but this family-owned and run spot is a long-time favorite in the Cultural District. The Italian fare is usually excellent and prepared using fresh ingredients. The ambience is superb—dark and romantic. Remember though, Italians feel dining

is an experience to be leisurely enjoyed, so don't choose Sardine's if you're in a hurry. Johnny Case, a talented jazz pianist, entertains nightly; on weekends his trio plays, and local musicians often join in for impromptu jam sessions. Dinner daily. (Southwest Fort Worth)

SZECHUAN CHINESE RESTAURANT
5712 Locke Avenue
Fort Worth
817/738-7300
$$
This award-winning, highly rated restaurant is tucked out of the way in a strip shopping center just off Camp Bowie Boulevard. Packed with loyal locals, it's a popular favorite for spicy Szechuan food that is expertly prepared and served. The décor is authentic, and most of the furnishings have been procured by family members who live in China. The walls are lined with countless pictures of celebrities who have visited, attesting to the classic quality of this long-established eatery. Lunch and dinner daily. ⅄ (Southwest Fort Worth)

TEXAS GRILL
6550 Camp Bowie Boulevard
Fort Worth
817/377-0270
$-$$
Standing-room-only crowds wait for the awesome burgers (20 to choose from) and homestyle fries. Locally owned and operated, the casual restaurant also serves great fried catfish, grilled chicken, salads, sandwiches, and homemade pies to drool over. Everything is well prepared and reasonably priced. Lunch and dinner daily. ⅄ (Southwest Fort Worth)

Ft Worth CVB

5

SIGHTS AND ATTRACTIONS

Some people come to soak up the ambience of the Old West, some to cheer the Dallas Cowboys or Texas Rangers, some to explore the fine museums and historical buildings, and some to shop until they drop. Whatever your reasons for coming to the Metroplex, you won't be disappointed by the number and diversity of sights and attractions.

Many attractions fit into more than one category. Many Metroplex attractions are museums listed in Chapter 6, Museums and Art Galleries. Many others are performing arts venues listed in Chapter 11, Performing Arts, and sports venues listed in Chapter 10, Sports and Recreation. Attractions for families are found in Chapter 7, Kids' Stuff. The attractions for shopaholics are listed in Chapter 9, Shopping.

DOWNTOWN DALLAS

CATHEDRAL SANTUARIO DE GUADALUPE
2215 Ross Avenue
Dallas
214/741-3954
Next to the Meyerson Symphony Center in the Arts District, this magnificent Catholic cathedral was located on the most elegant street in Dallas when it was dedicated in

1902. Daily 9-3:30. Free. ᕕ (Downtown Dallas)

DALLAS CITY HALL
1500 Marilla Street
Dallas
214/670-3011
The $43-million Dallas City Hall, designed by internationally renowned architect I. M. Pei, was dedicated in 1978 and is definitely one of the most distinctive buildings in the city. If you're interested in architecture,

DOWNTOWN DALLAS

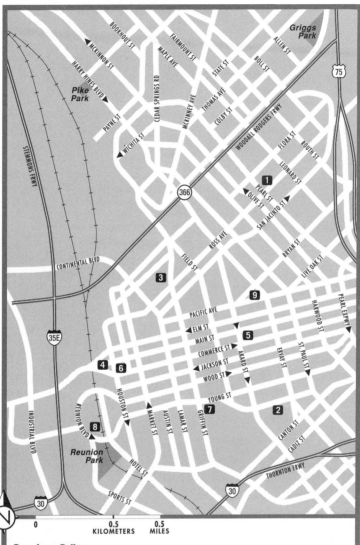

Downtown Dallas

1. Cathedral Santuario de Guadalupe
2. Dallas City Hall
3. Dallas World Aquarium
4. Dealey Plaza National Historic Landmark
5. Magnolia Building
6. "Old Red" Courthouse
7. Pioneer Plaza
8. Reunion Tower
9. Thanks-Giving Square

the way this structure was built makes for fascinating reading. The cantilevered building, sloping upward and outward, is balanced and held by a network of U-shaped cables. Enormous flagpoles fly the American, Texas, and Dallas flags on the four-acre plaza in front of the unique building. & (Downtown Dallas)

DALLAS WORLD AQUARIUM
1801 North Griffin Street
Dallas
214/720-2224, 214/720-1801
A privately owned aquarium in Dallas's West End began as Daryl Richardson's hobby. He enjoyed watching marine life, so he decided to share his enjoyment with others. You can walk through a 20,000-gallon tank—by tunnel of course—and view marine life from different destinations around the world. More than 80,000 gallons of saltwater in several large tanks exhibit stingrays, sharks, jellyfish, and hundreds of reef fish living in coral reef

ecosystems. There's also an Australian Great Barrier Reef exhibit and a monstrous glass-enclosed tropical rainforest. The penguins are adorable. Watch feeding demonstrations and educational films and use a brochure to take a self-guided tour. Daily 10-5. $10.95 adults, $6 seniors and children 3-12. & (Downtown Dallas)

DEALEY PLAZA NATIONAL HISTORIC LANDMARK
At intersection of Main, Commerce, and Elm Streets
Dallas
This small plaza was built as a Depression-era project and named for George Dealey, the founder of the *Dallas Morning News,* who donated the land to the city. Unfortunately, its notoriety results from the fact that President John F. Kennedy was assassinated while riding in a motorcade passing Dealey Plaza on November 22, 1963. There is a memorial plaque in the plaza, which is designated a National Historic

The Bass Family

The revitalization of Downtown Fort Worth is one of the most successful efforts of its kind in the country. The prominent Bass family played a huge role in these efforts. Fort Worth's Bass family owes its start to the late oilman and philanthropist, Sid Richardson, who left his vast fortune to his nephew, Perry Bass. Perry and his four sons invested in their city; The Worthington, Caravan of Dreams, the magnificent Performance Hall, and many of the trendy apartments, shops, and restaurants of Sundance Square can be attributed to the Basses. They have shared their wealth as enormous contributors to civic, cultural, and humanitarian projects in Fort Worth.

Landmark (see The Sixth Floor Museum, Chapter 6, Museums and Galleries). & (Downtown Dallas)

MAGNOLIA BUILDING
Akard, Commerce, and Main Streets
Dallas
Completed in 1922, the Magnolia Building housed the offices of Magnolia Petroleum Company, later Mobil Oil Company. The tallest structure in Dallas for more than 20 years, it was a symbol of the economically affluent city. In 1934, a revolving neon Flying Red Horse, the trademark for Magnolia Oil, was placed atop the building. The 15-ton horse became a landmark that is still seen today as a distinctive sight in the Dallas skyline. (Downtown Dallas)

"OLD RED" COURTHOUSE
Dallas County Historical Plaza
100 South Houston Street
Dallas
214/571-1300
This magnificent 1890-1892 example of Romanesque Revival architecture, built of Pecos red sandstone and Texas red granite, is the historic seat of the Dallas County government. Although it is one of Dallas's oldest remaining buildings, it's the sixth courthouse built on the site. The first floor now houses the state-of-the-art, high-tech Visitors Information Center. Mon-Fri 8-5, Sat-Sun 10-5. & (Downtown Dallas)

PIONEER PLAZA
Young and Griffin Streets
Dallas
The larger-than-life bronze sculptures of longhorn steers being herded by three cowboys on horseback along a cascading stream amid native plants is a magnificent sight.

The project, created by artist Robert Summers of nearby Glen Rose, will eventually have 70 figures, making it the largest bronze monument in the world. This Downtown, 4.2-acre mini-park, just north of the Dallas Convention Center and west of Dallas City Hall, commemorates the legendary cattle drives that allegedly forded the Trinity River near today's Hyatt Regency Hotel. Some scholars of western history say that a minor cattle drive could have possibly come near Dallas, but most were probably farther west toward Fort Worth. And so the rivalry continues. (Downtown Dallas)

REUNION TOWER
300 Reunion Boulevard
Dallas
214/651-1234
The 50-story tower in the southwest corner of Downtown has become the most identifying symbol in the Dallas skyline. (Never mind that Fort Worthians call it the "giant puffball in the sky.") A masterpiece of design and engineering weighing 23,600 tons, Reunion Tower opened in 1978. Visitors may take the elevator to the top in 68 seconds (or during a moment of temporary insanity, may climb the 837 steps) to The Lookout, a public observation deck atop the Tower, for a 360-degree panoramic view. Antares restaurant (see Chapter 4, Where to Eat) and The Dome cocktail lounge (see Chapter 12, Nightlife), both operated by the adjoining Hyatt Regency Hotel, offer spectacular views of the city as they slowly revolve at the rate of one revolution every 55 minutes. & (Downtown Dallas)

THANKS-GIVING SQUARE
Pacific, Bryan, and Ervay Streets

In Pioneer Plaza, life-size, bronze cowboys and steer commemorate Texas cattle drives

Dallas
214/969-1977
This tiny triangular park, an oasis of serenity in the midst of bustling Downtown, honors the universal spirit of Thanksgiving. Dominated by a 50-foot bell tower with three bronze bells, it includes a meditation garden, fountains, reflecting pool, and the white marble interfaith chapel with its spectacular horizontal stained-glass window. Chapel: Mon-Fri 9-5, Sat-Sun 1-5. Free. & (Downtown Dallas)

CENTRAL DALLAS

DALLAS MARKET CENTER COMPLEX
2100 North Stemmons Freeway (I-35E)
Dallas
214/655-6100
Located on 175 acres a few minutes northwest of Downtown on Stemmons Freeway, the world's largest wholesale trade center includes Market Hall, the World Trade Center, the Dallas Trade Mart, the International Apparel Mart, and the International Menswear Mart. Several other trade marts and the highly recognizable InfoMart are nearby and are considered part of the complex.

Market Hall is a privately owned exhibition hall that hosts boat shows, arts-and-crafts shows, antique shows, and so forth throughout the year that are open to the public. The InfoMart (1950 North Stemmons Freeway, 214/800-8000) is a $170-million, one-million-square-foot, lacy-looking, white metal and mirrored glass building designed after the Crystal Palace in London. It's the world's largest high-tech information resource center, and the public is welcome only to some offices, trade shows, computer classes, exhibits, and user group meetings. The rest of the buildings of the Market Center are not generally open to the public, although some trade shows and special events are public. & (Central Dallas)

The Dallas InfoMart is the world's largest high-tech exhibition and information center.

FREEDMAN'S MEMORIAL
Southwest corner of Lemmon Avenue and North Central Expressway (U.S. 75)
Dallas
214/670-3284
Freedman's Memorial marks the spot of a pre-Civil War African American burial ground. An old slave cemetery was discovered during road building and development. The remains of freed slaves, who founded Freedman's Town after the Civil War, were moved to adjacent property prior to widening a major freeway. Designated a state historic landmark, the memorial honors more than 7,000 early black pioneers. (Central Dallas)

SWISS AVENUE HISTORIC DISTRICT
Northeast of Downtown
Dallas
214/821-3290 (Historic Preservation League)
www.sahd.org
About two miles northeast of Downtown Dallas, the Swiss Avenue Historic District is one of the finest turn-of-the-century neighborhoods in the southwest. Named by an immigrant from Switzerland, Swiss Avenue became part of an exclusive residential area development and was paved in 1905. A 22-block area listed in the National Register of Historic Places represents more than one dozen architectural styles from English Tudor to Mediterranean. Approximately 200 carefully preserved and restored homes line Swiss Avenue with its lush evergreen median and broad sidewalks. The Historic District includes Swiss Avenue from Fitzhugh to La Vista and parts of Live Oak Street, Bryan Street, and La Vista Drive (Central Dallas)

EAST DALLAS

DALLAS AQUARIUM
First Avenue at Martin Luther King Boulevard (Fair Park)
Dallas
214/670-8443
Housed in one of the original Art Deco buildings in Fair Park, the Dallas Aquarium has been recently renovated. One of the largest inland aquariums in the nation, it's home to a diverse collection of nearly 5,000 wild and wonderful creatures, both freshwater and saltwater, from around the world. Everybody likes to watch the shark or piranha feedings Tuesday through Sunday at 2:30 p.m. Also on exhibit are reptiles and amphibians and cases of dazzling sea shells. Look behind the scenes through the viewing window into the breeding lab, where ongoing conservation programs help preserve endangered species. A special display, a 10,500-gallon Amazon Flooded Forest, exhibits fish of the Amazon River, including a prehistoric-looking catfish. Open daily 9-4:30. Admission: $3 adults, $1.50 children 3-11, under 3 free. & (East Dallas)

DALLAS ZOO
650 S. R.L. Thornton Freeway (I-35E)
Dallas
214/670-5656
www.dallas-zoo.org

About three miles south of Downtown, look for the tallest statue in the state, a 67-foot Plexiglas giraffe near the entrance. It's hard to miss! Home to more than 2,000 animals, including rare and endangered species such as the snow leopard and red panda, the Dallas Zoo also displays a nationally renowned reptile collection and interactive Reptile Discovery Center. The highly acclaimed "Wilds of Africa" exhibit features more than 80 species of African mammals, birds, and reptiles roaming in 25 acres of naturalistic re-creations of native habitat. The simulated rainforest features a walk-through aviary where you're surrounded by colorful, exotic birds. A recent addition is a chimpanzee habitat, replicating their native African habitat. To get a great look, take the specially designed Monorail Safari ($1.50 extra), a 20-minute ride with live narration. There's also a children's zoo, a restaurant, picnic areas, and a gift shop (see also Chapter 7, Kids' Stuff). Daily 9-5. $6 adults, $4 seniors, $3 children 3-11, free under 3. Parking $3 per car. ♿ (East Dallas)

FAIR PARK
3809 Grand Avenue
Dallas
214/670-8400
(Spanish 214/890-2911)
www.tgimaps.com/DALLAS/fairpark

Fair Park, an area two miles east of Downtown bounded by Parry Avenue, South Fitzhugh Avenue, Robert B. Cullum Boulevard, and the Union Pacific Railroad tracks, was built for the Texas Centennial Exposition of 1936, celebrating Texas' 100th anniversary of independence from Mexico. It has been designated as a National Historic Landmark for the spectacular Art Deco architecture, the oldest collection of Art Deco buildings in the United States.

More than 150 events take place in Fair Park annually, but the granddaddy of them all happens each fall when the 277-acre complex hosts The State Fair of Texas (see Chapter 1, Welcome, Calendar of Events), the largest Exposition in all of North

National Archives

The National Archives, Southwest Region (501 West Felix, Fort Worth, 817/334-5525) is located in buildings that housed the Quartermaster Depot during World War II. One of only a few in the country, the National Archives house a treasure trove of research information about everything from the nation's history to genealogy. A knowledgable staff is available to assist visitors.

GREATER DALLAS

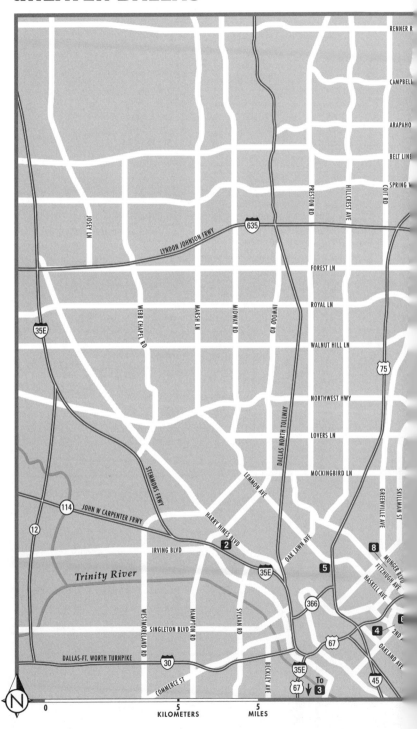

RENNER R

CAMPBELL

ARAPAHO

BELT LINE

SPRING V

PRESTON RD

HILLCREST AVE

COIT RD

635

LYNDON JOHNSON FRWY

JOSEY LN

35E

FOREST LN

ROYAL LN

WALNUT HILL LN

75

WEBB CHAPEL RD

MARSH LN

MIDWAY RD

INWOOD RD

NORTHWEST HWY

LOVERS LN

DALLAS NORTH TOLLWAY

MOCKINGBIRD LN

STEMMONS FRWY

LEMMON AVE

GREENVILLE AVE

SKILLMAN ST

114

JOHN W CARPENTER FRWY

12

HARRY HINES BLVD

8

MUNGER BLVD

IRVING BLVD

2

OAK LAWN AVE

FITZHUGH AVE

HASKELL AVE

Trinity River

35E

5

366

6

WESTMORELAND RD

HAMPTON RD

SYLVAN RD

SINGLETON BLVD

4

2ND

OAKLAND AVE

DALLAS-FT. WORTH TURNPIKE

30

BECKLEY AVE

35E

67

To

3

45

COMMERCE ST

67

N

0

5

KILOMETERS

5

MILES

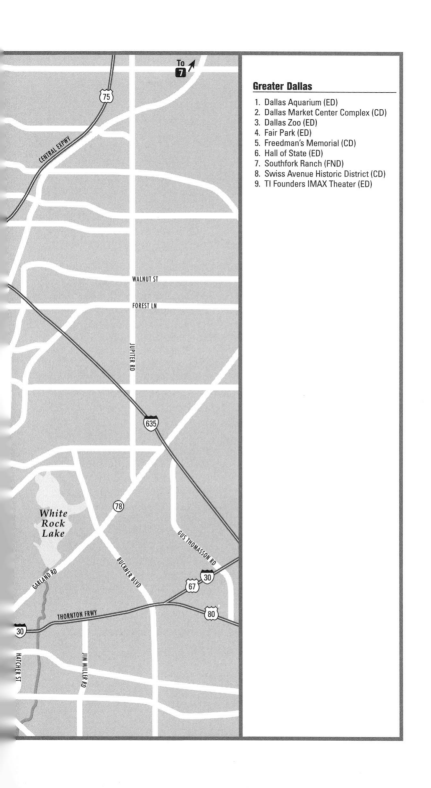

To 7 ↗

Greater Dallas

1. Dallas Aquarium (ED)
2. Dallas Market Center Complex (CD)
3. Dallas Zoo (ED)
4. Fair Park (ED)
5. Freedman's Memorial (CD)
6. Hall of State (ED)
7. Southfork Ranch (FND)
8. Swiss Avenue Historic District (CD)
9. TI Founders IMAX Theater (ED)

Armour & Swift

At the east end of Exchange Avenue in the Stockyards National Historic District is Armour & Swift Plaza, a Texas State Archaeological Landmark. The stairway and landscaped area mark the common entrance for the two meat-packing giants that greatly contributed to the economic success of the Stockyards. All that remains intact today is the Swift & Company's administrative office building at the crest of the hill, which now houses The Spaghetti Warehouse. A few ruins and part of a brick wall can be seen to the south.

America. The rest of the year, Fair Park is an attraction in its own right with the Hall of State (see following entry), the Dallas Aquarium (see previous listing), Starplex Amphitheater (see Chapter 11, Performing Arts), Cotton Bowl Stadium (see Chapter 10, Sports and Recreation), Fair Park Music Hall (see Chapter 11, Performing Arts), Dallas Horticultural Center (see Chapter 8, Parks, Gardens, and Recreation Areas), and the Museums of Fair Park: the African American Museum, the Age of Steam Railroad Museum, the Dallas Museum of Natural History, The Science Place, and the future Women's Museum (see Chapter 6, Museums and Art Galleries). Due to the large crowds, be cautious and use reasonable security precautions when visiting the Fair Park attractions and museums. See individual attraction listings for wheelchair accessibility. (East Dallas)

HALL OF STATE
3939 Grand Avenue (Fair Park)
Dallas
214/421-4500

www.dallashistory.org
The centerpiece of the 1936 Texas Centennial, this building is an exceptional example of Art Deco architecture. Costing $1.3 million, it was the most expensive of the buildings constructed for the Centennial and features marble floors and stenciled ceilings. The Great Hall showcases two enormous 95-foot murals depicting major events in Texas history and an immense gold seal with symbols of the six nations whose flags flew over Texas. Massive bronze entry doors open into the Hall of Heroes displaying larger-than-life statues of Texas heroes Stephen F. Austin, James Walker Fannin, Sam Houston, Mirabeau B. Lamar, Thomas J. Rusk, and William Barret Travis. Tue-Sat 9:30-5, Sun 1-5. Free except special exhibits. & (East Dallas)

TI FOUNDERS IMAX® THEATER
The Science Place (Fair Park)
Dallas
214/428-5555
www.scienceplace.org
The TI Founders IMAX® Theater,

with its scientifically designed seats and sound system, makes you feel like part of the experience. Located in The Science Place (see Chapter 6, Museums and Art Galleries), there's a nice museum shop and cafeteria. Daily 9:30-5:30. IMAX admission is separate; call for films and times. ＆ (East Dallas)

FAR NORTH DALLAS

SOUTHFORK RANCH
3700 Hogge Road
Parker
972/442-7800, 800/989-7800
www.foreverresorts.com
Dallas, the granddaddy of prime-time soaps, ran from 1978 to 1990 and has been shown in 96 countries. Although portraying an affluent Texas lifestyle, most of the show was filmed in California; however, the exterior shots of the Ewing mansion, Southfork, were of a real Texas home near Dallas, now possibly the most famous ranch in Texas. A few scenes were filmed in and around Dallas, and the opening credits scrolled over footage of Hereford cattle, oil wells, and wheat fields. The "Ewing family home" (that never was) is open daily, year-round for guided tours. An exhibit of memorabilia from the series is on display, a retail shop offers unique souvenirs, and Miss Ellie's Deli serves light lunches and snacks. Daily 9-5. $7.95 adults, $6.95 seniors, $5.95 children 4-12. (Far North Dallas)

MID-CITIES

HISTORIC DOWNTOWN
GRAPEVINE
Grapevine Visitor

Information Center
701 South Main
Grapevine
817/424-0561
www.ci.grapevine.tx.us
Listed in the National Register of Historic Places, Grapevine's attractive Downtown offers a variety of shops, eateries, winery tasting rooms, and historic walking tours. One of the oldest settlements in North Texas, Grapevine is proud of its heritage and has been actively restoring its buildings and sites for the last several years. The historical society and heritage foundation have worked to preserve and restore more than 40 sites, including the 1901 Cotton Belt Depot, the Palace Theater, and the pre-Civil War Torian Log Cabin. Watch artisans and craftsmen at the Heritage Center and shop for original art, antiques, clothing, gourmet cookware, gift items, and dozens of other fine choices. Sun-Fri 1-5, Sat 10-5 (Mid-Cities)

LAS COLINAS FLOWER CLOCK
Highway 114 at O'Connor Road
Irving
This colossal working clock is made of live flowers, which are planted several times a year to make sure there are always colorful, fresh flowers. (Mid-Cities)

MANDALAY CANAL WALK
AT LAS COLINAS
Highway 114 and North O'Connor
Road
Irving
The canal walk is part of a planned development of offices, restaurants, and retail shops. The walkway winds around the complex and the Omni Mandalay Hotel to the small Lake Carolyn and back. On a

level below the street, picturesque shops and eateries with red tile roofs line the banks of the winding canal. The whole area is slightly reminiscent of a European village. At one time water taxis (boats) offered scenic transportation along the canal, but as this book goes to press, they are no longer running. (Mid-Cities)

THE MOVIE STUDIOS AT LAS COLINAS
North O'Connor Road at Royal Lane
Irving
972/869-FILM
www.studiosatlascolinas.com

Lights! Camera! Action! Come see where movie magic is made right in the heart of Texas. The Studios Tour takes you "behind the scenes" of a working high-tech motion picture and television soundstage facility. Attractions include an interactive special effects display of a dangerous tornado or an erupting volcano; Starship Adventure, an interactive

outer space action in real Galactic Hollywood sets; Gold Mine Studios, where you can view a recording session, see a live audio recording, or even experience a remixing session; a priceless collection of famous costumes and memorabilia; and the National Museum of Communications (see Chapter 6, Museums and Art Galleries). Although part of the tour is not wheelchair accessible, wheelchair guests get a special treat to make up for it. Call for tour times. (Mid-Cities)

THE MUSTANGS OF LAS COLINAS
5205 North O'Connor Boulevard
Irving
972/869-9047

The world's largest equestrian sculpture shows nine larger-than-life galloping bronze mustangs splashing across a stream cut through a stone and granite plaza. Created by wildlife artist Robert Glen, it took seven years to make. In the lobby of the West Tower of Williams Square is the Mustang

Children of all ages love the Tarantula Steam Train at the Stockyards Depot

Ft Worth CVB

Sculpture exhibit, which includes a 20-minute film about the concept and creation of this imposing work. Exhibit: Tue-Sat 10-6. Free. (Mid-Cities)

TARANTULA STEAM TRAIN
709 South Main Street
Grapevine
817/251-0066
www.tarantulatrain.com
The Grapevine Terminal for the Tarantula Steam Train is the restored historic 1901 Cotton Belt Depot. The beautifully restored 1896 steam locomotive and its early-twentieth-century open touring cars and passenger coaches make roundtrip excursions between the Grapevine Depot and the Stockyards National Historic District in Fort Worth. At the Grapevine Depot, the engine is turned on a massive, 180-ton 1927 Santa Fe Railroad turntable for its journey to Fort Worth—what a sight to see! The one-way trip lasts about one hour and 15 minutes and, depending on seasonal schedules, there's usually a layover of a couple hours or so to explore the Stockyards area before the return trip to Grapevine. Schedule is seasonal; call for times. Roundtrip: $22 adult, $20 senior, $11 child 2-12; One-way: $13 adult, $13 senior, $10 child 2-12. & (Mid-Cities)

TEXAS STADIUM
2401 East Airport Freeway
Irving
972/438-7676
Irving's Texas Stadium, the home of the Dallas Cowboys National Football League team, has 63,855 covered seats, 388 luxury suites, 52 full concession stands, 40 specialty stands, 115 drinking fountains, and 86 restrooms. Tours leave from the Pro Shop, but no tours are given 24 hours before a game. You can bring a football and camera to take your photograph on the famous turf. In addition to the field, the 45-minute tour includes the press box, private luxury suite, locker room, and of course the gift shop. A one-of-a-kind showcase when it opened in 1971, the famous stadium with the hole in its roof is a popular venue for country-and-western concerts, festivals, and other events, as well as football games. Mon-Sat on the hour 10-3, Sun on the hour 11-3. $5 adults, $3 seniors and children 5-12, children 5 and under free (see also Chapter 10, Sports and Recreation). & (Mid-Cities)

ARLINGTON/ GRAND PRAIRIE

THE BALLPARK IN ARLINGTON
1000 Ballpark Way
Arlington
Ticket office: 817/273-5100
Tour information: 817/273-5099
This massive red-brick and granite

ballpark, home of the Texas Rangers baseball team, is one of the finest facilities ever built for baseball. An attraction in its own right, the building's facade features impressive architectural sculptures depicting scenes from Texas history. Sixty-seven murals picture some of the greatest players of the game. Thirty-five sculptured steer heads and twenty-one stars surround the stadium. The ballpark is the centerpiece of a 270-acre complex, which also includes the Legends of the Game Museum and the Children's Learning Center, a youth baseball park, a 12-acre lake, and parks along the perimeter. Take a fascinating tour of the ballpark and see the clubhouse, press box, batting cages, luxury suites, and dugout. Visit the Grand Slam Shop or the Timeless Treasures Gift Shop for souvenirs and specialty gifts. Tours are given year-round on non-game days: Mon-Sat 9-4, Sun 12-4. $5 adults, $4 seniors/ students with ID, $3 children 13 and under. Combination tickets available with Legends of the Game Baseball Museum admission (see also Chapter 10, Sports and Recreation; Chapter 6, Museums and Art Galleries; and Chapter 7, Kids' Stuff). க் (Arlington/Grand Prairie)

PALACE OF WAX AND RIPLEY'S BELIEVE IT OR NOT!
601 East Safari Parkway
Grand Prairie
972/263-2391 (metro)
www.tourtexas.com/ripleys
Visit two unusual and entertaining attractions in one exotic-looking, onion-domed building. In the Palace of Wax, come face to face with life-like figures from Hollywood, horrors, the Old West, history, childhood fantasy, and the life of Christ. Ripley's

has eight galleries displaying the most beautiful, bizarre, and fascinating oddities from around the world. All are authentic—believe it or not! There's a nice snack bar, gift shop, and game room. Mon-Fri 10-5, Sat-Sun 10-6. Combination tickets for both attractions: $12.95 adults, $9.95 children; one attraction only: $9.95 adults, $6.95 children. க் (Arlington/Grand Prairie)

SIX FLAGS HURRICANE HARBOR
1800 East Lamar Boulevard
Arlington
817/265-3356 (metro)
www.sixflags.com
/hurricaneharbordallas
Now part of the Six Flags family, this was the largest water park in the Unites States when it opened in 1983 as Wet'N Wild. Covering 47 acres, it offers an extensive variety of water rides and activities for everyone from the lazy floater to the daredevil. New in 1999 is Hook's Lagoon with three lagoons, a pirate ship, and exciting water rides. Body-surf in the million-gallon wave pool or relax at the beach with its shaded picnic area. There's a playground and kids' park, beach volleyball courts, music shows and videos, and a gift shop. Tube and raft rentals are available and professional lifeguards are on

ARLINGTON, GRAND PRAIRIE, & MID-CITIES

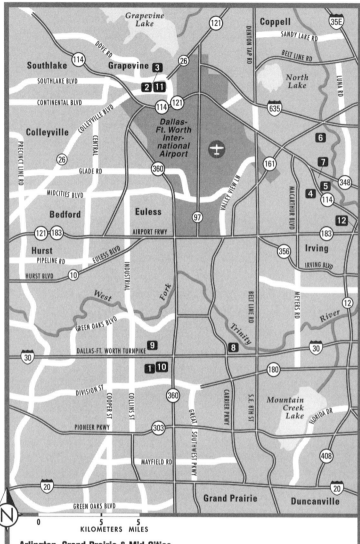

Arlington, Grand Prairie & Mid-Cities

1. The Ballpark in Arlington (AGP)
2. Grapevine Visitor Information Center (MC)
3. Historic Downtown Grapevine (MC)
4. Las Colinas Flower Clock (MC)
5. Mandalay Canal Walk at Las Colinas (MC)
6. The Movie Studios at Las Colinas (MC)
7. The Mustangs of Las Colinas (MC)
8. Palace of Wax and Ripley's Believe It or Not! (AGP)
9. Six Flags Hurricane Harbor (AGP)
10. Six Flags Over Texas (AGP)
11. Tarantula Steam Train (MC)
12. Texas Stadium (MC)

Famous Fort Worth Cemeteries

- **Greenwood Memorial Park** *(3100 White Settlement Road): The equestrian statues at the main entrance are replicas of a sculpture that has stood in St. Mark's Square in Venice, Italy, since 1204. In the circle of the drive is Turner's Oak, believed to be more than 700 years old. Legend says that following the Civil War, when the military and reconstruction government ordered the citizens of Fort Worth to surrender their property, Charles Turner, who lived at that spot, refused to give up his gold and buried it under this oak tree. The treasure was later used to finance businesses and citizens as they rebuilt the city. This impeccably maintained cemetery is the final resting place of dozens of prominent citizens from the twentieth century. Although not as old as Oakwood or Pioneer Rest cemeteries, tombstones bear the names Carter, Davis, Leonard, and Davey O'Brien, the Texas Christian University Heisman Trophy winner.*
- **Oakwood Cemetery** *(701 Grand Avenue): Opened in 1879 on 20 rolling acres donated by pioneer civic leader John Peter Smith, this tract is across the Trinity River from Downtown and has now grown substantially. A walk through its hallowed grounds is like a walk through Fort Worth history. The story of its division into sections for*

duty. Open daily mid-May to mid-Aug, weekends only early May to mid-Sep. Call for current admission fees (see also Chapter 7, Kids' Stuff). (Arlington/Grand Prairie)

SIX FLAGS OVER TEXAS
2201 Road to Six Flags (I-30 at Highway 360)
Arlington
817/640-8900 (metro)
www.sixflags.com/parks
Billed as the most popular tourist attraction in the state, Six Flags Over Texas opened in 1961 as the largest amusement park in Texas. Now more than 3 million visitors a year flock to the 205-acre park. The all-inclusive admission price includes everything but food, souvenirs, video games, and special events/concerts. The theme park is divided into areas representing Texas under six flags through history: Spain, France, Mexico, the Republic of Texas, the Confederacy, and the United States. There are rides for all ages and level of adventurer—you can zip, spin, fall, drop, whip, or twist until your heart throbs. One of the best known rides is the Texas Giant, the world's tallest wooden roller coaster, voted

blacks, whites, soldiers, and Catholics is a fascinating tale; Smith also donated land for a Jewish cemetery and several others. Brittle docket books in the Oakwood safe contain entries beginning in 1879. Historical markers abound alongside the gravestones of cattle and oil barons, cotton kings, business tycoons, bankers, writers, musicians, brave soldiers, gunslingers, and soiled doves. Notable "residents" include cattle baron Burk Burnett, frontier lawman "Longhair Jim" Courtright, cattle/oil baron W. T. Waggoner, legendary black businessman "Gooseneck Bill" McDonald, U. S. Senator and Texas Governor Charles A. Culberson, and dedicated pioneer and Oakwood founder, John Peter Smith.

- **Pioneer Rest Cemetery** (600 block of Samuels Avenue): This cemetery was founded in 1850, long before Fort Worth was a city, when two of Major Ripley A. Arnold's children died. Fort Worth's oldest cemetery is laden with historical markers and gravestones of many early settlers, including that of county namesake General Edward A. Tarrant.
- **Rose Hill Cemetery** (Lancaster at Rose Hill Drive): A lovely old cemetery on Fort Worth's east side, it's now famous as the final resting place of Lee Harvey Oswald, the assassin of John F. Kennedy.

several times as the top roller coaster in the world. Tamer rides include the narrow-gauge train and an old-fashioned carousel. Get a great view from the top of the three-hundred-foot Oil Derrick! A variety of shows delight audiences of all ages, and special live concerts at the Music Mill Amphitheater often feature top-name entertainers. Each season brings new rides and shows, and usually a rise in admission prices. Daily in summer, weekends only in spring and fall, and for special events like Halloween FrightFest in October and Holiday in the Park in late November and December. Call for schedule and current admission prices (see also Chapter 7, Kids' Stuff). & (Arlington/Grand Prairie)

DOWNTOWN FORT WORTH

CHISHOLM TRAIL MURAL
400 Main Street
Fort Worth
Covering the south side of the three-story 1907 Jett Building at 400 Main Street, these *trompe l'oeil* longhorns look as if they are bursting into Sundance Square. Created

TIP

On Wednesdays, admission to the Fort Worth Zoo is half price for all visitors.

by artist Richard Haas, the mural portrays Fort Worth's early days as a major stop on the Chisholm Trail. (Downtown Fort Worth)

NANCY LEE AND PERRY R. BASS PERFORMANCE HALL
Fourth and Commerce Streets
Fort Worth
Ticket office: 888/597-7827
Administrative office: 817/212-4200
Information Hotline: 817/212-4325
www.basshall.com
The city boasting the third-largest cultural district in the nation has a dazzling new crown jewel. The $67-million performing arts facility is named for Nancy Lee and Perry R. Bass (see sidebar on page 105). The 183,000-square-foot performance hall has 2,056 seats and serves as the permanent home to the Fort Worth Symphony Orchestra, Fort Worth Dallas Ballet, Fort Worth Opera, and Van Cliburn's International Piano Competition and Concert Series. In the hope of making the performing arts more accessible to the general public, numerous community organizations are permitted to use this fine facility. The multipurpose concert hall was designed for the ultimate in excellence. Built in the classic style of a nineteenth-century European opera house, it features state-of-the-art theatrical lighting and sound systems. Although it sits on a city block of land donated by the Bass family, a large

portion of the community contributed and supported the building of the facility. If you can't attend a performance, take a tour of the showpiece. Free public tours: Wed and Fri at 2:30 p.m. and Sat at 10:30 a.m., performance schedule permitting. Performance admission prices vary. Box office: Tue-Fri 10-6, Sat 10-4 (see also Chapter 11, Performing Arts). ♿ (Downtown Fort Worth)

SUNDANCE SQUARE
Bordered by Calhoun, Throckmorton, Second, and Fifth Streets
Fort Worth
817/339-7777
www.sundancesquare.com
Named for the "Sundance Kid" who, according to legend, hid out in the nearby Hell's Half Acre with his partner Butch Cassidy, Sundance Square is a 20-block area at the north end of downtown Fort Worth. With original red-brick streets and distinctive renovated buildings of early 1900s architectural design, it's now a lively entertainment district, home to upscale art galleries, theaters, restaurants, nightclubs, and specialty shops. Sundance West (on Throckmorton Street, just behind Caravan of Dreams) is the first of the fashionable downtown apartment buildings. Always bustling with activity, the Sundance Square area is surprisingly safe after dark, patrolled

DOWNTOWN FORT WORTH

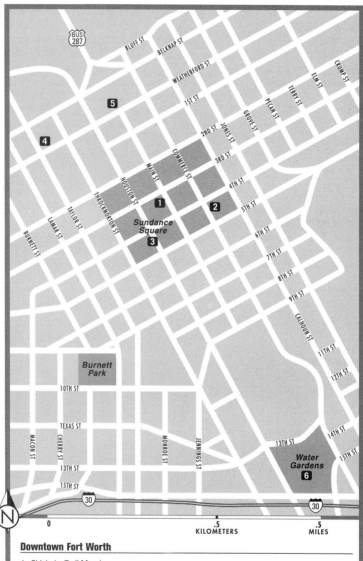

Sundance Square

Burnett Park

Water Gardens

BUS 287

BLUFF ST
BELKNAP ST
WEATHERFORD ST
1ST ST
2ND ST
3RD ST
4TH ST
5TH ST
6TH ST
7TH ST
8TH ST
9TH ST
10TH ST
11TH ST
12TH ST
13TH ST
14TH ST
15TH ST

JONES ST
GROVE ST
PECAN ST
TERRY ST
ELM ST
CRUMP ST
CALHOUN ST
COMMERCE ST
MAIN ST
HOUSTON ST
THROCKMORTON ST
TAYLOR ST
LAMAR ST
BURNETT ST
MACON ST
CHERRY ST
MONROE ST
JENNINGS ST

30

N

| 0 | .5 | .5 |
KILOMETERS
MILES

Downtown Fort Worth

1. Chisholm Trail Mural
2. Nancy Lee and Perry R. Bass Performance Hall
3. Sundance Square
4. Tandy Subway
5. Tarrant County Courthouse
6. Water Gardens

by a private security force. (Downtown Fort Worth)

TANDY SUBWAY
Fort Worth
817/336-5248
The only privately owned subway in the world runs between a free parking lot and Fort Worth Outlet Square in the Tandy Center. The underground electrical subway was the brainchild of brothers Marvin and O. P. Leonard, owners of Leonard's Bros., an early department store in downtown. Construction and excavation began in 1962; the tunnel had to be blasted through solid rock. Leonard's department store is long gone, but the Tandy Center/Fort Worth Outlet Square now uses the subway to carry shoppers to and from a 14-acre parking lot along the banks of the Trinity River, northwest of the central business district. Free. ♿ (Downtown Fort Worth)

TARRANT COUNTY COURTHOUSE
100 West Weatherford

Fort Worth's unique Water Gardens

Ft Worth CVB

Fort Worth
817/884-1111
One of the most beautiful courthouses in the state, built in 1893-1895 of native Texas pink granite and marble, it's one of Fort Worth's most beloved old buildings. Patterned after the Texas State Capitol in Austin and listed in the National Register of Historic Places, it stands proudly at the far north end of Main Street in downtown. North of the courthouse is the Paddock Viaduct, the Main Street bridge over the Trinity River, and the bluffs where the original army fort stood. ♿ (Downtown Fort Worth)

WATER GARDENS
Main Street between Commerce and Houston Streets
Fort Worth
817/871-7275
Given to the citizens of Fort Worth by the Amon G. Carter Foundation, this award-winning water garden features 19,000 gallons per minute of water cascading over multi-tiered concrete ledges. Designed by renowned architects John Burgee and Philip Johnson, who also designed the Amon Carter Museum, it was completed in 1974 at a cost of $7 million. The unusual 4.3-acre park near the Convention Center creates a secluded oasis amid the city bustle. You'll see lots of downtown workers with brown bag lunches at noontime enjoying the tranquility. And on a hot summer day, you can splash into this work of art to cool off. Sitting on land that was once part of the infamous "Hell's Half Acre," the garden has been used for scenes from the movie *Logan's Run* and as a backdrop for numerous productions and weddings. (Downtown Fort Worth)

NORTH FORT WORTH

FORT WORTH HERD
Information: 817/336-HERD
www.fortworthherd.com
On June 12, 1999, as part of Fort Worth's 150th birthday celebration, six mounted cowhands drove 15 longhorns through the Stockyards Historic District to the banks of the Trinity River. It was the first of what would become a daily event, the only one of its kind in the world. Each morning, genuine cowpunchers drive the Longhorn herd from their home in the Stockyards to the West Fork of the Trinity River, where they graze until mid-afternoon when they are driven back. Some of these magnificent animals have horn spans of six feet and weigh up to one ton. What a spectacle! Hear the cattle bawl! Hear the spurs jingle! Every detail of the cowboys' outfits and tack is authentic and historically accurate, giving observers a memorable glimpse into Fort Worth's past. For a good view, watch from the catwalk above the cattle pens, the lawn in front of the Livestock Exchange Building, or the outdoor seating areas of some of the Stockyards Station restaurants (see following entries). Daily; depending on weather in winter, 11:30 a.m. and 4:00 p.m. Free. (North Fort Worth)

FORT WORTH STOCKYARDS NATIONAL HISTORIC DISTRICT
Stockyards Visitor Center
130 East Exchange Avenue
Fort Worth
817/624-4741
www.ftworthstockyards.com
About two miles north of Downtown, the Stockyards National Historic District has been preserved, renovated, and restored as a tribute to Fort Worth's Western heritage and history as "Cowtown." Today, it's a bustling enclave of shops, galleries, dining establishments, saloons, and entertainment, all with a western flavor. The historic buildings and markers, the Stockyards Museum, and the Fort Worth Herd all safeguard the spirit of the Old West. (North Fort Worth)

LIVESTOCK EXCHANGE BUILDING
131 East Exchange Avenue
Fort Worth
817/625-5087
This imposing 1902 Spanish-style building was once the headquarters of one of the greatest livestock markets in the world, known as the "Wall Street of the West." Now it houses private offices of cattle brokers, marketing firms, lawyers, the Stockyards Museum (see Chapter 6, Museums and Art Galleries), and the North Fort Worth Historical Society. Mon-Fri 8-5, Sat 10-4 ♿ (North Fort Worth)

STOCKYARDS STATION
140 East Exchange Avenue
Fort Worth
817/625-9715, 972/988-6877 (metro)
www.stockyardsstation.com
Originally the hog and sheep pens of the largest stockyards in the Southwest, this area is now home to western-theme shops, galleries, and restaurants. The Tarantula Steam Train's Fort Worth depot is inside Stockyards Station (see following listing). Facilities are available for all sorts of group functions, meetings, and parties, both indoor and outdoor. On the east side is a small western-theme amusement park with a bronco and bull ride and 1932 carousel. Everyone will enjoy shopping and dining Texas-style (see

GREATER FORT WORTH

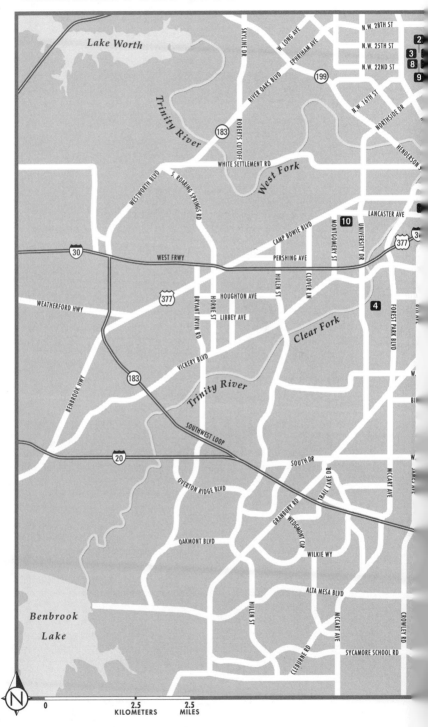

Lake Worth

N.W. 28TH ST
N.W. 25TH ST
N.W. 22ND ST
N.W. 16TH ST

2
3
8
9

SKYLINE DR
W. LONG AVE
EPHRIHAM AVE

199

RIVER OAKS BLVD

NORTHSIDE DR

Trinity River

183

ROBERTS CUTOFF

HENDERSON ST

WHITE SETTLEMENT RD

West Fork

WESTWORTH BLVD

S. ROARING SPRINGS RD

LANCASTER AVE

CAMP BOWIE BLVD

MONTGOMERY ST

UNIVERSITY DR

10

377

3

30

WEST FRWY

PERSHING AVE

HULEN ST

CLOVER LN

WEATHERFORD HWY

377

BRYANT IRVIN RD

HORNE ST

HOUGHTON AVE

LIBBEY AVE

4

FOREST PARK BLVD

Clear Fork

BENBROOK HWY

183

VICKERY BLVD

Trinity River

W.

BI

SOUTHWEST LOOP

20

OVERTON RIDGE BLVD

SOUTH DR

GRANBURY RD

TRAIL LAKE DR

WEDGMONT CIR

MCCART AVE

W.

JAMES AVE

OAKMONT BLVD

WILKIE WY

ALTA MESA BLVD

Benbrook
Lake

HULEN ST

MCCART AVE

CROWLEY RD

CLEBURNE RD

SYCAMORE SCHOOL RD

N

0   2.5   2.5
    KILOMETERS   MILES

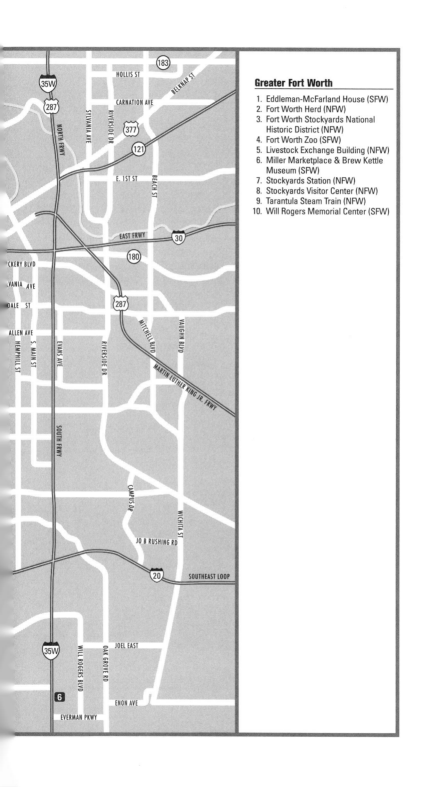

Greater Fort Worth

1. Eddleman-McFarland House (SFW)
2. Fort Worth Herd (NFW)
3. Fort Worth Stockyards National Historic District (NFW)
4. Fort Worth Zoo (SFW)
5. Livestock Exchange Building (NFW)
6. Miller Marketplace & Brew Kettle Museum (SFW)
7. Stockyards Station (NFW)
8. Stockyards Visitor Center (NFW)
9. Tarantula Steam Train (NFW)
10. Will Rogers Memorial Center (SFW)

Chapter 4, Where to Eat and Chapter 9, Shopping). Establishment hours vary. (North Fort Worth)

TARANTULA STEAM TRAIN
140 East Exchange Avenue
Fort Worth
817/251-0066
www.tarantulatrain.com
"All Aboard!" Yes, the conductor really shouts those words as the Tarantula Steam Train departs the Stockyards Depot for a nostalgic ride to Grapevine. The exquisitely restored 1896 steam locomotive pulls turn-of-the-century Victorian coach cars as well as open-sided touring coaches.

The 21-mile journey lasts about one hour and 15 minutes each way, and snacks are available on board. Explore the shops along Grapevine's historic Main Street, visit a vineyard or tasting room, and have lunch at one of the excellent local restaurants before returning to the Stockyards. Schedule is seasonal; call for times. Roundtrip: $22 adult, $20 senior, $11 child 2-12; One-way: $13 adult, $13 senior, $10 child 2-12. &
(North Fort Worth)

SOUTHWEST FORT WORTH

EDDLEMAN-MCFARLAND HOUSE
1110 Penn Street
Fort Worth
817/332-5875
Located on a bluff overlooking the Trinity River, this 1899 Queen Anne/Victorian home is one of the few remaining examples of Fort Worth's majestic "cattle baron" era. Listed in the National Register of Historic Places, it features finely crafted woodwork and exquisite architectural detail. Tours Tue and Thu at 10, 11, and 1 or by appointment. $2.50 (Southwest Fort Worth)

FORT WORTH ZOO
1989 Colonial Parkway
Fort Worth
817/871-7050
www.fortworthzoo.com

The spirit of the Old West is alive and well in the Stockyards National Historic District

Ft Worth CVB

Grapevine's Vineyards and Wineries

- *Delaney Winery & Vineyards*, 2000 Champagne Boulevard (Highway 121 at Glade Road), 817/481-5668; This ten-acre vineyard and winery has beautiful grounds, antique vats in a Grand Barrel Room, a tasting area, and a gift shop. Tue-Sat 10-5.

- *La Buena Vida Vineyards*, 416 East College Street, 817/481-9463; One of Texas' oldest producing wineries, with award-winning champagne, its tasting rooms includes a winery museum and picnic tables under a wisteria-covered arbor amid native Texas gardens and fountains. Mon-Sat 10-5, Sun noon-5.

- *Cap Rock Winery & Tasting Room*, 409 South Main Street, 817/329-WINE; The focal point of Grapevine's newest winery/tasting room is an 11-foot bar and painted murals of the winery in West Texas. Tue-Sat 11-4:30

- *Homestead Winery & Tasting Room*, 211 East Worth Street, 817/251-9463; Homestead is located in an historic home on Main Street and provides customers with personal attention and a fine selection of wines. Wed-Sat 11-5:30, Sun 1-5:30

- *La Bodega Winery & Tasting Room*, Terminal A, DFW Airport, 972/574-1440; The first-ever winery tasting room located in a major U.S. airport, La Bodega provides travelers a variety of wines from select Texas vineyards. Mon-Sat 7:30-10, Sun 11-10 (wine available after noon)

This exceptional zoo, ranked as one of the top five in the nation, is home to more than 5,000 native and exotic animals. Only a waterfall or river separates visitors from the animals at many of the "natural habitat" exhibits. See Sumatran tigers in Asian Falls, great ape species in a tropical rainforest, and a variety of condors and eagles in Raptor Canyon. Visit Koala Outback, Penguin Island, Flamingo Bay, and the top-notch Herpetarium, home to some of the rarest reptiles in the world. "Texas," an exhibit covering 11 acres, re-creates a nineteenth-century pioneer town complete with a working windmill and animals indigenous to the Lone Star State. Strollers and motorized carts are available for rent, and wheelchairs are complimentary for eligible visitors. There's a snack bar and an excellent gift shop. The longest miniature train ride in Texas begins opposite the zoo and winds through Forest and Trinity Parks. Daily 10-5, extended hours seasonally. $7 adult (over 13), $4.50 children (3-12), $3 seniors, free for toddlers 2 and under. Train $3 adults, $2.50 children. Parking $4 (see also Chapter 7, Kids' Stuff). & (Southwest Fort Worth)

MILLER MARKETPLACE & BREW KETTLE MUSEUM
7009 South Freeway
Fort Worth
817/568-BEER

If you're interested in the history of beer, then this is the place to go. A tour of the facilities will include the 5,000-year history of brewing and the 150-year history of Miller Brewing Company. The Brew Kettle Pub offers samples, and the Miller Marketplace has a variety of souvenir merchandise with the Miller logo printed on it as well as gift items and bar accessories for sale. Tue-Sat 11:30-5:30. Free. & (Southwest Fort Worth)

WILL ROGERS MEMORIAL CENTER
3401 West Lancaster
at University Drive
Fort Worth
817/871-8150

The original buildings of the Will Rogers Memorial Center were born of civic pride. When Dallas was chosen over Fort Worth as the site of the 1936 Texas Centennial, early Fort Worthians, not to be outdone by their rival to the east, had a celebration of their own. They built the Will Rogers Memorial Center to house the festivities. The complex now consists of several buildings and spaces; the Memorial Tower, Auditorium, Coliseum, and Livestock Barns are original. New additions include the Equestrian Center and Amon Carter Jr. Exhibit Hall, both added in the 1980s. The Southwestern Exposition and Livestock Show/Rodeo began in the stockyards in 1896 and was moved to the Will Rogers Coliseum in 1944, where it is still held from the end of January through mid-February each year. The 85-acre complex also hosts numerous equestrian and livestock exhibitions and competitions, regional athletic competitions, trade shows and fairs, graduations, concert performances, conventions, the Shrine Circus, and flea markets. The equestrian statue of Will Rogers on his horse, Soapsuds, was commissioned by Amon Carter to honor his great friend. & (Southwest Fort Worth)

Dallas CVB

6

MUSEUMS AND ART GALLERIES

Nowhere is the variety and diversity of the Metroplex more evident than in its museums. From highly acclaimed art museums and natural history museums to those devoted to cattle and dolls and airplanes and baseball, there's truly something for everyone.

Dallas maintains its cosmopolitan image with the world-class Dallas Museum of Art, yet pays tribute to one of the country's most tragic moments (President Kennedy's assassination) with the Sixth Floor Museum. As part of the revitalization of downtown, the Dallas Arts District was formed to centralize the scattered arts community. With major anchors the Dallas Museum of Art and the Morton H. Meyerson Symphony Center, the area is home to other art venues, performing arts buildings, and theaters. Just southeast of downtown is Fair Park, which is home to several museums and attractions on the grounds of the Texas Centennial Exposition of 1936.

"Cowboys and Culture" is an overused phrase, but none more accurately describes Fort Worth. The town is intensely proud of its Western heritage, but also world renowned for its Cultural District. In the Cultural District, within easy walking distance of one another are three extraordinary art museums (the Amon Carter Museum, the Kimbell Art Museum, and the Modern Art Museum) and the exceptional Fort Worth Museum of Science and History with its Omni Theater and Noble Planetarium, Scott Theatre, the Will Rogers Memorial Complex and Equestrian Center, and Casa Mañana Playhouse. Immediately to the south are the Fort Worth Botanic and Japanese Gardens.

Entertainment guide inserts in the Friday edition of both the Dallas Morning News and the Fort Worth Star Telegram list special exhibits, tours, and events. Ask about free lectures or tours. If you live in the area and plan to visit a particular museum frequently, check into a membership program that will offer discounts and other benefits.

Galleries throughout the Metroplex also offer an enormous variety. Look for traditional art on Fort Worth's west side along Camp Bowie Boulevard and in Downtown's Sundance Square. In Dallas, browse the galleries in the McKinney Avenue and Oak Lawn areas immediately north of Downtown. The Deep Ellum galleries on Dallas's east side offer what can only be called "alternative art."

ART MUSEUMS

AMON CARTER MUSEUM
3501 Camp Bowie Boulevard
Fort Worth
817/738-1933
www.cartermuseum.org
First, the bad news. This outstanding museum is closed until the summer of 2001 for a major expansion. Sample exhibits will be displayed in a cozy space downtown at 500 Commerce Street and on the Internet. While admitting he knew nothing about art, Amon Carter knew a great city needed art, and the devoted civic leader definitely wanted Fort Worth to be a great city. Thus, he assembled one of the country's finest collections of the work of Frederic Remington and Charles Russell, the premier artists of the American West. Since it opened in 1961 to house these collections, the Amon Carter Museum has become one of the nation's foremost showcases of American art. On display are exceptional paintings, sculpture, photographs, and graphic arts from the nineteenth and early twentieth centuries. The Carter's exhibits, educational programs, community events,

and publications support the museum's mission to promote the enjoyment and study of American art. Free. & (Southwest Fort Worth)

DALLAS MUSEUM OF ART
1717 North Harwood
Dallas
214/922-1200
www.dm-art.org
When this exceptional museum opened in 1984, the Dallas Arts District was born. Actually several museums in one, its collections are exhaustive. The "Art of the Americas" collection features significant treasures from the lost civilizations of Aztec, Anasazi, and Maya as well as noted twentieth-century artists. The "Art of Europe" collections include extensive works by the renowned European artists of the nineteenth and twentieth centuries. The "Arts of Africa" exhibits contain an astounding variety of paintings and sculpture of and from the African diaspora. Exquisite examples of decorative arts from China, Japan, and Southeast Asia, as well as Indonesian textiles, are featured in the "Arts of Asia and the Pacific." The Contemporary Art collection is outstanding. There's a Decorative Arts wing, a Sculpture Garden, a first-rate museum store, and two restaurants. The museum hosts exclusive traveling exhibits and special events. Docents and staff give talks and tours and sponsor art activities for children. Tue-Wed 11-4, Thu 11-9, Fri 11-4, Sat-Sun 11-5. Free (charge for special exhibits). & (Downtown Dallas)

KIMBELL ART MUSEUM
3333 Camp Bowie Boulevard
Fort Worth
817/332-8451

> The Dallas Museum of Natural History offers free admission on Mondays from 10 a.m. to 1 p.m.

www.kimbellart.org
Industrialist Kay Kimbell bequeathed his fortune to create the Kimbell Art Museum. The city's best-known museum is housed in a masterpiece of architectural art designed by Louis I. Kahn. Inspired by Renaissance designs, the vaulted skylights provide an innovative use of natural light to illuminate the galleries below. The award-winning building showcases a world-class collection of old masters, including Rembrandt, Caravaggio, Cezanne, and Picasso, as well as important examples of ancient, Pre-Columbian, African, and Asian art. The Kimbell is one of only a few American museums to regularly sponsor traveling exhibits from some of the world's great art collections. The Buffet at the Kimbell is one of the best lunch spots in town. Tue-Thu 10-5, Fri 12-8, Sat 10-5, Sun 12-5. Free. & (Southwest Fort Worth)

MEADOWS MUSEUM OF ART
6101 Bishop at Binkley (on the
SMU campus)
Dallas
214/768-2516
Texas oil financier and philanthropist Algur H. Meadows donated his world-class collection of Spanish art to Southern Methodist University. As a result, this museum displays the finest and most extensive collection of Spanish art outside Spain. The permanent collection includes masterpieces from the Middle Ages to the present, graphic works of Goya,

Baroque canvases, and Renaissance altarpieces. The Meadows presents public lectures and gallery talks by professors and visiting artists, as well as films and concerts throughout the year. Mon-Tue 10-5, Thu 10-8, Fri-Sat 10-5, Sun 1-5. Free & (Central Dallas)

MODERN ART MUSEUM
OF FORT WORTH
1309 Montgomery
Fort Worth
817/738-9215
www.mamfw.org
The city's oldest art museum features paintings and sculptures from every major movement in the twentieth century. The museum's permanent collection includes works by modern masters such as Pablo Picasso, Mark Rothko, Frank Stella, and Jackson Pollock. It hosts traveling special exhibits and offers free lectures throughout the year. Contemporary sculptures grace the museum grounds. Tue-Fri 10-5, Sat 11-5, Sun 12-5. Free. & (Southwest Fort Worth)

THE MODERN AT
SUNDANCE SQUARE
410 Houston Street
Fort Worth
817/335-9215
This branch of the Modern Art Museum of Fort Worth is located in Sundance Square downtown and features artworks from both the permanent collection and traveling

Sculpturesque folks chat outside the Modern Art Museum of Ft Worth

exhibits. It's housed in the historic 1929 Sanger Building, which is listed in the National Register of Historic Places. A nice museum store offers gifts and mementos. Mon-Wed 11-6, Thu-Sat 11-8, Sun 1-5. Free. & (Downtown Fort Worth)

SID RICHARDSON COLLECTION OF WESTERN ART
309 Main Street
Fort Worth
817/332-6554
www.sidrmuseum.org
Showcasing the spirit of the Old West, this permanent display features the largest single assemblage of works by Frederic Remington and Charles Russell, considered by many art-lovers to be the finest of the Western artists. The 60 paintings and bronzes were acquired by the late oilman and philanthropist Sid W. Richardson from 1942 until his death in 1959. The free self-tour guidebook adds interest and information, and a small gift shop sells mementos. Tue-Wed 10-5, Thu-Fri

10-8, Sat 11-8, Sun 1-5. Free. & (Downtown Fort Worth)

THE TRAMMELL AND MARGARET CROW COLLECTION OF ASIAN ART
2010 Flora Street
Dallas
214/979-6430
www.crowcollection.org
This amazing collection includes over 500 works of art and artifacts from China, Japan, Southeast Asia, and India, dating from 3500 B.C. to the early twentieth century. When the Crow Family Foundation decided to share one of the most extensive collections of its kind with the community, they built a 12,000-square-foot gallery adjacent to the Trammell Crow Center in downtown Dallas. In the heart of the Arts District, the entrance sets the mood with an oasis of cypress trees and a calming fountain framing the sculpture of a Chinese deity. The collections feature magnificent pieces from delicate Japanese scrolls to massive archi-

tectural pieces. One of the highlights is a selection of precious jade from China. Education and study of the Asian arts is a primary goal, so visitors will find an audio tour of selected pieces, a multimedia computer station in the lobby, and public tours on weekends (other times by arrangement). Tue-Sun 11-6, Thu 11-9. Free. & (Downtown Dallas)

SCIENCE AND HISTORY MUSEUMS

AGE OF STEAM RAILROAD MUSEUM
1105 Washington Street (in Fair Park)
Dallas
214/428-0101
Chug, chug! Toot, toot! Celebrate one of the most colorful eras in American history. The railroad reached Dallas in 1872 and ultimately made the city the center of commerce for the Southwest. Climb aboard pieces of history, such as luxurious Pullman sleeping cars, plush lounge cars, and the mighty steam locomotives. The Southwest Railroad Historical Society has preserved some nostalgic and unique vintage specimens in this outdoor, hands-on, interpretive museum, considered today to be one of the finest collections of historic railway equipment in the nation. The Switchman's Corner gift shop, located in

the restored 1905 Houston & Central Depot, offers a wide selection of gifts and a nice variety of books. Wed-Sun 10-5. $4 adults, $2 children 3-12, children under 3 free. & (East Dallas)

CATTLE RAISERS MUSEUM
1301 West Seventh Street
Fort Worth
817/332-8551
www.cattleraisersmuseum.org
Talking mannequins, life-size Longhorn cattle, multimedia visuals, and interactive exhibits bring to life the legends and lore of the cattle drives and cowboys. Visitors of all ages will enjoy reliving the spirit of this exciting period in the history and development of the Texas cattle industry. Outstanding collections of branding irons, spurs, and saddles are popular exhibits. The museum is a monumental project of the Texas and Southwestern Cattle Raisers Foundation, a nonprofit organization. Mon-Sat 10-5, Sun 1-5. $3 adults. & (Southwest Fort Worth)

DALLAS MEMORIAL CENTER FOR HOLOCAUST STUDIES
7900 Northhaven Road
Dallas
972/750-4654
Dedicated to the six million Jews who died during the WWII Holocaust, this museum's stated purpose is to remember, record, understand, explain, and enlighten

Sundance Square parking lots are free after 5:00 p.m. weekdays and all weekends.

future generations about this event unlike any other in history. Documentary films, photographs, artifacts, and exhibits are on display, as well as a library of more than two thousand books and periodicals. The museum's staff and members offer various programs, lectures, and slide/video presentations to schools and community groups. Mon-Fri 9:30-4:30, Sun 12-4, open Thu until 9 during the school year; closed Jewish and most national holidays. Free. ঙ (Central Dallas)

DALLAS MUSEUM OF NATURAL HISTORY
3535 Grand Avenue (in Fair Park)
Dallas
214/421-DINO
www.dallasdino.org
Displaying millions of years of Texas past and present is not an easy job. This museum contains extensive habitat displays and dioramas of native wildlife. Watch the working paleontology lab, where fossils are pieced together. See the Tenontosaurus, the first reconstructed Texas dinosaur. Dino World has bones, eggs, skeleton casts, and a simulated dig site. City Safari is a hands-on science discovery center for young children. The museum often hosts traveling exhibits and special events, and 40,000 school children participate in the educational programs. Daily 10-5. $5 adults, $3 seniors and children 3-18, children under 3 free. Free Mon 10-1. ঙ (East Dallas)

FIELDER HOUSE
1616 West Abram at Fielder
Arlington
817/460-4001
This museum, in a 1914 home, is dedicated to preserving the heritage of Arlington. Several rooms are furnished as turn-of-the-century rooms, a general store, and a barber shop. The museum hosts exhibits and events throughout the year. Another project of the Arlington Historical Society is The Heritage Center on

A prehistoric-sized sculpture at the Dallas Museum of Natural History

Dallas CVB

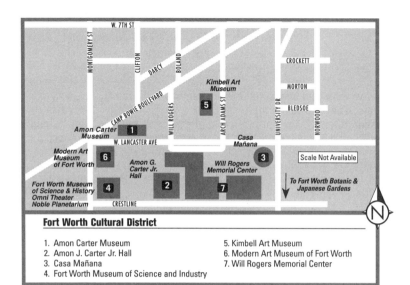

Fort Worth Cultural District

1. Amon Carter Museum
2. Amon J. Carter Jr. Hall
3. Casa Mañana
4. Fort Worth Museum of Science and Industry
5. Kimbell Art Museum
6. Modern Art Museum of Fort Worth
7. Will Rogers Memorial Center

Johnson Creek, which is located just down the street from Fielder House. It's a collection of two restored and furnished log cabins, a one-room schoolhouse, and an early barn exhibiting memorabilia from the days of the cotton industry. Colonel Middleton Tate Johnson, the Father of Tarrant County, is buried in the small cemetery. Wed-Sat 10-2, Sun 1:30-4:30. Free. (Arlington/Grand Prairie)

FIRE STATION NO. 1
Second and Commerce Streets
Fort Worth
817/732-1631
Fort Worth introduces itself at Fire Station No. 1, the site of the city's first fire station built in 1876 (the present one was built in 1907). This satellite exhibit of the Fort Worth Museum of Science and History is a great place to learn the most about the city in the least amount of time. It traces 150 years of Fort Worth history, including its heritage as an Army post and frontier town at the edge of West Texas. Find out how it got the nicknames "Cowtown" and "Panther City." Learn about the rivalry with Dallas and the legendary Amon Carter, the flamboyant newspaper publisher who put the slogan "Where the West Begins" on the *Fort Worth Star-Telegram*. Daily 9-7. Free. & (Downtown Fort Worth)

FORT WORTH MUSEUM OF SCIENCE AND HISTORY, OMNI THEATER, AND NOBLE PLANETARIUM
1501 Montgomery Street
Fort Worth
817/255-9300, 888/255-9300
www.fwmuseum.org
A favorite for the whole family, this exceptional museum attracts more than 1 million visitors a year. The largest attraction of its kind in the Southwest, it displays the wonders of nature through permanent collections and visiting exhibits. Of special interest are the History of Medicine, IBM Calculators and

Computers, and Man and his Possessions, six thousand years of human ingenuity. Kids love Rocks and Fossils, Kidspace®, and the DinoDig®, where they dig for dinosaur bones. Everyone can experience the legends and lore of the Lone Star State in the Texas History rooms. The museum also houses the **Omni Theater**, an 80-foot-high domed theater with sophisticated audio and video systems that dazzle your senses with spectacular film experiences. The **Noble Planetarium** offers entertaining astronomy and laser light productions, featuring advanced technology in a 30-foot domed theater. An excellent museum store is located in the lobby. Mon 9-5, Tue-Thu 9-8, Fri-Sat 9-9, Sun 12-8. $5 adults, $4 seniors, $3 children 3-12, children under 3 free. Additional charges for the Omni Theater and Noble Planetarium; combination tickets available. Call for schedules of performances. ᕼ (Southwest Fort Worth)

HERITAGE FARMSTEAD MUSEUM
1900 West 15th Street
Plano
972/424-7874
www.farmsteadmuseum.org
High-rise office buildings, hotels, and shopping centers surround this four-acre historic site, but when you walk through the entrance, you're transported into the last century. The Farrell-Wilson house, a stately 14-room home built in 1891, was one of the first homes in the county to get a telephone, electricity, and an indoor bathroom. The tour guide tells stories about the family and life as it was back then. Visit the one-room schoolhouse, barn, smokehouse, blacksmith shop, gardens, and farm animals. The Farmstead hosts edu-

cational programs and summer camps, holiday celebrations, and private gatherings. Call for hours and tour times. $3.50 adults, $2.50 seniors, $2.50 children 3-12. (Far North Dallas)

LOG CABIN VILLAGE
2100 Log Cabin Village Lane
Fort Worth
817/926-5881
Experience pioneer life on the Texas frontier! This living-history museum consists of seven authentic log homes built by Texas pioneers in the mid-nineteenth century. Guides dressed in period costumes tell the history of the cabins and the families that lived in them, and demonstrate pioneer crafts such as spinning, weaving, and candlemaking. One of the cabins has been converted to a grist mill and one is a reproduction of a working blacksmith shop. One cabin was the home of Isaac Parker, the uncle of Cynthia Parker who was captured by the Comanche as a young girl, later married Chief Nocona, and was the mother of Quanah Parker—the last Comanche war chief. Tue-Fri 9-5, Sat 10-5, Sun 1-5. $1.50 adults, $1.25 seniors and children 4-17, under 4 free. Free parking. (Southwest Fort Worth)

NATIONAL COWGIRL MUSEUM
AND HALL OF FAME
111 West Fourth Street, Suite 300
Fort Worth
817/336-4475 or 800/476-FAME
www.cowgirl.net
Begun in the Texas panhandle town of Hereford in 1975, this is the only museum in the world dedicated to honoring the women who distinguished themselves while exemplifying the pioneer spirit of the American West. The women in the

Freebies in Fort Worth

- *Amon Carter Museum*
- *The Contemporary Art Center of Fort Worth, Sundance Square*
- *Fire Station No. 1*
- *Fort Worth Botanic Gardens*
- *Fort Worth Water Garden*
- *Kimbell Art Museum*
- *Modern Art Museum*
- *The Modern at Sundance Square*
- *Sid Richardson Collection of Western Art*
- *Stockyards Museum*

National Cowgirl Museum and Hall of Fame are great women of spirit and courage who have carved paths in diverse areas of achievement. In order to increase its visibility, the founders moved the museum's contents from Hereford to Fort Worth in 1994, and have now broken ground for a new multi-million-dollar museum, scheduled to open in 2001, on a one-acre site in the heart of the Cultural District. For now you can visit the temporary offices in downtown Fort Worth, where a sample of the exhibits is on display, and proceeds from the gift shop contribute to the project. Mon-Sat 10-6. Free. &. (Downtown Fort Worth)

**OLD CITY PARK
HISTORIC VILLAGE
1717 Gano Street
Dallas
214/421-5141
www.oldcitypark.org**
This turn-of-the-century museum village of authentically restored buildings on 14 acres of Dallas's first city park tells the story of Dallas and north central Texas during the pioneer and Victorian days. Stroll the red-brick streets and visit more than 35 historic buildings dated from 1840 to 1910. Watch the potter, printer, and blacksmith work their crafts. Located on the edge of downtown, the vintage buildings are quite a contrast to the towering, glitzy Dallas skyline. A colorful museum shop, reminiscent of an old-time country store, is stuffed with handcrafted items, souvenirs, and old-fashioned candy. A restored late-1800s farmhouse is now Brent's Place, a restaurant serving tasty lunches. Grounds open daily sunrise to sunset. Visitors center Tue-Sat 10-4, Sun 12-4. $6 adults, $4 seniors, $3 children 3-12, children under 3 free. &. (Downtown Dallas)

**THE SCIENCE PLACE
AND IMAX® THEATER
Fair Park
Dallas
214/428-5555**

www.scienceplace.org
Kids of all ages head for The Science Place to learn how and why things work. Literally hundreds of hands-on exhibits and displays encourage kids to use their imagination and senses of touch, smell, sight, and hearing to discover the wonders of the universe.

A truly exceptional museum, it offers special programs and exhibits throughout the year. You'll feel as if you're part of the film experience in the TI Founders IMAX® Theater with its scientifically designed seats and sound system. There's a nice museum shop, a cafeteria, and in another building about one block away, The Science Place Planetarium. Combination tickets are available. Daily 9:30-5:30. Exhibit hall admission: $6 adults, $3 seniors and children 3-12, children under 3 free. IMAX admission is separate; call for films and times. & (East Dallas)

THE SIXTH FLOOR MUSEUM AT DEALEY PLAZA
411 Elm at Houston Street
Dallas
214/747-6660, 888/485-4854
www.jfk.org
November 22, 1963, was a tragic day in American history. For more than the three decades since the assassination of President John F. Kennedy, visitors from around the world have been drawn to the site of this event. Continued interest led to the development of the Sixth Floor Museum, which opened in 1989. Now Dallas's top visitor site, it's on the sixth floor of the former Texas School Book Depository Building, the location from which Lee Harvey Oswald allegedly shot the president. Designated a National Historic Landmark, along with Dealey Plaza, the museum contains an impressive array of photographs, artifacts, displays, and audiovisual presentations examining the life, times, death, and legacy of JFK. The adult and senior admission includes an audio guide available in seven languages; children's guides available in English only. Daily 9-6. $9 adults; $8 seniors, students, and children; children under 6 free. & (Downtown Dallas)

THE STOCKYARDS MUSEUM
131 East Exchange Avenue
Fort Worth
817/625-5087
Located in the historic Livestock Exchange Building, this collection is the culmination of efforts by members of the North Fort Worth Historical Society who worked diligently to restore the museum's antique display cases and now enthusiastically volunteer as hosts. The wide variety of artifacts and photographs relate to the history of the Stockyards, the meat packing industry,

TRIVIA

One of the world's longest-lasting light bulbs—burning since 1908—is housed in the Stockyards Museum. It was originally installed to light the backstage at the Byers Opera House, which later became the prestigious Palace Theater in Downtown Fort Worth.

The Sixth Floor Museum

and the railroads. A Native American exhibit focuses on Quanah Parker, the last Comanche war chief, who helped bring peace between the settlers and Indian tribes. Go if for no other reason than to see the lightbulb that has been burning since 1908. Mon-Sat 10-5. Free. ♿ (North Fort Worth)

THISTLE HILL
1509 Pennsylvania Avenue
Fort Worth
817/336-1212
This 1903 historic mansion is noteworthy as "one of the few remaining examples of Georgian Revival architecture in the Southwest," according to the National Register of Historic Places. Built as a wedding present from cattle baron W.T. Waggoner to his eccentric daughter, Electra, the house museum displays the lifestyle of the rich in the Quality Hill neighborhood during the 1900-1920 era.

On the guided tour, you'll learn that Electra was the first customer to spend $20,000 in one day at Neiman-Marcus, and that she returned from a European trip with a butterfly tattoo. She sold the house in 1911 to Winfield Scott, a cattle baron and civic leader. Only the downstairs is wheelchair accessible. Mon-Fri 10-3, Sun 1-4. Guided tours on the hour. $4 adults, $2 seniors and children 7-12. (Southwest Fort Worth)

OTHER MUSEUMS

AFRICAN AMERICAN MUSEUM
3536 Grand Avenue (in Fair Park)
Dallas
214/565-9026
Focusing on black culture, art, and history, this museum began in 1974 as part of Bishop College and now occupies a $6-million home in Fair Park across from the Music Hall. The building itself is a work of art—constructed of ivory stone in the shape of a cross with a 60-foot domed rotunda. Boasting one of

the largest collections of African American folk art in the United States, the museum also houses fine art by black artists from around the world as well as African masks, textiles, and sculptures. It hosts traveling and special exhibits, a fine lecture series, summer youth camps, and programs such as the Conference on African American History in Texas, Texas Black Literary Conference, and the Texas Black Women's Conference. Tue-Fri 12-5, Sat 10-5, Sun 1-5. Free but donations are appreciated. ♿ (East Dallas)

AMERICAN AIRLINES
C. R. SMITH MUSEUM
4601 Highway 360 at FAA Road
Fort Worth
817/967-1560
Located near the DFW Airport, this museum is a sight-and-sound, hands-on look at the world of flight from a first-class window seat.

Visitors of all ages will enjoy the large-screen film and video displays that present both historical and contemporary views of American Airlines and the commercial aviation industry. Learn about aerodynamics in a wind tunnel, see a cockpit and engine close-up, and, of course, visit the gift shop. Tue-Sat 10-6, Sun 12-5. Free. ♿ (Mid-Cities)

AMERICAN MUSEUM OF
THE MINIATURE ARTS
2001 North Lamar, Suite 100
Dallas
214/969-5502
Not everything in "Big D" is big. This Lilliputian collection was once a dollhouse museum in a Victorian home; now it fills a much larger location in the West End. Several completely furnished authentic miniature houses and shops are on display, as well as room settings,

Top Ten Sites of Western Heritage and Living
by Neil Ross, Sheriff, Fort Worth Westerners Corral of Westerners International

1. Cattle Raisers Museum
2. Exchange Avenue (Stockyards National Historic District)
3. Log Cabin Village
4. Amon Carter Museum
5. Billy Bob's Texas
6. Stockyards Museum
7. Thistle Hill
8. The Cattleman's Steakhouse
9. National Cowgirl Hall of Fame
10. Ryon's Saddle & Ranch Supply

dolls, and antique toys. Other collections include cars, planes, trains, and military models. A new addition offers special hands-on exhibits, a delightful children's library, a gift shop, and a party room. Wonder in amazement at the intricate attention to detail of the craftsmen. Tue-Sat 10-4:30, Sun 1-4. $7 adults, $5 seniors, $4 children under 12. ⛬ (Central Dallas)

ANTIQUE SEWING MACHINE MUSEUM
804 West Abram
Arlington
817/275-0971
The first of its kind in America, this unusual museum displays more than 150 sewing machines plus memorabilia depicting the history and development of one of the most important inventions of mankind. The collection includes 24 pre-Civil War machines and several models by Elias Howe, who patented the first sewing machine. Also displayed are antique buttons, bobbins, and dress patterns. In preparation for the Fourth of July parade in 1996, owner Frank Smith built a giant replica of an 1864 Civil War hand-cranked Shaw & Clark machine. The 16-foot-long, 10-foot-high replica actually works! But Smith had his arm in a sling when he uncovered the machine—he may be the only person to have ever broken an arm by falling off a sewing machine. He did make it into Ripley's Believe It or Not! for his efforts. Mon-Sat 10-5. $3 adults, $2 children 4-14, children under 4 free. (Arlington/Grand Prairie)

BIBLICAL ARTS CENTER
7500 Park Lane
Dallas
214/691-4661

www.biblicalarts.org
The theme here is nondenominational religious art from around the world that illustrates and interprets the Bible. The major attraction is the Miracle of Pentecost Presentation, a 30-minute light and sound demonstration showcasing the massive oil painting mural by Torger Thompson, which took almost three years to create. Tue-Sat 10-5, Thu 10-9, Sun 1-5. Art galleries free. Miracle of Pentecost Presentation $6 adults, $5.50 seniors, $5 children 6-18, children under 6 free. ⛬ (Central Dallas)

CAVANAUGH FLIGHT MUSEUM
4572 Claire Chennault
Addison
972/380-8800
Located on the east side of Addison Airport, this is one of the premier aviation museums in the country. Four hangars display a wonderful collection of "warbirds" from World War I to Vietnam, all of which have been restored to their original, flying condition. Because they are flown regularly, a maintenance hangar allows visitors a peek behind the scenes. A gallery enables visitors to trace the chronology of aviation with displays of memorabilia and art. With advance reservations (and an additional cost), you can take a spin in one of the restored military trainers. Mon-Sat 9-5, Sun 11-5; closed New Year's Day, Thanksgiving, and Christmas. $5.50 adults, $2.75 children 6-12, children under 5 free. ⛬ (Far North Dallas)

THE COCKROACH HALL OF FAME MUSEUM
2231-B West 15th Street
Plano
972/519-0355
www.pestshop.com

The *Mustangs of Las Colinas* is the largest equestrian sculpture in the world.

For bizarre museums, this one takes the prize. Owner Michael will tell you the story of its beginnings in The Pest Shop in Plano. He and his fancy-dressed roaches have appeared on numerous TV shows, and since his appearance on *The Tonight Show,* he has traveled around the country as a judge for "best-dressed roach" contests. His personal favorite is his own "Liberoache." With only the slightest encouragement from visitors, he will stage cockroach races and all sorts of other "entertainment". To be on the safe side, call first to make sure Michael is in the shop. Mon-Fri 12:30-5, Sat 11-3. Free. (Far North Dallas)

CONSPIRACY MUSEUM
110 South Market (inside the KATY building)
Dallas
214/741-3040
Called the "best place to become paranoid" by the *Dallas Observer,* this unique museum presents suspicions surrounding American political assassinations and coverups since 1835, including those of Presidents Lincoln, Garfield, and McKinley, with obvious emphasis on President John F. Kennedy, Robert Kennedy, and Martin Luther King Jr. Daily 10-6. $7 adults, $6 seniors, $3 children 9-12, children under 9 free. ♿ (Downtown Dallas)

DALLAS FIREFIGHTERS MUSEUM

3801 Parry at Commerce
Dallas
214/821-1500
Located in the 1907 Old No. 5 Hook and Ladder Company station near Fair Park, this museum houses a wonderful collection of old fire trucks, including "Old Tige," an 1884 horse-drawn steam pumper. Also on display are suits, helmets, extinguishers, and other mementos that tell the story of one hundred years of firefighting history. Opened in 1975 and staffed mostly by retired firefighters, it includes a gift shop with collectibles and souvenirs. Wed-Sat 9-4. $1 adults, $.50 children. (East Dallas)

FRONTIERS OF FLIGHT MUSEUM
Love Field Terminal Lobby,
Second floor
Dallas
214/350-1651
Exhibits in this flight museum trace the history of aviation from Greek mythology to da Vinci's dreams to the space shuttle. Some interesting items on display include Admiral Byrd's parka, a WWI Sopwith "pup" biplane, and silverware and china used aboard the Hindenburg airship. Love Field has a history of its own: Charles Lindbergh landed the Spirit of St. Louis there in 1927 while touring the country after his transatlantic solo flight. The Dallas Air Show is held at Love Field each September. Mon-Sat 10-5, Sun 1-5. Guided tours $2 adults, $1 children under 12. ♿ (Central Dallas)

INTERNATIONAL MUSEUM OF CULTURES
7500 West Camp Wisdom Road
Dallas
972/708-7406
The stated mission of this unusual

museum is "to be a window on indigenous people of the world and to create greater appreciation for ethnic and cultural diversity, thereby furthering mutual respect and peace between peoples." It's an interesting museum, capturing the imagination of children and adults alike with dioramas depicting life in far-away jungles or islands of the South Pacific and artifacts from exotic corners of the world. The museum has a nice gift shop and publishes a series of book in conjunction with SIL International, a linguistics institute. Tue-Fri 10-5, Sat-Sun 1:30-5. $2 adults, $1 children. & (East Dallas)

LEGENDS OF THE GAME
BASEBALL MUSEUM
1000 Ballpark Way
Arlington
817/273-5600
Located within The Ballpark in Arlington, this museum is a baseball lover's dream come true! The 17,000-square-foot museum features uniforms, baseballs, equipment, baseball cards, and photographs depicting the history of the sport. More than one hundred items on loan from the National Baseball Hall of Fame in Cooperstown, New York, include Babe Ruth's jersey, Lou Gehrig's bat, and Joe DiMaggio's glove. Exhibits include "Women in Baseball" and "Negro League" showcases. Fans can create a video dubbed with their voice calling a play-by-play Rangers game. Upstairs is the Children's Learning Center (see Chapter 7, Kids' Stuff). Apr-Oct Mon-Sat 9-6:30, Sun 12-4; Nov-Mar Tue-Sat 9-4, Sun 12-4. $6 adults, $5 seniors and students with ID, $4 children 4-18. Combination tickets for museum admission and ballpark tour: $10 adult, $8 seniors and students with ID, $6 chil-

dren 4-18 (see also Chapter 5, Sights and Attractions). & (Arlington/Grand Prairie)

NATIONAL MUSEUM
OF COMMUNICATIONS
Dallas Communications Complex
North O'Connor at Royal Lane
Irving
972/869-FILM
When Samuel Morse tapped out his first message in 1839, today's world of telecommunications would have been a far-fetched fantasy. Exhibits here trace the evolution of communications through the ages. Displayed are collections of vintage radios, televisions, phonograph machines, and memorabilia, including an eighteenth-century wooden printing press, the microphone used by Walter Cronkite during his final newscast, and a hand-cranked movie camera used by Charlie Chaplin to make silent films. But mostly, it's a hands-on museum to let visitors experience, rather than observe. This place is for visitors of all ages to have fun and/or reminisce. Unfortunately, it's now the waiting area for the Movie Studio tours of Las Colinas (see Chapter 5, Sights and Attractions) and cannot be viewed separately. Sun-Fri 12-4, Sun 10-4. Admission included in cost of Studio Tour. & (Mid-Cities)

PATE MUSEUM
OF TRANSPORTATION
U.S. Highway 377
817/396-4305
www.classicar.com/museums
/pate/pate.htm
A few miles southwest of Fort Worth, the Pate Museum has become a foremost attraction. It began humbly as a private collection by A.M. Pate Jr., with a handful of

automobiles, one airplane, and a private rail car. Now, the museum boasts an impressive array of classic, antique, and special-interest automobiles, a fine exhibit of aircrafts, plus an antique private railroad car, a Minesweeper boat, and a 1,500-volume transportation library. Enjoy the myriad means of transportation that played a vital role in building America. Tue-Sun 9-5. Free. (Southwest Fort Worth)

THE WOMEN'S MUSEUM
Fair Park
Dallas
512-459-1167, 888-337-1167
www.thewomensmuseum.org
Scheduled to open in the fall of 2000, this 70,000-square-foot, three-story museum will showcase women's place in history and their contributions to the world. The Smithsonian-affiliated museum will use high-tech, interactive exhibits to tell the inspiring stories of outstanding women. State-of-the-art gadgetry will enable you to have a virtual conversation with Cleopatra or Joan of Arc. An exciting bonus resulting from the plan is the preservation and restoration of a condemned building, built in 1909, in Fair Park.(East Dallas)

GALLERIES

AFTERIMAGE GALLERY
2828 Routh Street,
The Quadrangle, #115
Dallas
214/871-9140
www.afterimagegallery.com
This world-renowned photography gallery is one of the oldest and most prestigious in the country. Popular Texas photographer Keith Carter

had his first gallery show here, and Ansel Adams exhibited in the early days. The success of the gallery is a result of the efforts of founder and owner Ben Breard, who has also created an exceptional web site for those who can't visit in person. (Central Dallas)

THE EDGE OF GLASS GALLERY
4911 Camp Bowie Boulevard
Fort Worth
817/731-8388
An unusual gallery featuring the works of blown and handmade glass artists from around the world. (Southwest Fort Worth)

EDITH BAKER GALLERY
2404 Cedar Springs, Suite 300
Dallas
214/855-5101
One of the oldest contemporary art galleries in Dallas, the Edith Baker Gallery represents primarily Texas artists. Legendary in Dallas art circles, Mrs. Baker has contributed her talents for decades in the areas of teaching and charitable work with underprivileged artists. (Central Dallas)

EVELYN SIEGEL GALLERY
3700 West Seventh Street
Fort Worth
817/731-6412
A premier showcase for original art, this gallery offers fine paintings and prints, ceramics, sculpture, photography, and glass from more than 50 artists. (Southwest Fort Worth)

GALERIE KORNYE WEST
1601 Clover Lane
Fort Worth
817/763-5227
Featuring traditional masterworks of fine art, this intimate gallery of-

Dallas' Arts District is connected to an area of antique galleries and eateries by the McKinney Avenue trolley, with its refurbished, authentic cars from the early 1900s.

fers a variety of academic and impressionistic arts. The art-historian owner is usually on hand to visit and share knowledge with clients. Appraisals, restorations, and framing are also available. (Southwest Fort Worth)

GERALD PETERS GALLERY
2913 Fairmount Street at Cedar Springs Road
Dallas
214/969-9410
Noted as one of Dallas's premier high-snob-quotient galleries, it features an impressive list of mid-career contemporary artists. Mr. Peters also has galleries in Santa Fe and New York. Openings are "events," and any show here is worth seeing. Mon-Fri 12-6, Sat 12-5. (Central Dallas)

KITTRELL-RIFFKIND ART GLASS
5100 Belt Line Road, #820
Dallas
972/239-7957
Tie up the kids and clasp your hands before you enter this magical fantasy world of sparkling glass objets d'art. Hundreds of treasures, both decorative and useful, range from exquisite to whimsical. This gallery features an ever-changing selection of outstanding work by more than three hundred artists. (Far North Dallas)

RODEO PLAZA GALLERY
2511 Rodeo Plaza in the Stockyards
Fort Worth
817/625-1025
Watch artists create at this working studio featuring more than 20 artists and sculptors. (North Fort Worth)

SOUTHWEST GALLERY
4500 Sigma Road at Welch
Dallas
972/960-8935
This premier gallery moved to this 16,000-square-foot showroom from its long-time location in Preston Forest Shopping Center. It needed the space because it provides framing, art restoration, and limited consulting services, as well as showing a huge variety of artwork. The name is misleading because the gallery displays contemporary and traditional works as well as Western and Southwestern, specializing in late-nineteenth- and twentieth-century American and European paintings and sculpture. (Far North Dallas)

STOCKYARDS STATION GALLERY
140 East Exchange Avenue
Fort Worth
817/624-7300
Located in the Stockyards National Historic District, this gallery exhibits a fine collection of Western original oils and bronzes, as well as Remington and Russell prints and

bronzes. Other items include Western-oriented photographs, travel bags, gift items, charms, books, posters, and Indian jewelry.

THOMAS KINKADE GALLERY
302 Main Street
Fort Worth
817/335-2060, 888/242-0650
The soft-hued works of Thomas Kinkade are showcased here. Visitors can immerse themselves in the misty and pastoral canvases of America's most collected living artist. Other locations include The Parks Mall in Arlington (817/419-9535), Hulen Mall in Fort Worth (817/292-3166), and Vista Ridge Mall in Lewisville (972/316-1212).(Downtown Fort Worth)

VALLEY HOUSE GALLERY
6616 Spring Valley Road
Dallas
972/239-2241
This lovely gallery and its serene five-acre sculpture garden began life as a rural, secluded home where artist Donald Vogel could paint. The city has grown around it, but there's still a feeling of sereneness and solitude. The gallery is now owned by Donald's son, Kevin, and his wife Cheryl, who have continued Donald's legacy by remaining active in the art scene and hosting impressive shows and events. (Far North Dallas)

WILLIAM CAMPBELL CONTEMPORARY ART GALLERY
4935 Byers Avenue
Fort Worth
817/737-9566
For 26 years,this exceptional, upscale gallery has offered eclectic, lively, and bold art in a variety of media, including painting, sculpture, paper, photography, ceramic, and mixed media. The gallery also contains a specialty framing business. (Southwest Fort Worth)

Dallas CVB

7

The term "kids" can encompass young people from toddlers to teenagers, adults going through their "second childhood," and those perpetually young at heart. All of these groups have diverse tastes and different ideas about what's fun or interesting. Enough description is given for each listing so you can decide if your family will enjoy these attractions or activities. Please see Chapter 5, Sights and Attractions and Chapter 6, Museums and Galleries because many of those listings will appeal to children as well.

The vast area known as The Metroplex has just as vast a variety of activities for kids of all ages. Energetic youngsters will enjoy amusement parks, water parks, and racetracks. Those with more subdued interests can choose from a tremendous medley of museums in the area, most of which have special programs and exhibits for children. Whether you're interested in dolls or baseball, tigers or toys, you'll find places to meet your needs. Many area stores offer a delightful array of merchandise for future "shopaholics," and performances at children's theaters delight audiences of all ages.

Watch the action of professional sports teams, rodeos, or racing. Participate in favorite sports such as tennis, bowling, or swimming. Take lessons to learn hockey, horseback riding, or ice-skating. Visit the zoo, the great outdoors, and area lakes and parks. Whatever you choose, remember to have fun!

ANIMALS AND
THE GREAT OUTDOORS

ADVENTURE WORLD
7451 Starnes
North Richland Hills
817/581-5760
This is the largest handicapped-accessible park in Texas, using a wood fiber material that is hard enough for wheelchairs to move easily, yet soft enough to minimize kids' falls. Ramps instead of stairs lead to equipment, and "access points" allow children to access the equipment from wheelchairs. Several playground areas are geared for children of different ages. This park is part of a future one-hundred-acre park project development by the city. & (Mid-Cities)

BURGER'S LAKE
1200 Meandering Road
Fort Worth
817/737-3414
Anyone who grew up in Fort Worth knows Burger's Lake, which is an institution among area residents. The spring-fed lake with two sandy beaches provides old-fashioned family fun. It's not a slick, modern water park; it's just an ol' swimming hole. There's a diving board, a water slide, plenty of shallow water for the little ones, picnic tables, and a volleyball court. Take your own lawn chairs, floats, or water toys. A concession stand sells basic

Giraffe Statue at the Dallas Zoo

refreshments. No pets or alcohol are allowed. Open in summer, daily 9-dark. (Southwest Fort Worth)

DALLAS ZOO
650 S. R.L. Thornton Freeway
(I-35E)
Dallas
214/670-5656
www.dallas-zoo.org
Look for the tallest statue in the state—a 67-foot Plexiglas giraffe—near the entrance. It's hard to miss! The Dallas Zoo is home to more than two thousand animals, including rare and endangered species. Kids love the nationally renowned reptile collection. The interactive Reptile Discovery Center has informative

---

TRIVIA

The "welcome" statue at the Dallas Zoo is the tallest statue in Texas (by the length of a tongue), soaring 67.5 feet tall. Naturally, it's a giraffe.

Calendar for Kids

Metroplex cities have special events throughout the year that children would enjoy. Some of the dates to mark on your calendar include:

- **January:** *Kidfilm (an international children's film festival)*
- **March:** *St. Patrick's Day Parade and Irish Festival; Metroplex Doll Club Show; Texas Storytelling Festival; Very Special Arts Festival (tailored for children with special needs); Dino Day*
- **April:** *Imagination Celebration; Spring Break Family Fun Fair; Scarbrough Faire Renaissance Faire (continues through June); Easter Egg Hunts*
- **May:** *Artfest for Kids; Mayfest; Kid's World Exposition; Folklore Festival; Playfest*
- **June:** *Pioneer Heritage Festival; Texas Scottish Festival and Highland Games*
- **July:** *Fourth of July celebrations; Ringling Brothers Barnum & Bailey Circus*
- **September:** *Pepsi KidAround; National Championship Indian Pow-Wow; Kidsport Triathlon; Plano Hot Air Balloon Festival*
- **October:** *Oktoberfest; State Fair of Texas; Great Dallas Duck Race; Haunted Houses and Fright Nights*
- **November:** *American Indians Art Festival and Market*
- **December:** *Holiday in the Park at Six Flags Over Texas; lots of holiday parades and festivities*

displays that aim to help people be less fearful of reptiles. Walk through the Rainforest Aviary, where you're surrounded by colorful, exotic birds. The highly acclaimed "Wilds of Africa" exhibit features African mammals, birds, and reptiles roaming in naturalistic re-creations of their native habitat. Take the specially designed Monorail Safari ($1.50 extra), a 20-minute ride with live narration. At the Children's Zoo, kids can pet tame and baby animals, enjoy other hands-on exhibits, and learn how to select a family pet. There's a restaurant, a picnic area, and a gift shop (see also Chapter 5, Sights and Attractions). Daily 9-5. $6 adults, $4 seniors, $3 children 3-11, children 2 and under free. Parking $3 per car. ♿ (East Dallas)

FORT WORTH NATURE CENTER & REFUGE
9601 Fossil Ridge Road
Fort Worth
817/237-1111

Ten miles from Downtown Fort Worth, prairies, forests, marshes, and the Trinity River remain much as they were 150 years ago in the largest city-owned nature center in the United States. The 3,500 acres provide a sanctuary for native wildlife and plants, and a 25-mile trail system provides visitors with a good opportunity to view white-tailed deer, buffalo, and live armadillos. Nature programs, workshops, and story hours are held at the Hardwicke Interpretive Center. Maps, interpretive exhibits, a gift shop, and a nature library are found in the center, which is wheelchair accessible (see also Chapter 8, Parks, Gardens, and Recreation Areas). Daily 9-5. Free. (North Fort Worth)

FORT WORTH ZOO
1989 Colonial Parkway
Fort Worth
817/871-7050
www.fortworthzoo.com

You can easily spend a day at this exceptional zoo, ranked as one of the top five in the nation. Home to more than five thousand native and exotic animals, the zoo is renowned

---

TOP TEN TOP TEN TOP TEN TOP TEN TOP TEN TOP TEN TOP TEN TOP TEN TOP TEN TOP TEN TOP TEN TOP TEN

Top Ten Activities to Share with Preschool Children
by Steve Coxsey, MS, LPC, and co-owner of The Knowledge Store Child Care Center in Bedford

1. Fort Worth Museum of Science and History
2. Fort Worth Zoo
3. Dallas Zoo
4. Clubhouse for Kids Only
5. Casa Mañana
6. Ice Skating
7. The Science Place at Fair Park
8. CATS (Creative Arts Theater and School)
9. Tarantula Steam Train
10. Water Parks

Bonus #11: Six Flags Over Texas—There are separate areas with rides and play areas for preschoolers. Cartoon characters walking around are naturally a favorite, and some of the shows are especially planned to entertain the younger crowd.

Cute Koala at the Fort Worth Zoo

for creating "natural habitat" exhibits, where only a waterfall or river separates visitors from the animals. Colorful birds fly freely in the tropical rainforest, and rare snakes and lizards live in the acclaimed Herpetarium. In late spring, a popular annual event called "Zoo Babies" showcases the zoo's baby animals. Strollers and motorized carts are available for rent. There's a snack bar and an excellent nature gift shop. The longest miniature train ride in Texas (seasonal schedule, additional fee) begins opposite the zoo and winds five miles through Forest and Trinity Parks to the duck pond and back (see also Chapter 5, Sights and Attractions). Daily 10-5, extended hours seasonally. $7 adults 13 and over, $4.50 children 3-12, $3 seniors, toddlers 2 and under free. Parking $4. ♿ (Southwest Fort Worth)

SAMUELL FARM
100 East Highway 80 at Belt Line Road
Mesquite
214/670-7866

Experience life on a working farm of the nineteenth and early twentieth century! The farm's 340 acres offer a lot to see and do, including ponds for fishing, hiking and riding trails, hayrides, picnic tables, and a barnyard with friendly farm animals. Horseback riding and hayrides are available for additional fees. Something is always going on at Samuell Farm, from birthday parties to day camps to numerous holiday festivals. Thanks to the generosity of Dr. W. W. Samuell, who willed the farm to the city of Dallas, city kids can glimpse the rural heritage of this country. Daily 9-5. $3 adults 12 and over, $2 children 3-11, children under 3 free. (East Dallas)

SPRING CREEK FARM
On Plano Road between Campbell and Renner Roads
Richardson
972/235-7191

Do you eat Owens Country Sausage for breakfast? When C. B. Owens perfected his brand of country sausage, his farm was on the far outskirts of Dallas. Now surrounded by the city's growth, it's in the suburb of Richardson. But the 15-acre farm still gives visitors a peek into rural life around the turn of the century. Outdoors, see Belgian draft horses similar to those that pulled the wagons that delivered the fresh sausage in the olden days. Learn the history of the fine Belgian horses and visit the ducks, rabbits, ponies, and sheep—a thrill for city kids. A museum houses reproductions of a blacksmith shop, a general store, a butcher shop, and a fully-equipped early 1900s kitchen. The butcher shop displays some of the antique tools Owens used to make the now-famous sausage. (Far North Dallas)

MUSEUMS

AMERICAN MUSEUM OF THE MINIATURE ARTS
2001 North Lamar, Suite 100
Dallas
214/969-5502
Not everything in "Big D" is big. This Lilliputian collection was once a dollhouse museum in a Victorian home; now it fills a much larger location in the West End. Several completely furnished authentic miniature houses and shops are on display, as well as room settings, dolls, and antique toys. Collections more interesting to boys include cars, planes, trains, and military models. The intricate attention to detail of the craftsmen's work is absolutely amazing. A new addition offers special hands-on exhibits, an excellent children's library, a gift shop, and a party room (see also Chapter 6, Museums and Art Galleries). Tue-Sat 10-4:30, Sun 1-4. $7 adults, $5 seniors, $4 children under 12. & (Central Dallas)

FORT WORTH MUSEUM OF SCIENCE AND HISTORY
1501 Montgomery Street
Fort Worth
817/255-9300, 888/255-9300
www.fwmuseum.org
Everybody loves this museum, which attracts more than one million visitors a year. Family-friendly, hands-on exhibits are playful and interesting ways to discover electricity, magnetism, acoustics, weather, and biology. Kids love Kidspace®, ExploraZone®, and DinoDig®, where they dig for dinosaur bones. Everyone can experi-

ence the legends and lore of the Lone Star State in the Texas History rooms. The museum also houses the **Omni Theater**, an 80-foot-high domed theater with sophisticated audio and video systems. The **Noble Planetarium** offers entertaining astronomy and laser light productions, featuring advanced technology in a 30-foot domed theater. An excellent museum store is located in the lobby (see also Chapter 6, Museums and Art Galleries). Mon 9-5, Tue-Thu 9-8, Fri-Sat 9-9, Sun 12-8. $5 adults, $4 seniors, $3 children 3-12, children under 3 free. Additional charges for the Omni Theater and Noble Planetarium; combination tickets available. Call for schedules of performances. & (Southwest Fort Worth)

LEGENDS OF THE GAME BASEBALL MUSEUM AND CHILDREN'S LEARNING CENTER
The Ballpark in Arlington
1000 Ballpark Way
Arlington
817/273-5600
"Take me out to the ballgame." What special words for most American kids. If you want to see the Texas Rangers play baseball, see Chapter 10, Sports and Recreation, for information. The outstanding museum and learning center located within The Ballpark exhibits memorabilia such as uniforms, equipment, photos, and baseball cards that show the history of this all-American sport. One of the most popular attractions is a booth where fans can create (for an extra fee) a video of a play-by-play Ranger game using an overlay of their own voices. The **Children's Learning Center** features interactive exhibits about baseball and how it relates to other fields. For

example, a huge U. S. map has major team logos on the map and geography-related baseball questions on the computer. Another computer touch-screen allows kids to experiment with how wind, altitude, and speed affect where the baseball will go when hit (physics). Catch a pitch from Nolan Ryan, and learn how baseballs are made. The Dugout is a special play/learning area for tots under five (see also Chapter 5, Sights and Attractions; and Chapter 6, Museums and Art Galleries). Apr-Oct Mon-Sat 9-6:30, Sun 12-4; Nov-Mar Tue-Sat 9-4, Sun 12-4. $6 adults, $5 seniors and students with ID, $4 children 4-18. Combination tickets for museum admission and ballpark tour $10 adult, $8 seniors and students with ID, $6 children 4-18. & (Arlington/Grand Prairie)

RIVER LEGACY
LIVING SCIENCE CENTER
703 NW Green Oaks Boulevard
Arlington
817/860-6752
www.ci.arlington.tx.us/nature.html
The Living Science Center features interactive exhibits and displays, including aquariums and terrariums. Take a thrilling ride down the Trinity River on a simulated raft ride using the latest technology. The Science Center is located in River Legacy Parks, which include a plethora of

hiking and biking trails, river overlooks, nature trails, and picnic areas along the banks of the Trinity River (see also Chapter 8, Parks, Gardens, and Recreation Areas). Tue-Sat 9-5. & (Arlington/Grand Prairie)

THE SCIENCE PLACE
AND IMAX® THEATER
Fair Park
Dallas
214/428-5555
www.scienceplace.org
Billed as "an amusement park for your brain," The Science Place is a fun place to learn how and why things work. Literally hundreds of hands-on exhibits and displays encourage kids to use their imagination and senses of touch, smell, sight, and hearing to discover the wonders of the universe. Kid's Place is primarily for children seven and under where they can make music on a walk-on piano, try out computers, or see technology displays in the special surround-sound theater. The Science Place Planetarium is in another building about one block away. This truly exceptional museum offers special programs and exhibits throughout the year (see also Chapter 6, Museums and Galleries). Daily 9:30-5:30. Exhibit hall admission: $6 adults, $3 seniors and children 3-12, children under 3 free. IMAX® admission is

Although the OMNI and IMAX® theater experience is thrilling to adults and older children, it may be too intense for younger children because it can cause motion sickness.

separate; call for films and times. ⅋ (East Dallas)

TRAINSCAPE
Dallas Children's Medical Center
1935 Motor Street
Dallas
214/920-2000
One of the largest permanent model train exhibits in the country is on display at Children's Medical Center in Dallas. The two-story, G-scale, eight-train system chugs along more than one thousand feet of track, through the Colorado Rockies, the Arizona desert, and (of course) past the Dallas skyline—all in the main entrance lobby of the hospital. The exhibit took about six months to build under the direction of Dallas artist Malcolm Furlow, who is known for his work on Disney movie sets and his model train layouts at F.A.O. Schwartz toy store in New York. The idea came from the hospital's CEO, George Farr, who has loved trains since he was a child. Open daily. Free. ⅋ (North Dallas)

PUPPETS AND THEATER

CASA MAÑANA
CHILDREN'S PLAYHOUSE
3101 West Lancaster
Fort Worth
817/332-2272
www.casamanana.org
/children.htm
A huge geodesic dome marks the spot. Since it was built, this theater-in-the-round has been home to shows and concerts. Many of the productions have now moved downtown to the new Bass Performance Hall, allowing Casa Mañana room to expand its exceptional Children's Playhouse program. A full season of plays geared for young audiences, based on fairy tales, nursery rhymes, and holiday themes are performed by a professional theater troupe from October through May. For little more than the cost of a movie, children (and adults) can see delightful stage presentations of such plays as *Rumpelstiltskin, Tom Sawyer, Robin Hood,* and *The Princess and the Pea.* Call for show schedule and prices. ⅋ (Southwest Fort Worth)

CREATIVE ARTS THEATRE
AND SCHOOL (CATS)
1100 West Randol Mill Road
Arlington
817/265-8512 (metro)
This performing arts school for young people offers performances on weekends during the school year and in the summer. Children are prominently featured as actors in the productions geared to preschool through early elementary age. Backstage tours are available by reservation. Call for performance schedule. $7 adults, $6 children. ⅋ (Arlington)

DALLAS CHILDREN'S THEATER
2215 Cedar Springs
Dallas
214/978-0110
The Dallas Children's Theater presents exciting performances for the whole family by experienced actors and acting students. They present serious plays as well as storybook tales at both the El Centro College Theater (Main at Market) and the Crescent Theater (2215 Cedar Springs at Maple). Dallas Children's Theater works extensively with area schoolchildren, offering special matinee performances and classes. Call for performance schedule and prices, usually in the $12 to $14 range. ⅋ (Downtown Dallas)

Storytelling

Traditionally, "Storytelling Under the Stars" is held during the summer months at parks around the Metroplex. Children of all ages can gather to hear local storytellers free of charge. Check the local newspapers for dates and times.

DALLAS PUPPET THEATER
Valley View Mall, Upper Level
Dallas
972/361-1416
These talented puppeteers entertain kids and adults at the Puppet Theater near the Disney Store on the upper level of Valley View Mall. The puppet company also performs at schools, festivals, and birthday parties. A popular attraction in the mall, the theater draws crowds of all ages when a performance is being held. Performances consist of mostly storybook tales on weekend afternoons and an annual production of *A Christmas Carol* over the holiday season. Schedule varies. Free. ও (Far North Dallas)

PAWNEE BILL'S
WILD WEST SHOW
Cowtown Coliseum
121 East Exchange Avenue
Fort Worth
817/625-1025
Return to the days of Buffalo Bill and Annie Oakley with this historical re-creation of a genuine touring Wild West Show. The Coliseum hosted many a Wild West Show in the early 1900s, but eventually the rodeos became more popular. Pawnee Bill's is rip-roarin' family fun every weekend during the summer. Trick shooters, ropers, riders,

and all sorts of colorful characters perform and entertain you with their talent and antics. You may even see a stagecoach hold-up! Memorial Day-Labor Day Sat-Sun at 2:30 and 4:30. $7 adult, $4 children 12 and under. ও (North Fort Worth)

STORES/RESTAURANTS KIDS LOVE

BUCKAROO'S SODA SHOPPE
140 East Exchange Avenue
Fort Worth
817/624-6631
The Riscky's folks (see Chapter 4, sidebar) have opened up a bright, cheery, kid-friendly spot in Stockyards Station. There's a saddled life-size horse model and "saddle seats" at the counter and at some of the stand-alone tables. Kid cuisine features hamburgers, hot dogs, shakes, and ice cream. The food is standard all-American tourist offerings, and the grown-up-sized portions are monstrous. A sinful chili cheese dog with chili, Cheddar, mustard, and onion sells for $3.75, and their excellent onion rings are $2.95. Just call the diet a goner. Blue Bell ice cream (Texas-made and the best ice cream on the planet according to most Texans) is served in cones, sundaes, and

banana splits. Open daily. & (North Fort Worth)

DISNEY STORE
Hulen Mall
4800 South Hulen Street
Fort Worth
817/370-7199
A favorite of kids everywhere, the Disney Store has all sorts of merchandise featuring favorite Disney characters. The only problem is getting the kids to leave. Other locations are at North Park Center in Dallas, Valley View Mall in Dallas, Collin Creek Mall in Plano, The Parks Mall in Arlington, and North-East Mall in Hurst. & (Southwest Fort Worth)

THE ENCHANTED FOREST BOOKS FOR CHILDREN
6333 East Mockingbird, Suite 231
Dallas
214/827-2234, 800/BOOKS-56
Kids will love this inviting bookstore with its lively trees painted on the windows and an enchanted "forest" of books and toys inside. The kid-friendly store has a stage and play area, special programs and guests, a summer "camp," and other activities throughout the year. & (Central Dallas)

FAO SCHWARTZ
307 NorthPark Center
Dallas
214/750-0300
www.fao.com
This enormous toy store delights children of all ages. It's packed with stuffed animals (wild and domestic), mechanical toys, games and books of all descriptions, exclusive toy collections, robots, sleds, kid-sized cars, Furby babies, and much, much more. & (Central Dallas)

JEKYLL & HYDE CLUB
3000 Grapevine Mills Parkway, #518
Grapevine
972/691-1300
Be on the look out for this part-restaurant, part-adventure kids club is located in Grapevine Mills Mall; just look for the screaming gargoyles at the entrance, where you'll be greeted by some strange characters and ushered into a gothic chamber-of-horrors dining area. The "entertainment" is a bit much, although it's probably thrilling for an eight-year-old kid. Animal heads on the wall scream, screech, and squawk in all sorts of unusual voices, and live costumed entertainers put on skits and annoy diners. Surprisingly, the food ranges from very good to excellent, except for the canned tea. Most dishes are in the $12 to $16 price range, with a kid's menu of burgers, chicken strips, and pizza, all for $6.95 including a soft drink. Save room for the chocolate crème brûlée, an awesome treat at $5.50. Lunch and dinner daily. & (Mid-Cities)

THE NATURE COMPANY
317 NorthPark Center
Dallas
214/696-2291
A favorite of kids and parents alike, this store is filled with nature-related toys, books, games, and cool T-shirts with tarantulas, wolves, and other critters on them. They also have a nice mail-order catalog. & (Central Dallas)

RAINFOREST CAFÉ®
Grapevine Mills Mall
3000 Grapevine Mills Parkway
Grapevine
972/539-5001

Shopping for souvenirs at Stockyards Station

Experience an encounter with talking trees, animatronic birds and animals, and recorded jungle noises amid cascading waterfalls and giant aquariums at this wild store/restaurant. The true-to-nature rainforest includes beautiful resident parrots, and the staff will gladly answer questions about the birds. A fiber optic "starscape" creates a realistic star-filled night sky. The Rainforest Café® has an international menu of Mexican, Italian, American, and Cajun fare and an amazing drink selection. The huge gift shop out front offers a wild array of unusual gifts and souvenirs. Be prepared to wait during busy hours on weekends. Open for lunch and dinner daily. & (Mid-Cities)

WARNER BROS. STUDIO STORE
The Parks at Arlington
3811 South Cooper Street
Arlington
817/557-1136
All of your favorite Looney Tunes characters adorn T-shirts and all

sorts of wearing apparel, tote bags, mugs, keychains, mouse pads, and almost anything else you can imagine. Tasmanian Devil slippers look like they would keep your feet warm while you cuddle up with a life-size Tweety Bird. Another location at NorthPark Center in Dallas. & (Arlington/Grand Prairie)

THEME PARKS

LONE STAR FAMILY FUN PARK
1000 Lone Star Parkway
Grand Prairie
972/263-7223
Adjacent to the Lone Star Race Track, this family-oriented park features picnic gazebos, a petting zoo, pony rides, and a giant playground (see also Chapter 10, Sports and Recreation). (Arlington/Grand Prairie)

NRH2O FAMILY WATER PARK
9001 Grapevine Highway
(Highway 26)

North Richland Hills
817/656-6500

The big attraction here is the world's longest uphill watercoaster! The Green Extreme defies all the laws of gravity: it's a seven-story, 1,161-feet monster of twists and turns with water propelling the riders at 19 feet per second. Other attractions are water slides, a wave pool, the Endless River, and the Tad Pole Station, an activity center for children under 54 inches tall. The Ocean and Ocean Beach provide fun for all ages, and Professor Frogstein's Forest has picnic tables. Open summers only. $12.95 children over 54 inches tall, $10.95 children under 54 inches tall, children under 2 free. (Mid-Cities)

SANDY LAKE AMUSEMENT PARK
I-35E at Sandy Lake Road

Carrollton
972/242-7449

A favorite swimming spot for Dallas kids for many years, the enormous pool at Sandy Lake has a deep area with a diving board but also shallow areas, one of which has a slide for youngsters. Shaded tables and other slides and play areas are also situated around the pool. Watch peacocks, ducks, and geese while you sun. In addition to the pool, the park offers a challenging miniature golf course, amusement rides, paddleboats, and concessions. Most areas, except the miniature golf course, are wheelchair accessible. Sandy Lake Park is the site of numerous school events and festivals throughout the year. Usually open Apr-Sep, but hours vary. General admission $1.50 for ages 4 and up,

---

TOP TEN

Top Ten Activities to Share with School-Age Kids

by Steve Coxsey, MS, LPC, and co-owner
of The Knowledge Store Child Care Center in Bedford

1. Tour the Ballpark in Arlington
2. Tour Texas Stadium
3. Six Flags Over Texas
4. Six Flags Hurricane Harbor
5. Fort Worth Museum of Science and History
6. Ice Skating at the Star Center
7. Tour The Movie Studios at Las Colinas
8. Fort Worth Zoo
9. Dallas Zoo
10. Dinosaur Valley State Park in Glen Rose

additional charge for activities. (Far North Dallas)

SIX FLAGS HURRICANE HARBOR
1800 East Lamar Boulevard
Arlington
817/265-3356 (metro)
Wear the kids out with acres of sun and fun at the Southwest's largest water park. This 47-acre tropical getaway features dozens of heart-pounding rides, pools, and attractions that are drenched with excitement. The Black Hole (a heart-stopping, 500-foot drop through wet black tubes) was voted the number-one water ride in the world, and the Sea Wolf is billed as the longest and tallest water raft slide in America. A one-million-gallon wave pool and a children's area add to the fun. Lockers, tube and towel rental, retail shops, and food services are available. Daily mid-May to mid-Aug, weekends only early May to mid-Sep. Admission including tax $26.93 adults, $13.47 seniors and children under 48 inches tall, children under 2 free. Parking $5 per car. (Arlington/Grand Prairie)

SIX FLAGS OVER TEXAS
2201 Road to Six Flags (I-30 at Highway 360)
Arlington
817/640-8900 (metro)
www.sixflags.com/parks
Bugs Bunny and his Looney Tunes pals welcome you to this thrilling amusement park with exciting shows and world-class rides, including the "Texas Giant," a massive wooden roller coaster that has been voted the top roller coaster in the world three times. New in 1998, Mr. Freeze, billed as the state's tallest and fastest roller coaster, which launches riders to a height of 236 feet and speeds of 70 miles per hour in less than four seconds, is not for the faint of heart. New in 1999, Batman The Ride is arguably the most innovative coaster design of the twentieth century. Theme areas cover 205 lavishly landscaped acres and feature more than one hundred thrilling rides, games, shows, and attractions. Open daily in summer, weekends in spring and fall, and for special events such as the Texas Heritage Crafts Festival in September, the Halloween FrightFest in October, and Holiday in the Park in late November and December. Call for schedules and current admission prices. (Arlington/Grand Prairie)

RECREATION

AIR COMBAT CENTER
921 Six Flags Drive, #117
Arlington
817/640-1886
www.aircombatschool.com
Zoom through the virtual sky! Experience the thrill of being a real military fighter pilot! Simulators are actual jet aircraft cockpits mounted on hydraulic motion bases that the virtual pilots control. Flights start with a short ground school and mission briefing before you get to suit up in complete flight gear and begin your mission. The experience takes about one and one-half hours. Minimum height requirement is four feet eight inches, and reservations are highly recommended. Mon-Sat 10-3. $40. (Arlington/Grand Prairie)

ARLINGTON SKATIUM
5515 South Cooper Street
Arlington
817/784-6222
Claiming to be the largest skating

center in Texas, this notable facility features a hardwood maple floor and offers the ultimate skating experience. In-line skates are welcome. There's also a video arcade and full concession stand. Tue 7-9 p.m., $4 children, parents skate free with paid child; Fri 7-11 p.m., $6; Sat 11 a.m.-10 p.m., $6; Sun 1-6 p.m., $5; skate rentals $1-3. (Arlington/Grand Prairie)

CELEBRATION STATION
4040 Towne Crossing Boulevard (I-30 at LBJ)
Mesquite
972/279-7888
Give them a treat inside the 16,000-square-foot indoor facility packed with entertaining games, shows, and video games, as well as a restaurant serving pizza, hot dogs, and other kid-friendly foods. Outdoors on the six-acre park are go-carts, batting cages, bumper boats, carnival rides, and two miniature golf courses. Seasonal schedule. No admission fee; games and rides are priced individually. (East Dallas)

CLUBHOUSE FOR KIDS ONLY
6550 Camp Bowie Boulevard
Fort Worth
817/763-0707
This play center is geared toward kids ages 2 to 12. The main focus of the village is the treehouse, around

which are the grocery store, medical center, library, craft center, and other community buildings. Kids can climb the climbing walls, get their faces painted, and participate in Karaoke or a dozen other activities. Second location at 2200 Airport Freeway, 817/355-5060. $6.95 children 2-12, $4.95 children 1-23 months, adults free. (Southwest Fort Worth)

DISCOVERY ZONE
4860 SW Loop 820
Fort Worth
817/738-4386
Parents can leap, slide, crawl, and play with their kids. This indoor family play center, with its brightly colored tunnels, bridges, slides, and ball pools, is geared for younger children. Pizza and snacks are available; it's a popular place for parties. Open daily. Other locations at 9100 North Central Expressway, Dallas, 972/739-4386; 3301 West Airport Freeway, Irving, 972/256-1900; and 1118 West Arbrook Boulevard, Arlington, 817/472-9973). (Arlington/Grand Prairie)

DR PEPPER YOUTH BALLPARK
Behind The Ballpark in Arlington
1000 Ballpark Way
Arlington
817/273-5269
Just north of The Ballpark in Arling-

ton (see Chapter 5, Sights and Attractions), this state-of-the-art baseball facility,is designed specifically for children age 12 and under. The replica stadium is the site of Texas Rangers camps and clinics (information: 817/273-5297) throughout the year, teaching the fundamentals of baseball to all ages. Instructors include current Texas Ranger players and coaches, as well as college coaches and former players. The facility is also rented out for youth ballgames, birthday parties, and group events. All children age 13 and under may join the Dr Pepper Jr. Rangers, the official youth fan club (information: 817/273-5143). For $12, members receive lots of goodies, including free game tickets, a tour of the ballpark, a membership card, a logo pin, posters and newsletters. (Arlington/Grand Prairie)

DYNO-ROCK INDOOR CLIMBING GYM
608 East Front Street
Arlington
817/461-3966
www.dynorock.com
Become a "wall crawler" in a climbing gym that offers a safe, controlled environment for climbers of all ages and skill levels. With more than 14,000 square feet of artificial rock climbing surface, as well as sheer climbing walls, it provides a lot of challenging fun. Mon-Tue 3-10, Wed-Fri 11-10, Sat 6-11, Sun 1-9. $9, rentals extra; monthly and annual passes available. (Arlington/Grand Prairie)

GAMEWORKS
3000 Grapevine Mills Parkway
Grapevine
972/539-6757

GameWorks was created as the ultimate entertainment destination. From fantasy concepts to interactive reality, players can compete in a dynamic series of thematic environments. Sun-Thu 11-1, Fri 11-2, Sat 10-2. Games priced individually. (Mid-Cities)

KID'S TOWN
751 Central Expressway
Richardson
972/231-2345
This place is way cool! The playscapes represent a real town, including a medical center, a grocery store, a TV station, an airport, a theater, and other community buildings. Kids can shop in the toy store, play doctor at the medical center, and climb on the fire engine. (Far North Dallas)

MALIBU SPEEDZONE®
11130 Malibu Drive
(I-35 at Walnut Hill)
Dallas
972/247-7223
www.speedzone.com
Speed! Race! Zoom! Any kind of "fast" word applies to this speedy place. Customized, scale Formula One racers let you race against the clock, and three-hundred-horsepower dragsters take you from 0 to 70 miles per hour in three seconds. Test your driving skills on the "Slick Trax" or "Turbo Track." For those who prefer less adrenaline-based fun, you'll find more than one hundred of the fastest racing and action video games in Electric Alley or 36 racing-theme holes of miniature golf. When you need a rest, enjoy a cold drink, a snack, or a full meal in the Speedzone Café. Sun-Thu 11 a.m.-11 p.m., Fri-Sat 11 a.m.-1 a.m. (Central Dallas)

NASCAR SILICON MOTOR SPEEDWAY
Dallas Galleria
Dallas
972/490-RACE
This is the place to race! The Galleria's newest entertainment complex features racecar simulators powered by 700-horsepower engines capable of reaching 200 miles per hour. (Far North Dallas)

NORTH RICHLAND HILLS ENTERTAINMENT DISTRICT
8851 Grapevine Highway
(Highway 26)
North Richland Hills
Approximately one mile north of Loop 820 on Highway 26 is a concentration of kid-friendly attractions such as NRH2O Family Water Park, Mountasia FunCenter, Mountasia Hockey, Texas Indoor Speedway, Midcities Combat Zone Paintball, and Southwest Golf. (Mid-Cities)

PUTT-PUTT GOLF AND GAMES
2004 West Pleasant Ridge Road

Arlington
817/467-6565
Don't think of the miniature golf courses of years ago. Yes, Putt-Putt still offers championship putting courses, but it now also features state-of-the-art game arcades, outstanding go-cart tracks, batting ranges, and concession areas. Other locations at 17717 Coit Road, Dallas, 972/248-4966; and 1701 East Division, Arlington, 817/277-6501. Daily 10 a.m.-1 a.m. Games priced separately. (Arlington/Grand Prairie)

TILT ADVENTURE MOTION THEATER
603 Munger
Dallas
214/720-7276
This West End entertainment center features the TILT Adventure Motion Theater, which is a thrilling experience for all, as well as the latest video games, simulators, and shooting galleries. TILT sites are located in most of the major malls in the Metroplex. (Downtown Dallas)

Witold Skrypczak

8

PARKS, GARDENS, AND RECREATION AREAS

The city of Dallas maintains 406 neighborhood, community, and regional parks covering nearly 23,000 acres and more than 50 miles of jogging and biking trails. It provides recreational facilities and activities at more than 250 tennis courts, 125 soccer fields, 40 football fields, 100 baseball and softball diamonds, 100 swimming pools, 225 playgrounds, 42 recreational centers, 6 golf courses, and much more.

In addition, the Dallas park system includes the Dallas Arboretum, Dallas Horticulture Center, Dallas Zoo, Dallas Aquarium, Fair Park, and Samuell Farm. For a complete listing of Dallas parks, see the "Community Pages" in the front of the Dallas Yellow Pages. For activities in the parks, call 214/670-7070.

Arlington has an extensive network of 46 city parks offering facilities for hiking, in-line skating, biking, boating, fishing, swimming, picnicking, golf, tennis, and a variety of other sports and activities.

Fort Worth's park network is second in total acreage only to Chicago. Two major city parks run along the Trinity River southwest of Downtown: Trinity Park, north of I-30, and Forest Park, south of I-30. Stretching for almost 2 miles along the Clear Fork of the river, Trinity Park contains the Fort Worth Botanic Gardens, Japanese Gardens, and Conservatory, as well as nearly 10 miles of jogging and biking trails, and an outdoor fitness course. Forest Park to the south is home to the Fort Worth Zoo, its miniature train ride, and Log Cabin Village historical park.

Numerous smaller neighborhood parks that offer a wide variety of activities are scattered throughout the city; a complete listing of Fort Worth parks and their facilities appears in the "Community Pages" in the front of Fort Worth's Yellow Pages.

The Dallas Arboretum and Botanical Garden has the largest public selection of azaleas in the United States.

Nearly all the cities in the Metroplex have well-maintained park systems and facilities for recreational activities. For a list of the Parks and Recreation Department phone numbers for various cities, please see the sidebar on page 167.

ARBOR HILLS NATURE PRESERVE
6701 Parker Road
Plano
972/941-7250
This unique natural escape from suburban sprawl includes a mammoth playground structure of bridges and ramps and slides and rocks. Hiking and biking trails and paths lead through woods of native trees and wildlife. (Far North Dallas)

BACHMAN LAKE PARK
3500 Northwest Highway
Dallas
214/670-6374
Bachman Lake is a scenic, 205-acre lake within the city limits of Dallas encircled by a jogging/in-line skating track. There's a soccer field, a playground, multipurpose fields, and picnic tables with grills. On a sunny day, you may see the rowing club out on the lake; motorboats and swimming are not allowed. Sometimes concessions rent paddleboats and skates. Bachman Recreation Center offers facilities and activities for those age six and up with special mental or physical needs. Staffed with therapeutic recreational professionals, the facilities are color-coded and include a pool, a hot tub, a full gym-

nasium, a weight room, an arts-and-crafts room, a theater, and an adjacent fishing pier on the lake. Staying in the park after dark is not advisable. Free. (Central Dallas)

CEDAR HILL STATE PARK
1570 West FM 1382 at Highway 67
Cedar Hill
972/291-6641
Cedar Hill State Park is a 1,826-acre urban nature preserve located on Joe Pool Reservoir. The scenic beauty of the area contrasts with the surrounding flat plains. The park complements the extremely popular lake, which has more than one hundred miles of shoreline and a profusion of water-based recreation. More than 350 wooded campsites with hookups are located within walking distance of restrooms and hot showers. Park facilities include more than two hundred picnic tables, two lighted fishing jetties, two concrete four-lane boat ramps, a swimming beach, four playgrounds, and a stocked perch pond for the youngsters. Off-road biking trails and courses for all levels of riders are among the best in the area. There are also scenic hiking and walking trails where bikes are not allowed.

This pastoral area's proximity to the Metroplex draws weekend campers and day users. The convenient location and excellent camping facilities attracts tourists who use the park as a base for longer stays to explore the entire area. In fact, the park now ranks first in visitation of all the Texas State Parks. Within the park is the **Penn Farm Agricultural History Center** (972/291-0209), affording a glimpse into history with reconstructed and historic buildings from the mid-nineteenth through mid-twentieth centuries. Penn Farm is home to a variety of farm animals and an organic vegetable garden. Open daily, it is staffed by volunteers, and the tour is self-guided. For lake facilities, see Chapter 10, Sports and Recreation. (East Dallas)

THE DALLAS ARBORETUM AND BOTANICAL GARDEN
8525 Garland Road at Buckner Boulevard
Dallas
214/327-8263

On the eastern shore of White Rock Lake, The Dallas Arboretum is an oasis in the heart of one of Dallas's oldest neighborhoods. Acres of towering trees, fragrant gardens, and lush lawns transport you from the city's "fast lane" into a serene and tranquil world. More than five thousand different varieties of plants ensure colorful blooms year-round, from fresh blooms of springtime to vivid colors of fall. The Palmer Fern Dell, cool and misty as an English country glade, gently moistens its shade-loving ferns and rhododendrons with a unique micro-mist fog. Displaying rainbow colors all year, the Jonsson Color Garden has the largest collection of azaleas in the Southwest that bloom in spring and 15,000 chrysanthemums that bloom in the fall. The Hunt Paseo de Flores (walkway of flowers) traverses the length of The Arboretum and ends at the Fogelson Fountain, which was donated by Greer Garson in memory of her late husband, Buddy Fogelson.

The DeGolyer House, a spectacular 1939 Spanish Colonial Revival mansion listed in the National Register of Historic Places and a Recorded Texas Historic Landmark, was the center of the DeGolyer

A young visitor to the Dallas Arboretum & Botanical Garden

Dallas CVB

estate. Tours of the home are conducted regularly, and several special events are held throughout the year. Open daily except Thanksgiving Day, Christmas Day, and New Year's Day. Mar-Oct 10-6; Nov-Feb 10-5. $6 adults, $5 seniors, $3 children 6-12, children under 6 free. Parking $2. (Central Dallas)

DALLAS HORTICULTURAL CENTER
3601 Martin Luther King Boulevard (Fair Park)
Dallas
214/428-7476
This 7.5-acre center is home to one dozen gardens, including an antique rose garden, a Xeriscape garden of native plants, a medicinal/culinary garden, an iris garden (more than three hundred varieties), and a classic French landscape garden with a 50-foot fountain surrounded by colorful plants. Visit the two-story conservatory and greenhouse complex. Tue-Sat 10-5, Sun 1-5. Free. (East Dallas)

DALLAS NATURE CENTER
7171 Mountain Creek Parkway
Dallas
972/296-1955
Part of this wilderness preserve is the highest point in Dallas County and offers magnificent views of Joe Pool Lake. A habitat for native plants and wildlife, facilities include seven miles of hiking trails, picnic areas, a visitor center, and a butterfly garden. Open daily 7-sunset. Free. (East Dallas)

DEBUSK PARK/ KIDQUEST
1625 Gross Road at Peachtree
Mesquite
972/216-6260
KidsQuest is a community playground project featuring 12,000 square feet of adventure. Kids climb and crawl all over a wooden pirate ship, practice their circus act on a rubber tightrope, and slide through tubes and assorted passageways. (East Dallas)

The Esplanade at Fair Park

Dallas CVB

Parks and Recreation Departments:

- *Addison, 972/450-2851*
- *Arlington, 817/459-5474*
- *Benbrook, 817/249-3000*
- *Dallas, 214/670-4100*
- *Farmers Branch, 972/919-2620*
- *Fort Worth, 817/871-7275*
- *Garland, 972/205-2750*
- *Grand Prairie, 972/237-8100*
- *Grapevine, 817/481-0351*
- *Irving, 972/721-2501*
- *Mesquite, 972/216-6260*
- *North Richland Hills, 817/581-5760*
- *Plano, 972/941-7250*
- *Richardson, 972/238-4250*

FOREST PARK
1500-2000 Colonial Parkway at
University Drive
Fort Worth
817/927-9386
Forest Park is south of I-30 on the opposite bank of the Clear Fork from Trinity Park on the north side of I-30 (see following listing). It's most noted for Log Cabin Village and the Fort Worth Zoo with its miniature train ride through the parks. There's an outdoor swimming pool, playgrounds, picnic areas, and shelters. It's almost impossible to tell where one park ends and the other begins, and it doesn't really matter. Train ride $3 adults, $2.50 children. (Southwest Fort Worth)

FORT WORTH BOTANIC GARDEN
3220 Botanic Garden Boulevard

Fort Worth
817/871-7686
24-hr. Recorded Information:
817/871-7689
Located in Trinity Park, the Botanic Garden consists of several different gardens spread over 114 acres of beautifully landscaped grounds. Created in 1933 during the Great Depression, the rose gardens were the first public relief project in Tarrant County and began the oldest botanic garden in the state of Texas. Now more than 2,500 native and exotic plant species are displayed in restful natural settings. Still the centerpiece, the Rose Gardens reach their peak of spectacular blooms in late April and again in October. Stroll through the 10,000-square-foot Conservatory filled with lush tropical plants from around the

TRIVIA

Seven state parks are located within one hour's drive of Dallas.

world and visit the highly acclaimed Japanese Garden (see following listing). The Exhibition Greenhouse contains exquisite orchids and an enormous collection of begonias. The Gardens restaurant offers light lunch fare Tuesday through Saturday, and the gift shop sells garden and nature-related items. Gardens open daily 8-sundown. Free. Conservatory open Mon-Fri 10-9, Sat 10-4, Sun 1-4, extended hours in summer; $1 adults, $.50 seniors and children 4-12, children under 4 free. & (Southwest Fort Worth)

FORT WORTH JAPANESE GARDEN
3220 Botanic Garden Boulevard
Fort Worth
817/871-7686

Nature is held in great esteem in Japan, as evidenced by the ambience throughout these gardens. A stroll among the waterfalls and pools where Oriental Koi swim and the tranquility of harmonic natural beauty should relax even the most frenzied soul. Abundant praise has been lavished on Fort Worth's Japanese Garden. Originally the site of a gravel pit, it's now a serene place filled with beautiful spring blooms and fall foliage. The Meditation Garden is patterned after a temple garden in Kyoto, and the Mikoshi was a gift from Fort Worth's sister city, Nagaoka, Japan. There's a pagoda, a teahouse, and an exceptional gift shop in a fine waterside building surrounded by complementary landscaping. April-Oct daily 9-7; Nov-March Tue-Sun 10-5. $2 adults

weekdays, $2.50 weekends; $1 children 4-12; children under 4 free. & (Southwest Fort Worth)

FORT WORTH NATURE CENTER & REFUGE
9601 Fossil Ridge Road
Fort Worth
817/237-1111

The Fort Worth Nature Center is the largest municipally-owned facility of its kind in the United States. Only ten miles from downtown Fort Worth, prairies, forests, marshes, and the Trinity River remain much as they were 150 years ago. The 3,500-acre Nature Center & Refuge provides a sanctuary for native wildlife and plants, and a 25-mile trail system provides visitors with a good opportunity to view deer, buffalo, and live armadillo. For more than 30 years, Nature Center educational programs have exposed thousands of school children to the basics of ecology and environmental responsibility. The Hardwicke Interpretive Center has nature programs, maps, interpretive exhibits, and a gift shop and nature library and is wheelchair accessible. Daily 9-5; Visitors center: Tue-Sat 9-5, Sun noon-5 (North Fort Worth)

HEARD NATURAL SCIENCE MUSEUM AND WILDLIFE SANCTUARY
1 Nature Place (Hwy. 5 on FM 1378)
McKinney
972/562-5566
www.heardmuseum.org

The legacy of Miss Bessie Heard, this 275-acre wildlife sanctuary is dedicated to preserving wildlife and teaching nature conservatism to the community. You'll spot furry critters as well as pretty wildflowers along the wandering self-guided nature trails. The Heard Raptor Center treats and releases orphaned or injured birds of prey, supported in part by the Wild Child Adoption program. The 16,250-square-foot museum has exhibit halls, live animal displays, and collections of natural science, such as rocks, minerals, shells, and fossils. An additional eight thousand square feet holds classrooms, and the educational program is phenomenal, involving thousands of students each year. Bring your camera and binoculars.

A gift shop offers a nice variety of nature-oriented merchandise. Located about 25 miles from downtown Dallas; call for exact directions. Tue-Sat 9-5, Sun 1-5. Museum free, self-guided trail $2 adults, $1 children. (Far North Dallas)

HERITAGE PARK
Bluff and Main, north of Tarrant County Courthouse
Fort Worth
817/871-7275
Located both on the bluffs above the Trinity River and on the river below, this park is the approximate site of the original Camp Worth. From the bluff, there's a great view of the Trinity River Valley to the north, but the biggest part of the park is down along the river where you can walk or rent a canoe, pedal boat, or bicycle from the Boat and Recreation Center in the Tandy Parking Lot. The park is not the safest place to be after dark. (Downtown Fort Worth)

KIEST PARK
3080 South Hampton Road
Dallas
214/670-4100
This 255-acre park contains a neighborhood swimming pool, various sports courts and fields, more than two miles of trails, and picnic

Jogging along the Trinity River

Ft Worth CVB

areas. The nearby recreation center has 16 tennis courts. (East Dallas)

LAKE ARLINGTON
6300 West Arkansas Lane
Arlington
817/451-6860
In the southwest corner of the city, this 2,250-acre lake is popular for fishing, boating, sailing, and skiing. Bowman Springs Park and Richard Simpson Park are on its shoreline, as well as the Lake Arlington Golf Course. (Arlington/Grand Prairie)

LAKE LEWISVILLE STATE PARK
Access via Highway 121, then FM 423 north of The Colony
This 721-acre park on a peninsula on the eastern shore of Lake Lewisville is extremely popular among Metroplex residents for sailing, water skiing, and especially fishing. The park offers boat ramps, picnic areas, camping facilities, shelter restrooms, showers, a playground, and bait and tackle concessions. (Far North Dallas)

LAKE WORTH
Northwest end of city off Texas Highway 199
Fort Worth
Fishing, boating, other watersports are among the activities to be enjoyed at this 3,500-acre, city-owned lake. There are picnic areas and some scenic points along Meandering Drive. The Fort Worth Nature Center adjoins it on the northwest. (North Fort Worth)

L. B. HOUSTON PARK AND NATURE AREA
Off Highway 114 near Irving
Dallas
972/670-6374
An ideal destination for nature lovers

and bird watchers is this 475-acre wilderness preserve. It's near the crossing along the Elm Fork of the Trinity River, which was used by many people who were going to California during the Gold Rush. Park facilities include more than eight miles of trails and 100 picnic tables. The L. B. Houston Tennis Center has 12 lighted courts. (Central Dallas)

PECAN VALLEY PARK
Benbrook Lake
Benbrook
817/249-3000
This park at Benbrook Lake, southwest of Fort Worth, is a well-established park with a host of recreational activities including boating, swimming, camping, picnicking, and equestrian trails. (Southwest Fort Worth)

RANDOL MILL PARK
1901 West Randol Mill Road
Arlington
817/459-5474
One of Arlington's oldest parks features tennis and basketball courts, playgrounds, picnic areas, and a swimming pool. Fishing is permitted in Randol Mill Pond. (Arlington/Grand Prairie)

RIVER LEGACY PARKS
701 NW Green Oaks Boulevard at Cooper

TRIVIA

Only one species of armadillo lives in Texas—the nine-banded (*Dasypus novemcinctus*). All of an armadillo's litter are the same sex.

Arlington
817/860-6752
www.riverlegacy.com
A long-term goal in the Metroplex is to link Dallas and Fort Worth via trails along the Trinity River. This combined 958-acre park is part of the plan. Whether or not that ever happens, Arlington's River Legacy Parks are some of the most beautiful natural landscape in the area. Winding along the Trinity River, the parks feature wooded hiking and biking trails, nature trails, scenic overlooks, and picnic areas. Birders come to enjoy the thick forests and open greenbelt. River Legacy Parks are also the home of the Living Science Center (see also Chapter 7, Kids' Stuff). (Arlington/Grand Prairie)

Dallas's skyline beyond White Rock Lake

SAUNDERS PARK
Stockyards National Historic District
Fort Worth
Along the banks of Marine Creek, Saunders Park is a landscaped oasis where cowboys and tourists can enjoy a restful respite from the hustle and bustle of the Stockyards. (North Fort Worth)

TRINITY PARK
2401 University Drive at I-30
Fort Worth
817/871-7698
Trinity Park runs about two miles along the Clear Fork of the Trinity River north of I-30 and adjoins Fort Worth's Cultural District. Full of natural splendors, the sprawling park contains the Fort Worth Botanic Garden and Japanese Garden, eight miles of jogging and biking trails, and an outdoor fitness course. Scattered throughout the beautiful park are playgrounds, picnic tables, water fountains, and

restrooms. Trinity Park is also the scenic site of Shakespeare in the Park performances each summer. (Southwest Fort Worth)

TRINITY RIVER TRAILS
Northside Drive and
Samuels to Foster Park
Fort Worth
817/871-PARK
This scenic paved trail winds along the Trinity River through Heritage Park (just north of Downtown), Trinity Park, past the Fort Worth Zoo and miniature train in Forest Park, then through Overton Park to Foster Park at South Drive. It's 32 miles roundtrip, but you can pick up the trail almost anywhere along the route. (North Fort Worth to Southwest Fort Worth)

WHITE ROCK LAKE PARK
8300 Garland Road
Dallas
214/670-4100
White Rock Lake is the focal point of this park. The lake was built as a city water supply in 1910, and by the

1930s, it was the "in" place for swimmers and sunbathers. Although swimming is no longer allowed, the lake is still a popular gathering place. Probably one of the prettiest lakes in the area, it's as close to nature as you can get inside the city limits. Park facilities include a variety of sports fields, play areas, shaded picnic tables, and a scenic hiking and biking trail that follows the water's edge. Sailboats dot the lake on pretty days, and you may spot an occasional canoe or kayak gliding by. Fishermen will be hoping for bass and catfish, and the wide variety of birds may be hoping for the same. The Dallas Arboretum adjoins the park on the east. Nearby, Flagpole Hill Park has a newly designed playground for disabled children. It also has a spectacular view of White Rock Lake and is a great place to fly kites. Many Dallasites remember Flagpole Hill as "the sledding hill." Free. (North Dallas)

9

SHOPPING

Dallas boasts more shopping centers per capita than any other major U.S. city. Ever since the five Sanger brothers, immigrants from German Bavaria, rode the Houston & Texas Central Railroad to Dallas in 1873 and established Sanger Brothers Department Store, Dallas has been a retail center. Subsequently, a former Sanger employee, Herbert Marcus, and his brother-in-law, A. L. Neiman, opened an "exclusive woman's ready-to-wear store" in 1907. As they say, the rest is history. Dallas became a mecca for shoppers as home to not only Neiman Marcus but also America's oldest shopping center, Highland Park Village.

From that strong foundation, Dallas's reputation as a leading retail center grew, attracting quality merchants and buyers from all parts of the country. Many great names in retail have come to Dallas: Macy's, Marshall Fields, Saks Fifth Avenue, Lord & Taylor, Nordstrom's, Tiffany & Co., Calvin Klein, and Ralph Lauren. Dallas is also the headquarters of J.C. Penney department store.

Most of these stores are found as anchor stores in large regional malls, such as The Galleria, NorthPark Center, Hulen Mall, and Vista Ridge Mall. Visits to the area's smaller neighborhood centers can be greatly rewarding if your interests tend toward the unusual or unique shops and boutiques. Recognized as America's first shopping center, Highland Park Village's Spanish-inspired architecture is a unique attraction close to the heart of the city. The Shops and Galleries of the Crescent and the antique shops along Knox Street and McKinney Avenue/Uptown also offer an enormous variety of specialty merchandise and are fun places to browse.

The Fort Worth area offers Hulen Mall on the south side, Ridgmar Mall on the west side, and North East Mall and mega-mall Grapevine Mills in the Mid-Cities. The fine Western wear shops along Exchange Avenue in the

Stockyards District are the places to get your cowboy and cowgirl duds. Although Fort Worth has some excellent, stylish shopping areas, this is one category where Dallas shines brighter. But then, it's supposed to because shopping is one of its major tourist attractions.

A Metroplex shopping spree is not limited to expensive merchandise, either. The latest trend is discount shopping. There seems to be something for everybody, from discount chain stores to factory outlet stores to the megamall of them all, Grapevine Mills. And for the extremely economical shopper, "flea markets" can be found somewhere in the area every weekend. The listings here are just a sampling of the variety of choices.

SHOPPING DISTRICTS

Camp Bowie Boulevard

A variety of tempting, unique shops and galleries stretch along "old red-brick Camp Bowie" and Seventh Street on either side of the Cultural District. The close proximity to some of the best art museums in the country invites the eclectic shopper to explore the area. Being able to park close to the shops is another plus. (Fort Worth)

BACKWOODS
3212 Camp Bowie Boulevard
Fort Worth
817/332-2423
www.backwoods.com
For more than 25 years, the friendly and knowledgeable staff at Backwoods has been outfitting customers for life's adventures. An authorized Scott & Sage fly fishing dealer, this store has a huge selection of clothing, gear, and equipment for the camper, fisher, hunter, and outdoorsperson of any kind.

NORMA BAKER ANTIQUES
3311 West Seventh Street
Fort Worth
817/335-1152
Norma carries one of the largest selections of antique estate silver in the Metroplex, as well as new silver patterns and pieces. She also has a fabulous collection of American cut glass, plus a general line of antiques.

THE MARKET
3429 West Seventh Street
Fort Worth
817/334-0330
What a selection of home furnishings! This combination gift shop, gallery, furniture store, antique store, and interior decorating shop has something that will appeal to everyone. They have silk flowers, kitchen items, candles, and an immense variety of home decorating items. It's always lavishly and elegantly decorated for the holidays.

Highland Park Village

Two early entrepreneurs hired the designer of Beverly Hills to design a beautiful town, and Highland Park was "born" in 1907. Then they decided the town needed a town square/shopping area, so the developers traveled to Spain and Mexico, returned to Highland Park, and hired architects to create an extraordinary Mediterranean Spanish-style village like no other. The resulting Highland Park Village (Preston Road at Mockingbird, Dallas, 214/521-0050, www.hpvillage.com) debuted as the first shopping center in America. The first stores opened in 1931, and the Village Theater, the first luxurious suburban theater, opened in 1935. But interrupted by the Depression and WWII, it took nearly 20 years to complete the center. Although the Village has now been modernized and renovated, it still retains its original Spanish architecture, terra cotta roofs, stucco walls, intricate iron work, and serene center courtyard surrounded by brick walkways and lush landscaping.

The shops are now upscale, high-quality, stylish establishments with an international flavor. Most people recognize the names of Calvin Klein, Polo/Ralph Lauren, Ann Taylor, Harolds, and Williams-Sonoma. Some lesser known establishments include Heritage Rare Coins, Wolford Boutique, St. John Boutique, William Noble Rare Jewels, and Gerald Tomlin Antiques. Amid the fine shops are Café Pacific (Mediterranean bistro), Mi Cocina (Tex-Mex), Patrizio (Italian), and the requisite Starbucks. (Central Dallas)

Historic Downtown Grapevine
Grapevine's Main Street is lined with interesting shops, galleries, and eateries. Browse to your heart's content and don't miss the side streets and Barton Street (one block west of Main Street). (Mid-Cities)

BARTON STREET STAINED GLASS
334 South Barton Street
Grapevine
817/488-0187
This delightful stained glass studio

and gallery displays a great selection, but if you don't see what you want, the artist will create something especially for you.

BRITISH EMPORIUM
130 North Main Street
Grapevine
817/421-2311
Featuring imported foods, teas, and other items from the old British Empire countries, this delightful shop was opened about six years ago because the owner said she was tired of having to drive to Dallas to purchase her British favorites.

GRAPEVINE ART GLASS
334 South Barton Street
Grapevine
817/251-5193
Drool over these exquisite hand-blown objets d'art. The beautiful art glass bracelets make a unique souvenir.

OFF THE VINE
324 South Main Street
Grapevine
817/421-1091
Who could visit Grapevine without stopping in this wine shop with its selection of more than 175 wines and wine-related gift items?

PUEBLO CONNECTION
334 South Main Street
Grapevine
817/481-7724
This shop displays a lovely assortment of quality Native American

TRIVIA

Dallas has more shopping centers per capita than any other major U.S. city.

items, jewelry, and artwork. Say "hi" to the cigar-store Indian as you enter.

SPECIAL EFFECTS
120 South Main Street
Grapevine
817/329-7276
Enter and smell fresh potpourri, hear soft piano music drifting from a heavenly source, and "ooh" and "aah" at the lovely home décor accents, fancy gifts, and candles.

Historic Downtown Plano
If you like quaint, artsy places and antique shops, visit Historic Downtown Plano just a few minutes north of Dallas (East 15th Street between Avenue M and Avenue G). Walk the red-brick streets and discover a fine array of antique malls, specialty and gift shops, galleries, boutiques, and eateries. Pottery and art glass, antique sporting collectibles and wildlife carvings, Victorian clothing and jewelry, needlework, dolls, baskets, fine gifts, and dozens of antique shops suit a wide variety of tastes. To satisfy other tastes, there are two restaurants, a tearoom, and a bakery. (Far North Dallas)

Inwood Village
Shopping Center
On the edge of prestigious Highland Park and University Park, this shopping center (Lovers Lane at Inwood Road, Dallas, 214/745-1701) was one of the city's first deluxe neighborhood shopping centers when it opened in 1949. Still a nice, upscale group of shops include Bookstop, St. Bernard Sports, Voyagers and numerous shops with jewelry, art and antiques, collectibles, apparel, and gifts. Inwood Village is also the site of several acclaimed restaurants. (Central Dallas)

Knox Street Area
On the southeastern edge of Highland Park, this shopping area attracts those who are tired of the malls and are looking for the unusual. Boutiques, antique and specialty shops, a furniture store, an electronic/video store, and a 37,000-square-foot Crate and Barrel offer a variety of merchandise in this upscale neighborhood. A myriad of fine restaurants and clubs are also located in the Knox Street vicinity. (Central Dallas)

McKinney Avenue/Uptown
This lively, dynamic neighborhood offers a fascinating array of antique shops offering treasures from elegant to eccentric, art galleries, specialty shops, and some of the finest dining spots in town. The

TRIVIA
Abraham Lincoln Neiman, his wife Carrie, and brother-in-law Herbert Marcus opened a store in Dallas that immediately established a reputation for high quality at a high price. In 1928, after clashes with Herbert and Herbert's son Stanley, A. L. Neiman sold his share of the business to Marcus for $250,000. About the same time, he and Carrie divorced. When Neiman died at the age of 95, in the Masonic Home in Arlington, he was utterly destitute, his only possession a cufflink that he kept in a cigar box.

McKinney Avenue Trolley (see Chapter 2, Getting Around) connects much of the area to downtown Dallas. (Downtown Dallas)

Plaza of the Americas

In the Dallas Arts District, this small, yet elegant shopping mall (700 North Pearl Street, Dallas, 214/720-8000) surrounds a 15-story atrium with giant palm trees. The interior is striking with French marble floors and mahogany woods. Classical white marble statues adorn the entrances of the two office towers that flank the shopping area on the north and south. About 40 shops, restaurants, and services are located in the two-story plaza, as well as a popular ice skating rink. (Downtown Dallas)

Shops and Galleries of the Crescent

The Hotel Crescent Court (see Chapter 3, Where to Stay) is the centerpiece of this complex, but a few exclusive and expensive shops surround a three-level open atrium. The diminutive shopping village (200 Cedar Springs at Maple Avenue, Dallas, 214/871-8500 or 871-3200) offers a truly distinctive collection of specialty items, antiques, art, and fine apparel. Controlled by Caroline Hunt, daughter of oil baron H. L. Hunt, it reflects her tastes and fascination with the English countryside. (Downtown Dallas)

LADY PRIMROSE'S SHOPPING ENGLISH COUNTRYSIDE
Shops and Galleries of the Crescent
Dallas
214/871-8333
Choose from a variety of imported antiques, unusual decorative accessories, and gifts. On the second

level is an assemblage of "thatched cottages," individual shops selling such items as luxurious christening gowns, linens, English silver, and jewelry. Lady Primrose's Thatched Cottage Pantry serves lunch and afternoon tea.

STANLEY KORSHAK
Shops and Galleries of the Crescent
Dallas
214/871-3600
Catering to the rich and famous, this award-winning store offers the finest men's and women's apparel as well as exclusive cosmetics, home furnishings, linens, gift items, jewelry, and a full bridal service. The spacious store proudly offers personal service and attention to detail by a highly trained staff.

BOEHM PORCELAIN GALLERY
Shops and Galleries of the Crescent
Dallas
214/855-7999
An amazing collection of porcelain birds, flowers, and animals are on display, as well as crystal. Be careful browsing because some items have five-figure price tags.

CATHY'S ANTIQUES
Shops and Galleries of the Crescent
Dallas
214/871-3737
Cathy's offers a fine selection of antique furniture, estate jewelry, linens, porcelain, and silver.

Snider Plaza

In the center of University Park, this older shopping area at Lovers Lane and Hillcrest (www.sniderplaza.net) has seen many stores come and go. Establishments face each other across the plaza, so it's a great place for browsing. The galleries and upscale shops are always interesting. Kuby's Sausage House, a popular German deli, and Peggy Sue's Bar B Que are described in Chapter 4, Where to Eat (see also the Kuby's listing in the Notable Stores section. (Central Dallas)

THE ELLIOTT YEARY GALLERY
Snider Plaza
Dallas
214/265-1565
Offering artwork for all tastes and budgets, this gallery specializes in master ceramics. The décor creates the ambience of galleries along the French Riviera.

HENRY JACKALOPE
Snider Plaza
Dallas
214/692-8928
This is the place to find "Dallas chic" Western wear, such as handmade alligator boots and contemporary southwestern designer fashions.

Stockyards National Historic District
Part of the fun of visiting the Stockyards is dudin' yourself up to be a cowboy or cowgirl and taking home all the Old West souvenirs you can carry. You'll find some of the best Western fashions anywhere along Exchange Avenue, as well as handmade boots and custom cowboy hats. Most of the shops and boutiques offer merchandise (from T-shirts to artwork to home furnishings) with a Western flair. (North Fort Worth)

FINCHER'S WESTERN WEAR
115 East Exchange Avenue
Fort Worth
817/624-7302
Not a new, urban cowboy store, Fincher's has offered fine Western wear in Cowtown since 1902. You'll find Western apparel and accessories for the whole family, from infants to adults. A custom shirt can be ordered for your hard-to-fit cowboy. You can get a hat hand-creased in the gigantic hat department, and pick up a few souvenirs while you're there. The east half of the building was originally the Stockyards National Bank until 1933, and you can still see the vaults.

FROM THE HIDE
117 West Exchange Avenue
Fort Worth

817/624-8302

The Old West is still alive in this truly unique store. You'll smell leather and hear cowboy music when you walk in. The décor could be called Western kitsch. Hard to describe, this establishment contains a little bit of anything, from fine leather goods and jeans to jackalopes and stuffed armadillos and jewelry made from rattlesnake rattles to lots and lots of relics. It's a great place to browse.

HOUSE OF BLADES
114-A East Exchange Avenue
Fort Worth
817/626-1713

This distinctive knife shop was built in the hallway of the building it occupies, which explains its narrowness. But it's crammed with hundreds of knives of every conceivable description, from common pocket knives to rare custom-designed pieces with hand-carved handles.

LUSKEY'S/RYON'S
WESTERN STORE
2601 North Main Street
Fort Worth
817/625-2391, 800/725-RYON
www.luskeys.com

One of the leading Western stores since 1919, Windy Ryon moved his Saddle and Ranch Supply Store to this building in the 1950s. It's changed ownership since then, but it still specializes in custom-made saddles; you can watch the craftspeople work right in the store. There's also a gigantic selection of anything Western, including boots, apparel, and accessories in all price ranges.

M. L. LEDDY & SONS
BOOT & SADDLERY
2455 North Main Street

Fort Worth
817/624-3149

Since 1922, Leddy's has sold superb custom-made boots, saddles, and chaps. Still family owned, they have some unusual Texas-type items such as quill ostrich attaché cases and bar glasses with famous cattle brands. For the ultimate souvenir, Leddy's will put golf spikes on any pair of cowboy boots for you. Fore, y'all!

MAVERICK FINE WESTERN WEAR
& SALOON
100 East Exchange Avenue
Fort Worth
817/626-1129

Originally the Maverick Hotel, this 1905 building is one of the Stockyard's oldest and has had a long, colorful history. Now Maverick Fine Western Wear offers high-quality leather apparel, boots, custom hats, Double D Ranchwear, silver jewelry, and accessories. And there's a nice assortment of gift items, specialty foods, books, and the like. The authentic 50-foot bar supplies the "saloon" qualification. You can order a longneck beer or sasparilla and wait while the little woman (or man) tries on all the fancy duds.

PURE-D-TEXAS
116 East Exchange Avenue
Fort Worth
817/626-9077

"Pure-D" means gin-u-wine. Every item in this store has been made (manufactured or handcrafted), assembled, or grown in Texas. A great place to shop for souvenirs, the shop has everything from Texas wines to Texas toys.

STOCKYARDS STATION
130 East Exchange Avenue

Fort Worth
817/625-9715
Without destroying the architectural integrity of the original sheep and hog pens of the stockyards, the authentic but modernized setting now houses a variety of Western-oriented shops, galleries, and restaurants. You can still see the original fences and brick floors throughout the retail area.

For Western clothing, try Circle R Ranchwear (817/626-9966), Destination Fort Worth (817/625-1254), Leather Trading Company (817/624-4993), and Stockyards Station Trading Post (817/624-4424).

For art, jewelry, and gifts, stop by New West Arts (817/626-6633), Stockyards Station Gallery (817/624-7300), Silver Feather (817/624-4413), Moondance (817/626-6861), or the Old West Country Store (817/625-2422).

Specialty shops include the Ernest Tubb Record Shop (817/624-8449), The Candy Barrel (817/626-5536), Texas Hot Stuff (817/625-1221), and Wines Texas Style (817/335-9463). Inside the Tandy Leather Company (817/624-6337), which began in Fort Worth, you'll find an interesting, unique leathercraft museum.

Sundance Square
This unique downtown shopping and entertainment district (817/339-7777) offers variety and style from museum gallery gift shops to fashionable clothing to gift items to jewelry. (Downtown Fort Worth)

MAIN STREET OUTFITTERS
501 Main Street
Fort Worth
817/332-4144 or 888/99-TROUT
Practically anything by Orvis can be found here. From high-end outdoor

apparel, knives, and binoculars, to travel accessories. The fully stocked fly shop has the finest in fly fishing equipment, fly-tying materials, and rods and reels.

THE NATURE COLLECTION
406 Houston Street
Fort Worth
817/335-0999
www.earth-home.com
A haven for the shopping-weary, the unusual chain-store is comfortable, with towering trees, warm wood appointments, soft bubbling waters cascading over dozens of decorative fountains, and the tinkle of wind chimes. It's a nice place to browse awhile. Gifts for the nature lover include CDs with music from around the world, bubbling fountains, aromatherapy candles and oils, animal figurines, science and nature toys for all ages, natural bath and body products, and a good selection of books. They also sell lots of goodies for gardens and gardeners, including birdfeeders, fountains, and wind chimes.

An angel overlooking Sundance Square

Ft Worth CVB

PARFUMERIE MARIE ANTOINETTE
101 West Second Street
Fort Worth
817/332-2888 or 800/634-1538
This fragrant shop offers lotions and potions for bath and body care. A special souvenir is "Bluebonnet" fragrance, billed as the "captured scent of the Texas Hill Country."

University Park Village

Aptly named for its proximity to Texas Christian University (TCU), this relatively new upscale shopping area (817/654-0521) has a nice variety of merchants such as Talbot's, Harold's, Ann Taylor, John L. Ashe, Banana Republic, Victoria's Secret, The Gap, and Barnes & Noble. Several other unusual stores include Voyagers, Williams-Sonoma, Uncommon Angles, Toys Unique, Into the Garden, Omaha Steaks, Simple Things, Wolf Camera, the Pottery Barn, and a huge Hallmark Showcase. Eateries include Blue Mesa Southwestern Grill, Chili's, Water Street Seafood, and Starbucks. (Southwest Fort Worth)

UNCOMMON ANGLES
1616 South University Drive,
Suite 303

Fort Worth
817/335-9933
The ultimate in uncommon, this shop features the artistic creations of more than 150 artisans from around the world. Owners Bill and Judy Shelton have searched far and wide to find unique items for their discriminating clientele. You'll see exquisite works of hand-blown glass, paintings, hand-turned woodcarvings, kaleidoscopes, and the finest handcrafted jewelry.

VOYAGERS, THE TRAVEL STORE
1600 South University Drive,
Suite 608
Fort Worth
817/335-3100
It's easy to spot the flags of many nations flying outside this store. Even if you're not planning a trip at the moment, this shop is fascinating. Look down and upside-down at the satellite photo of the world woven into the carpet and up at the globe suspended from the ceiling. The shop offers everything for the traveler from gadgets to expensive lug-gage to a travel agency. Find maps, journals, guidebooks, foreign exchange calculators, and all sorts of bags, backpacks, and totes. Travel agents are on duty to help plan that trip you didn't know you were taking. Another location at Inwood Village Shopping Center in Highland Park.

West End Marketplace

Built as the Brown Cracker and Candy Factory in the early 1900s, this historic red-brick building at 603 Munger Avenue at Market Street (214/748-4801) now houses the West End Marketplace, a huge shopping and entertainment center with four floors of shopping, eateries, and entertainment venues (see Chapter 12, Nightlife). Building hours (shop hours vary) are Monday through Thursday 11 a.m. to 10 p.m., Friday and Saturday 11 a.m. to midnight, and Sunday noon to 6 p.m. (Downtown Dallas)

ALAMO FLAGS
West End Marketplace,
Second Floor

Fort Worth's University Park Village features upscale shops and restaurants

Ft Worth CVB

Dallas
214/220-2122
See and buy flags from around the world, as well as flag-related items such as T-shirts, caps, pins, patches, coffee mugs, and personalized items.

CATS, CANINES, AND CRITTERS
West End Marketplace,
Second Floor
Dallas
214/740-0256
The perfect shop for critter lovers!

FREEFLIGHT GALLERY
West End Marketplace,
Third Floor
Dallas
214/720-9147
Handmade artwork, including jewelry, wood, art glass, kinetic sculptures, pottery, and kaleidoscopes, are exhibited in this fine collection of museum-quality art.

THE OFFICIAL DALLAS COWBOYS PRO SHOP
West End Marketplace
Third Floor
Dallas
214/979-0500
Here's the place to find Dallas Cowboy apparel, including hats, shirts, jackets, sweatshirts, and even a tiny Cowboys cheerleader outfit for a future fan. There are mountains of memorabilia of all descriptions from keychains to coffee mugs and authentic autographed merchandise.

PURPLE PARADISE
West End Marketplace,
Second Floor
Dallas
214/855-5229
If your passion is purple, then you've found paradise!

WILD BILL'S WESTERN STORE
West End Marketplace
Third Floor
Dallas
214/954-1050
www.wildbills1.com
Wild Bill's has a huge selection of Western apparel for the whole family, even little buckaroos. You'll find all the major brands, but if you can't find exactly what you're looking for, custom-made boots and clothing are available. Choose Western gifts from affordable to extravagant for that special someone.

NOTABLE BOOKSTORES

ANTIQUARIAN OF DALLAS
2609 Routh Street
Dallas
214/754-0705
Browsers beware! You could spend hours amid the myriad rare, out-of-print, first editions, and leather-bound books in this enthralling store.

Categorized as a general bookstore, it features an excellent selection of everything from poetry to Texana, from war to religion. The noteworthy children's section offers entertaining and educational volumes for all ages. You'll find some nice prints and Texas maps, too. (Downtown Dallas)

BARNES & NOBLE
7700 W. Northwest Hwy.
Dallas
214/739-1124
This well-known chain bookstore has a dozen locations throughout the Metroplex, six in the Dallas area and six in the Fort Worth/Arlington/Mid-Cities area. Each has a large selection of new books and periodicals, an excellent children's selection, and an upscale coffee bar/café. They feature numerous author appearances, children's story times, and other literary events. All are open seven days a week. (Central Dallas)

BOOK SHOPPE
1822 W. Berry
Fort Worth
817/926-8208
www.thebookshoppe.com
Enter and be personally greeted by Simon and Schuster! The two "adopted" center-of-attention cats

think it's their bookstore. If so, they should be commended. This extremely well-organized shop has thousands of gently-used books—fiction and non-fiction, hardback and paperback, classics, rare editions, and out-of-print volumes dating from the early 1800s. More current selections include best sellers and books on tape. (West/Southwest Forth Worth)

BORDERS BOOKS & MUSIC
10720 Preston Rd.
Dallas
214/363-1977
With four locations in the Metroplex, this bookstore chain boasts a variety of over 200,000 titles of books, music, and videos. An Expresso café offers refreshments during a browsing break and numerous chairs and sofas scattered around the store provide a comfortable atmosphere to peruse your potential selections. The stores have knowledgeable staffs and feature frequent author booksignings, poetry readings, story times, and special events. Other locations: 5500 Greenville Ave., Dallas, 214/739-1166; 2403 S. Stemmons, Lewisville, 972/459-2321; 4613 S. Hulen, Fort Worth, 817/370-9473. (Central Dallas)

CONNECTIONS BOOKSTORE
2416 Forest Park Blvd.
Fort Worth
817/923-2320
One of the rare remaining independent bookstores, this one is noteworthy for its personal service. The friendly, helpful owner and staff will gladly special order if you can't find what you're looking for. It's a general bookstore featuring a thoughtful collection of books, unusual greeting cards, and an excellent selection of

TRIVIA

Dallas's Highland Park Village, built in 1931 under single ownership, was the first planned shopping center with a unified architectural style and stores facing in toward an interior parking area.

children's books. (Southwest Fort Worth)

HALF PRICE BOOKS
770 Road to Six Flags
(in Lincoln Square)
Arlington
817/274-5251
This large bargain bookstore chain has 13 locations around the Metroplex, each with an enormous selection of new and used books, used records, CDs, cassettes, videos, and magazines. No telling what you'll find. And they're all open seven days a week. (Arlington/Grand Prairie)

THE HISTORY MERCHANT
2723 Routh Street
Dallas
214/742-5487
A mini-paradise for anyone interested in history, this is a comfortable store with chairs around a stone fireplace and a friendly, helpful staff. Discover such items as rare books by and about Winston Churchill, exclusive portrait bronzes of historical figures, commemorative first edition items, as well as framed photographs, prints, and autographs. Established in 1969, The History Merchant specializes in fine, rare, and out-of-print books on World War II, history, literature, and biographies. (Downtown Dallas)

MAJORS SCIENTIFIC BOOKSTORE
802 Montgomery Street
Fort Worth
817/731-0281
www.majors.com
Here you'll find specialty books and multimedia of interest in the fields of medicine, nursing, allied health professions, consumer health, dental, veterinary, fire/police, technology, and science as well as textbooks in the same categories. It also has a selection of medical related gift items, scrubs and labcoats, anatomical charts, and instruments. A second location is in Dallas at 2137 Butler, 214/631-4478. (Southwest Fort Worth)

75 PERCENT OFF BOOKS
5152 Rufe Snow
North Richland Hills
817/498-2872
Blessed bliss for bargain seekers, this discount store sells publishers' overstock, and slightly damaged/blemished books at a huge savings. Thousands of books cover tabletops—a nice arrangement for wheelchair-bound and short people who can't reach high shelves. Dozens of new titles are put out daily and there's no telling what you'll find from day to day. There are two additional locations in the Metroplex, at 13020 Preston Rd., Dallas, 972/702-0414 and 1717 E. Spring Creek Parkway, Plano, 972-423-8120. (Mid-Cities)

NOTABLE STORES

BASS PRO SHOPS
OUTDOOR WORLD
2501 Bass Pro Drive
Grapevine
972/724-2018
www.outdoor-world.com
This enormous 200,000-square-foot store, located across the street from Grapevine Mills Mall, is filled to capacity with the newest in fishing, hunting, boating, golfing, and camping equipment. It's sort of a Disneyworld for sporting enthusiasts, with stuffed bears ready to pounce from faux mountains, a waterfall splashing into a 30,000-gallon

Top Ten Places to Shop for Western Wear

by Bill and Linda McKinley, owners Sundowner Trailers of Texas

1. **Best Hats,** 2739 North Main, Fort Worth, 817/625-6650

2. **Cavender's Boot City,** 2515 Centennial Drive at Highway 360, Arlington, 817/640-8899 (other Metroplex locations in Fort Worth, Hurst, Dallas, Plano, Mesquite, and Lewisville)

3. **Justin Boot Outlet,** 717 West Vickery Boulevard, Fort Worth, 817/654-3103

4. **Maverick,** 100 East Exchange Avenue, Fort Worth, 817/626-1129

5. **M. L. Leddy's Boot and Saddlery,** 2455 North Main, Fort Worth, 817/624-3149

6. **Oxbow Saddlery,** 9812 Highway 80 West, Fort Worth, 817/244-7199

7. **Ryon's Western Wear,** 2601 North Main, Fort Worth, 817/625-2391

8. **Sean Ryon Western Store and Saddle Shop,** 2707 North Main, Fort Worth, 817/626-5390

9. **Sergeant's Western World,** 4905 South Cooper, Arlington, 817/784-6464 (also 13600 Stemmons Freeway, Farmers Branch, 972/406-9464), www.sergeantswestern.com

10. **Western Warehouse,** 3000 Grapevine Mills Parkway (in Grapevine Mills Mall), Grapevine, 972/355-8312 (other Metroplex locations in Dallas and Arlington)

aquarium, and assorted displays sitting and hanging around the store. The gigantic selection of any kind of equipment, clothing, or gifts related to sports staggers the mind. If you tire of shopping, there's a bow and gun range (instruction and hunter safety classes are available), a golf driving range and a putting green (a PGA professional is on staff), and a shooting arcade. If you get hungry, visit Big Buck Brewery & Steakhouse. If you get tired, there's even an Outdoor World Embassy Suites Hotel. This store is worth a visit just to see its grand scale. (Mid-Cities)

CAVENDER'S BOOT CITY
5248 South Hulen Street
Fort Worth
817/294-4400
With more than 10 stores in the Metroplex, Cavender's offers a tremendous selection of name-brand Western wear. (Fort Worth)

DALLAS FARMERS MARKET
1010 South Pearl Street
Dallas
214/939-2806
Not exactly a shop, but great fun! One of the largest farmers markets in the country was established in 1941 and now covers 12 acres of downtown Dallas. Every day, you'll find hundreds of farmers selling fresh vegetables, fruits, nuts, honey, herbs, and flowers. Seasonally, you'll find poinsettias, Christmas trees, pumpkins, and other holiday offerings. Special events include cooking classes (by some top chefs) and educational classes throughout the year. Closed on Christmas and New Year's days. Free parking. (Downtown Dallas)

ELLIOTT'S HARDWARE
4901 Maple Avenue at Motor Street
Dallas
214/634-9900
www.elliottshardware.com
Definitely not your ordinary hardware store, Elliott's advertises "100,000 Things You Can't Live Without." In business in Dallas since 1947, it exhibits a staggering variety of merchandise. An entire section has nothing but replacement parts and pieces for grills of all shapes and sizes. The center of attraction is in the center of the store: an incredibly huge selection of cabinet hardware, especially restoration and reproduction hardware. Select from dozens of glass doorknobs, Victorian shower rings and soap holders for clawfoot tubs, ornate door knockers, and knobs and pulls galore. They stock lots of hard-to-find items. A second location is in Grapevine at 108 N. Northwest Hwy, 817/424-1424. (Downtown Dallas)

GARDNER'S RIBBONS AND LACE
2235 East Division
Arlington
817/640-1436
Gardner's off-the-beaten-track location doesn't keep ladies from finding it; they come from all over north central Texas. Bridal laces, specialty ribbons, bead, silk embroidery, and more buttons than you can imagine pack the shelves and showcases. They have a few specialty fabrics, but the real attraction is the amazing selection of fancy trimmings. (Arlington/Grand Prairie)

KAY FABRIC CENTER
518 West Arapaho, #113
Richardson
972/234-5111
If you sew or quilt, leave your husband in front of a TV and come to this paradise of fabrics, buttons and bows, ribbons and lace! Locally owned and operated by the Molnar family since 1971, this gigantic store is stuffed with fabrics, including such hard-to-find items as one-hundred-percent cashmere, silks, velvets, lames, lingerie materials, swimwear lining, ultrasuede, and ultraleather. Browse rows of bridal fabrics and dozens of pearl, beaded, and lace tiaras and headpieces. The selection of notions is mind-boggling, including belting, buckles, buttons, tassels, frogs, fringe, eyelets, ribbons, and lace. A display exhibits dozens of sequined appliques, rhinestone trims, lace and beaded collars, and appliques. Need feathers? Choose from ostrich, chandelle, or maribou. Voted the Best Fabric Store in Dallas in a 1999 "Best of Dallas" poll, this store is definitely worth a visit. (Far North Dallas)

NEIMAN AND MARCUS

Once upon a time there were two men, named Neiman and Marcus. . . . The flagship Neiman Marcus Downtown store has a fifth-floor museum in which the shopping legend's 90-year history is presented in high style. New displays are added regularly.

KUBY'S SAUSAGE HOUSE
6601 Snider Plaza
Dallas
214/363-2231
www.kubys.com
Okay, so Kuby's is a German restaurant (see Chapter 4, Where to Eat), but it's also an "Old World" specialty store offering an extensive selection of imported gourmet products. Browse among the mustards, olive oils and marinades, jams, jellies, coffees and teas, European chocolates, breads, dumplings, seasonings, pickles and sauerkraut, Marzipan and gummies, and imported gift items. The authentic meat market offers homemade sausages and cold cuts as well as wild game and fresh meat cuts. (Central Dallas)

THE LEATHER FACTORY
3831 East Loop 820 South
Fort Worth
817/496-4874
The Leather Factory is a national supplier of leather products and leather-working tools for both the professional and the hobbyist. The warehouse showroom is crammed with everything from whole cowhides to starter leather-working kits for kids. If you do work with leather, the selection of tools, conchos, buckles, studs, and tack supplies is awesome. They also have an exhaustive mail-order catalog. (Southwest Fort Worth)

LONE STAR CIGARS
13305 Montfort at LBJ (I-635)
Dallas
972/39CIGAR
Advertising Dallas's largest selection of premium cigars, this store has a 1,750-square-foot humidor, which is fully stocked with literally hundreds of brands of fine cigars. In addition, they carry an extensive collection of humidors and accessories. (Far North Dallas)

MAPSCO
5308 Maple Avenue
Dallas
214/521-2131 or 800/950-5308
www.mapsco.com
This store is fascinating whether you want to get around Dallas or the planet. It specializes in maps, atlases, high-quality globes, and the famous MAPSCO street guides. Cutting-edge technological offerings include a variety of global positioning satellite (GPS) units and travel-related and mapping computer software. (Central Dallas)

NEIMAN MARCUS
1618 Main Street
Dallas

214/741-6911
www.neimanmarcus.com
When Herbert Marcus, Sr. and his sister and brother-in-law, Carrie and A.L. Neiman, opened an "exclusive woman's ready-to-wear store" in Dallas in 1907, they put Dallas on the national fashion map. It was said that shoppers would have to visit 40 New York stores to find the variety of quality merchandise and designer labels represented by the Neiman Marcus store.

As years passed, national and international retailers joined Neiman Marcus to form a variety of fashion choices that would impress any shopper. The first Neiman Marcus mail-order catalog in 1915 was a six-page brochure. The famous His & Hers gifts for the socially-conscious billionaires began in 1960. Still the reigning queen of local merchants, this historic, original, flagship downtown store is a "must" for serious shoppers. The renowned Zodiac Room restaurant is located on the sixth floor and features a mostly ladylike menu. Locations also in NorthPark Center and Prestonwood Mall in Dallas and in Ridgmar Mall in Fort Worth. (Downtown Dallas)

SERGEANT'S WESTERN WORLD
4905 South Cooper Street
Arlington
817/784-6464, 800/383-3669
www.sergeantswestern.com
Headquartered in Farmer's Branch, with another store in Lewisville, Sergeant's Western World is an immense Western store featuring a truly comprehensive selection of Western apparel, show clothing, saddles, tack, and horse equipment.

The Arlington location is the new "superstore." Sergeant's is the exclusive retail outlet for Silver Mesa show clothing and custom saddles, handcrafted by artisans and acclaimed as some of the best in the world. Sergeant's "traveling store" attends prestigious equestrian shows around the country. An award-winning catalog is available, as is online catalog shopping. (Arlington/Grand Prairie)

STANLEY EISENMAN'S
FINE SHOES
6333 Camp Bowie Boulevard
Fort Worth
817/731-2555
A favorite for more than 50 years, this family-owned business is still the place to shop for fine footwear. Known for its large range of hard-to-find sizes, they carry high-quality, brand-name shoes in sizes 3 to 12 and in AAAAA to B widths. The staff is helpful and knowledgeable. This extraordinary shoe store has three locations in the Metroplex. If you wear a hard-to-find size shoe, then this store is a "must" for you. Other locations at 3000 South Hulen Street, Fort Worth, and Village by the Parks Mall, Arlington. (Southwest Fort Worth)

TRIVIA

World-famous Neiman Marcus got its start in Downtown Dallas, where the flagship store continues to thrive.

TEXAS TREASURE HUNTING HEADQUARTERS
5604 River Oaks Boulevard
Fort Worth
800/444-4289
Definitely an unusual and fun place to browse. Family-owned and operated, it's been a full-line metal detecting and mining equipment store since 1979. You just might get the "fever" if you hang around long enough. Good luck! (Southwest Fort Worth)

WOODCRAFT SUPPLY
6954 Green Oaks Road
Fort Worth
817/569-0777
This store carries absolutely everything you can imagine for the woodworker, and the knowledgeable sales staff members are woodworking enthusiasts, too. Wander through the vast selection of quality tools (hand and power), fine hardwoods and exotic woods, and more than 500 how-to books and videos. The store offers dozens of classes, demonstrations, and seminars monthly. Another location is in Brookhaven Shopping Center, 14380 Marsh Lane, Addison, 972/241-0701. (Southwest Fort Worth)

THE WOODEN SPOON
1617 Avenue K
Plano
972/424-6867, 800/2-NORDIC
A visit to The Wooden Spoon is a double delight. A special Scandinavian shop and cultural center, which is located in the lovingly restored historic Foreman home (circa 1867), it is a Plano Historic Landmark. The shop specializes in Scandinavian imports such as candles, dolls, linens, kitchen utensils, handmade crafts, flags, crystal, tiles, jewelry,

pewter, clothing, CDs, videos, books, and food items. The Wooden Spoon Art Studio offers a variety of classes, including painting (oils, acrylics, and pastels), Rosemaling, Nordic knitting, tatting, and language classes in Norwegian, Swedish, Finnish, and Danish. In addition to the gift shop and art studio, The Teaspoon Deli serves a smorgasbord of treats on the downstairs level of the house. It's a delightful place to visit. (Far North Dallas)

MAJOR SHOPPING MALLS

COLLIN CREEK MALL
North Central Expressway
(Highway 75) between
exits 28 and 29
Plano
972/424-7691
www.collincreekmall.com
Built to cater to those in Plano and the bedroom communities farther north, Collin Creek Mall isn't as crowded as some of those closer in to town. Anchored by Foley's, Dillard's, Sears, Mervyn's, and J.C. Penney, the two-story mall has about 150 specialty shops, including the requisite ones. But you'll also find some more upscale or unusual shops such as Natural Wonders, Eddie Bauer, Brookstone, the KERA Store of Knowledge, and Godiva Chocolatier. A nice-sized food court offers the usual fast food; there's also a Luby's Cafeteria and Tino's Mexican Restaurant. Mon-Sat 10-9, Sun noon-6. (Far North Dallas)

GALLERIA
LBJ (I-635) at
Dallas Parkway North
Dallas

972/702-7100
www.dallasgalleria.com
World-class shopping at its very best! Many shopaholics swear this galleria offers the best shopping on the planet. The center covers 1.8 million square feet and houses more than two hundred quality shops, many of which are exclusive to Dallas. The shops and 30 eateries on three levels surround a sparkling ice-skating rink under a vaulted skylight. Architecturally, the mall is patterned after Milan, Italy's Galleria Vittorio Emanuelle, which was built in 1867.

The anchor stores are Macy's, Nordstrom's, and Saks Fifth Avenue; other fine shops include Talbots, Abercrombie & Fitch, Versace Jeans Couture, Cartier, Tiffany & Co., Bachendorf's Crystal, The Old World, Crate & Barrel, Papyrus, Coach, and Gucci. Kids love The Disney Store, KERA Store of Knowledge, Noah's Ark, and the five-theater General Cinema.

The Galleria is especially lovely when decked out in its Christmas finery. But there's more: The complex also includes three office towers and the four-star Westin Hotel. Although parking is available for nearly ten thousand cars, traffic congestion can be dreadful, especially during the holidays. Open Mon-Sat 10-9, Sun noon-6. (Far North Dallas)

HULEN MALL
4800 South Hulen Street
at Loop 820
Fort Worth
817/294-1200
Boasting the widest range of merchandise in the city under one roof, the recently expanded Hulen Mall houses more than 150 specialty shops and restaurants. Dillard's, Foley's, and Montgomery Ward anchor, surrounded by such stores as Casual Corner, Petite Sophisticate, Victoria's Secret, The Gap, Laura Ashley, Coach, Crabtree & Evelyn, Brookstone, a Thomas Kincaide Gallery, and a Godiva Chocolatier.

The mall offers a Premier Shoppers Club with perks such as discounts, bonuses, and prizes throughout the year. To tempt the little ones, there's The Disney Store, Warner Bros. Studio Store, Natural Wonders, and KERA Store of Knowledge. Its convenient location plus the fact that it's the only mall on the southwest side of Fort Worth means it's very crowded. For some reason, it seems as if the parking lot is more congested than inside the mall. Perhaps it's because Hulen Street is lined with gazillions of other shops, restaurants, and strip centers for several blocks both to the south of the mall and on the north side of Loop 820.

T I P

NorthPark Center is the only major shopping center in the Dallas area that is directly accessible by DART. The shopping center offers a complimentary shuttle to and from DART's Park Lane station.

Mon-Sat 10-9, Sun noon-6. (Southwest Fort Worth)

IRVING MALL
**3880 Belt Line Road
at Highway 183
Irving
972/255-0571**

This older mall has been thoroughly renovated and expanded to more than 150 stores, anchored by Foley's, Dillard's, Sears, Mervyn's, and J.C. Penney. The variety and selection is excellent. Other stores include Barnes & Noble, Bath & Body Works, Casual Corner, GAP (Baby GAP and GAP Kids), Old Navy, Truly Texas, and Victoria's Secret. In addition to the plethora of shops, a 14-screen mega-theater offers the latest movies in a modern facility with stadium seating, digital sound, an oversized video game room, and a full service café. The mall's location is convenient (east of DFW Airport and west of Texas Stadium) but in a highly congested area. Belt Line Road is lined with strip centers and individual stores and restaurants both north and south of Airport Freeway (Highway 183). Mon-Sat 10-9, Sun noon-6. (Mid-Cities)

NORTH EAST MALL
**1101 Melbourne Road
Hurst
817/284-3427**

Undergoing a gargantuan expansion in 2000, this mall is anchored by two Dillard's (one for men, one for women), as well as Sears, J.C. Penney, and Montgomery Ward. New anchors scheduled to open are Saks Fifth Avenue and Nordstrom's. An excellent variety of more than 110 specialty shops offers everything from aromatherapy to yo-yos. The mall offers MallPerks, a frequent shopper program that awards points for dollars spent, which are then converted to discounts and bonuses. This mall plays a big part in the HEB (Hurst-Euless-Bedford) community, hosting special events such as safe Halloween parties, fire and police department education programs, and health and safety fairs. Mon-Sat 10-9, Sun noon-6. (Mid-Cities)

NORTHPARK CENTER
**Northwest Highway at North
Central Expressway (Highway 75)
Dallas
214/361-6345**

In 1965, NorthPark Center opened as the first enclosed shopping center, the most elegant and the largest air-conditioned such facility in the country. It has been setting the standard for shopping excellence ever since. Shoppers view paintings, prints, and sculptures by famous artists while strolling the mall. It attracts so many international visitors that the mall directory is in five languages. Anchored now by Neiman Marcus, Dillard's, and Foley's, 2001 promises Nordstrom's. Other fine stores include Burberry, Talbots, Liz

TRIVIA

Leonard's Department Store (1918-1974) covered a half-dozen city blocks. Fort Worth Outlet Square shoppers now ride the former Leonard's M&O Subway

Claiborne, Brooks Brothers, Rand McNally Travel and Bookstore, Coach, Tiffany & Co., Abercrombie & Fitch, Dooney & Bourke, and The Market. If kids could love a mall, this would be it; penguins play at an indoor pool and stores for the youngsters include FAO Schwartz, the Disney Store, Warner Bros. Studio Store, Noah's Ark, and the Nature Company. Choose from a variety of restaurants such as La Madeleine French Bakery & Café, Maggiano's Little Italy, El Fenix Mexican Café, or the Zodiac Room at Neiman Marcus. There's also fast food, a cafeteria, and snacks if you're in a hurry. You'll find courtesy strollers, wheelchairs, and electric carts at NorthPark Center Concierge, which also answers questions, gives directions, and sells gift certificates and stamps. Valet parking is available. A shuttle runs between NorthPark and the nearest DART station. Mon-Sat 10-9, Sun noon-6. (Central Dallas)

THE PARKS AT ARLINGTON
3811 South Cooper at I-20
Arlington
This colossal 1.3-million-square-foot mall serves a huge population on the south side of the Metroplex, making it one of the leading shopping centers. Anchored by Dillard's, Mervyn's, Sears, J.C. Penney, and Foley's, the enclosed two-level mall houses more than 160 specialty shops and eateries. A great selection of stores includes County Seat, Miller's Outpost, Victoria's Secret, Eddie Bauer, The Gap, The Limited, and The Bombay Company; kids' favorites include The Disney Store, Warner Bros. Studio Store, Kay Bee Toy & Hobby Shop, Natural Wonders, and the Dallas Cowboy Pro

Shop. The satellite area around the mall is packed with dozens more stores. Located at a highly congested intersection, the mall itself is spacious and never seems too crowded. Mon-Sat 10-9, Sun noon-6. (Arlington/Grand Prairie)

RIDGMAR MALL
2060 Green Oaks Road at I-30
Fort Worth
817/731-0856
Ridgmar Mall has been undergoing a $60-million renovation since being acquired by the Shopco Group in September 1997. Home to Tarrant County's only Neiman Marcus store, other anchors are Foley's (with a 180,000-square-foot showplace), Dillard's, Sears, and J.C. Penney. Currently, this mall doesn't have the wide range of choices offered by some of the others, but the extensive renovation will add more than 30 stores and the AMC Ridgmar 20 megaplex movie theater. Mon-Sat 10-9, Sun noon-6. (Southwest Fort Worth)

TOWN EAST MALL
Town East Boulevard at LBJ
(I-635)
Mesquite
972/270-2363
One of the first enclosed shopping centers in the area, Town East opened in the city of Mesquite in 1971. You can shop at more than two hundred stores in this three-level mall, with anchor stores Dillard's, Foley's, Sears, and J.C. Penney. Plenty of parking is available, and this mall is usually less crowded than some of the others except during the holidays. Specialty stores include American Eagle Outfitters, Casual Corner, The Limited, The Gap, Miller's Outpost, Victoria's Secret,

The Disney Store, World of Science, Love From Texas, Crabtree & Evelyn, and the San Francisco Music Box Company. To entertain the kids, there's Aladdin's Castle, a Tilt Family Entertainment Center, and a gigantic food court. Mon-Sat 10-9, Sun noon-6. (East Dallas)

VALLEY VIEW MALL
LBJ (I-635) at Preston Road
Dallas
972/661-2424
Opened in 1973 as the first shopping center north of LBJ Freeway, Valley View was renovated in 1993 and now the two-level mall houses about 175 stores surrounding a lovely atrium. It's anchored by Foley's, Dillard's, Sears, and a huge J.C. Penney that occupies the 233,000-square-foot space of a former Bloomingdale's. The mall also includes the ubiquitous mall stores, food court, and new in 2000 is AMC Valley View 20 Theaters. Mon-Sat 10-9, Sun noon-6. (Far North Dallas)

VISTA RIDGE MALL
I-35E at FM 3040
Lewisville
972/315-0015
The area's newest super-mall, Vista Ridge offers 1.1 million square feet of prime shopping. Anchored by Foley's, Dillard's, Sears, and J.C. Penney, it contains more than 160 specialty stores, a food court and a cafeteria, and a 12-screen movie theater. The mall itself is beautiful, with two levels of shops around atriums, fountains, and wide walkways. In the area surrounding the mall are located dozens of satellite stores, such as Linens 'N Things, MJD Designs, Comp USA, Target, Toys 'R' Us, Garden Ridge, Service Merchandise, Best Buy, Office

Depot, Haverty's Furniture, and literally scores of restaurants and fast food spots. Mon-Sat 10-9, Sun noon-6. (Far North Dallas)

FACTORY OUTLET CENTERS

FORT WORTH OUTLET SQUARE
Third and Throckmorton Streets
Fort Worth
817/415-3720 or 800/414-2817
www.fwoutletsquare.com
Around and above a public ice-skating rink, about 40 stores offer a variety of clothing and Western wear, shoes, luggage, toys, gifts, and food. Outlets stores include Mikasa, London Fog, Spiegel, Samsonite Luggage, Haggar, Dress Barn, and Radio Shack. Park free and ride the subway (see sidebar, Chapter 2) or park in the Sundance Square lots. Mon-Thu 10-7, Fri-Sat 10-9, Sun noon-6. (Downtown Fort Worth)

GRAPEVINE MILLS MALL
3000 Grapevine Mills Parkway at Highway 121 North
Grapevine
972/724-4900 (metro)
888/645-5748
www.grapevinemills.com
You've probably heard that everything in Texas is BIG! Well, this Megamall is really big at nearly two million square feet! It's home to more than two hundred famous-name manufacturer and retail outlets, off-price retailers, specialty stores, eateries, video arcades, and a 30-screen movie complex. It has great selection and tremendous values, with such stores/outlets as Off Fifth (Saks Fifth Avenue outlet), Burlington Coat Factory, Old Navy, Dockers Outlet, Levis Outlet, London Fog, J.C. Penney Outlet Store,

TRADERS VILLAGE

The famous Texas-sized flea market, Traders Village (2602 Mayfield Road, Grand Prairie, 972/647-2331, www.tradersvillage.com) features more than 2,000 vendors spread across a 106-acre site. They sell their wares every Saturday and Sunday, year-round. There's a little bit of everything imaginable offered supposedly at bargain prices. It's best to know your merchandise and prices because there's a lot of cheap stuff, too. There are kiddie rides and arcade games for the children. There's an onsite ATM machine and a wide variety of food vendors so you can spend the day. More than 2.5 million visitors a year visit Traders Village for family fun, food, bargains, and dozens of special events and festivals throughout the year. A top-rated RV Park is adjacent to the site. Sat-Sun 8-dusk. Free admission, parking $2 per vehicle.

Naturalizer Shoes, Samsonite, Bose, OshKosh B'Gosh, Mikasa Factory Store, Western Warehouse, Brookstone, and Bed Bath & Beyond. The kids will love the Warner Bros. Studio Store and Sega Gameworks, an arcade full of cutting-edge video and virtual reality games. A Texas-sized food court can please any palate, and the themed restaurants—Rainforest Café, Jekyll & Hyde Club (see Chapter 7, Kids' Stuff) and Dick Clark's American Bandstand Grill—are great fun. A visit here is an adventure itself! Mon-Sat 10-9:30, Sun 11-8. (Mid-Cities)

HORCHOW FINALE
3400 Preston Road
Plano
972/519-5406
High-priced jewelry, linens, china, and apparel from the famous Horchow Collection are sold here at deep discounts. (Far North Dallas)

INWOOD TRADE CENTER
1300 Inwood Road
Dallas
214/521-4777
Just north of Downtown Dallas two blocks south of Stemmons Freeway (I-35E), this shoppin center is a cluster of individual outlet stores with in-front-of-the-store parking. Stores include the Crate & Barrel Outlet, Everyware, Shoe Fair, Accessory Mart, Suzanne's, Uniform Outlet, Seventh Avenue Plus Size Outlet, Maternity Designers Outlet, Royal Optical Outlet, and Simmons Mattress Outlet, as well as a variety of others. (Central Dallas)

PLANO OUTLET MALL
1717 East Spring Creek Parkway
Plano

972/578-1591

Anchored by Garden Ridge, this relatively small outlet mall contains many of the usual shops, such as L'eggs/Hanes/Bali, Dress Barn, Famous Footwear, T.J. Maxx, Bruce Allen Bags, 75 Off Books, and Bugle Boy. Nostalgia Crafts & Antiques has up to three hundred vendors who sell fine antiques, furniture, crafts, and collectibles. Reza's Café serves lunch. Mon-Sat 10-9, Sun noon-6. (Far North Dallas)

FLEA MARKETS

**FLEA MARKET
AT THE CATTLE BARNS
3401 Burnett-Tandy Dr.
Fort Worth
817/332-0229**

The cattle barns behind Will Rogers Memorial Complex turn into a huge indoor flea market each weekend. Between 100-150 dealers set up shop offering all sorts of collectibles, antiques, and general "stuff." It's been a popular place for bargain-shoppers and browsers for nearly 25 years. Sat-Sun 8-5; closed during the Stock Show (mid-January through mid-February). Free admission, free parking. & (Southwest Fort Worth)

**TRADERS VILLAGE
2602 Mayfield Road
Grand Prairie
972/647-2331 (metro)
www.tradersvillage.com**

Don't even attempt to visit unless you have a good pair of sturdy walking shoes and a lot of time. The famous Texas-sized flea market features more than two thousand vendors spread across the 106-acre site. They sell their wares every Saturday and Sunday, year-round. There are also kiddie rides, arcade games, and a wide variety of festival foods. More than 2.5 million visitors per year visit Traders Village for family fun, food, bargains, and dozens of special events and festivals throughout the year. A top-rated RV park is located adjacent to the site. Sat-Sun 8-dusk. Free admission, parking $2 per vehicle. & (Arlington/Grand Prairie)

Dallas CVB

10

SPORTS AND RECREATION

Texans love their sports! Dallas was selected by The Sporting News as one of the nation's top three "sports cities" in both 1998 and 1999. The DFW Metroplex is one of the few in the country with at least one team from every major sports league. There are six professional teams: the Dallas Cowboys (NFL football), the Dallas Mavericks (NBA basketball), the Texas Rangers (American League baseball), the Dallas Stars (NHL hockey), the Dallas Burn (outdoor soccer), the Dallas Sidekicks (indoor soccer), plus the Texas Motor Speedway (NASCAR racing), Lone Star Park (horse racing), championship professional rodeo, and two annual PGA golf events.

In 1998, Dallas voters approved a $230-million downtown arena, which will serve as the new home for the Stars and the Mavericks. That arena is expected to open in the fall of 2000. Until then, the Stars and the Mavericks continue to play at Reunion Arena in downtown Dallas.

Collegiate sports action is provided by the region's numerous colleges and universities, including Southern Methodist University (SMU) and Texas Christian University (TCU), both in the Western Athletic Conference. One of the biggest games of the year is the "Red River Shootout" between the universities of Texas and Oklahoma, which is played in the Cotton Bowl. Sitting on the original site of the State Fair Stadium that was built in 1921 entirely of wood, the Cotton Bowl underwent a multi-million-dollar renovation in 1994 for the World Cup competition.

The residents of the Metroplex enjoy recreational sports as much as spectator sports. The area has a profusion of outdoor facilities, including hiking and biking trails, recreational lakes, parks, tennis courts, swimming pools, and naturally, countless golf courses because golfers can usually play year-round. See also Chapter 8, Parks, Gardens, and Recreation Areas.

PROFESSIONAL SPORTS

Auto Racing

TEXAS MOTOR SPEEDWAY
I-35W at Highway 114
P.O. Box 500
Fort Worth
817/215-8500
www.texasmotorspeedway.com
Completed in 1997, Texas's newest
and largest racetrack is the site of
both major NASCAR (National Association for Stock Car Auto Racing)
and Indy Racing League events.
With permanent grandstand seating
for 154,861 and 194 luxury suites with
seating for 13,192, it's the second-
largest sports facility in America.
The Speedway Campgrounds provide more than 6,000 spaces and a
5,100-square-foot restroom facility.
You may take a behind-the-scenes
tour, and if there's no speedway activity, you'll get to take a lap around
the oval track in one of the tour vans.
Tours may be changed or cancelled
due to weather or speedway activ-

ity. Speedway World, the official
store of the Texas Motor Speedway,
is stuffed with souvenir merchandise
and racing apparel featuring favorite
NASCAR Winston Cup drivers. The
track has also become a popular
venue for huge rock and country
music concerts. If you attend an
event, go early because traffic will
be horrendous. Tickets to events
vary from $10-100. Tour hours: Mon-
Fri 9-4, Sat 10-4, Sun 1-4. $6 adult, $4
seniors and children 12 and under. ⅋
(North Fort Worth)

Baseball

TEXAS RANGERS
The Ballpark in Arlington
1000 Ballpark Way
Arlington
Ticket information: 817/273-5100
www.texasrangers.com
The Texas Rangers play about 80
home games in the season from
late March until October. Whether
it's because of the new stadium or
the winning seasons, baseball has

Fast cars and big crowds at the Texas Motor Speedway

Dallas CVB

won its way into the hearts of Metroplex fans. The American League West Division Champion Texas Rangers attracted nearly 3 million fans in 1999. The 49,292-seat Ballpark in Arlington is a tribute to America's national pastime and an attraction in itself (see also Chapter 5, Sights and Attractions; Chapter 6, Museums and Galleries; and Chapter 7, Kids' Stuff). Tickets $5-30. &. (Arlington/Grand Prairie)

Basketball

DALLAS MAVERICKS BASKETBALL
Reunion Arena

777 Sports Street
Dallas
972/988-DUNK
www.nba.com/mavericks
An NBA franchise since 1980, the Mavericks bring exciting basketball games to their fans from November through April. It was feared that football-loving Dallas wouldn't support the Mavericks, but even though their roller-coaster winning/losing seasons have driven fans crazy, they still come to Reunion Arena to watch their team. A new $230-million, 750,000-square-foot arena is scheduled to open in the fall of 2000 that will be the new downtown home of the Mavericks. Tickets $10-50. &. (Downtown Dallas)

Equestrian

WILL ROGERS EQUESTRIAN CENTER
One Amon Carter Square
Fort Worth
817/871-8150
The Will Rogers Equestrian Center has become recognized as one of the nation's premier equestrian

Dallas Cowboys in the Pro Football Hall of Fame

Bob Lilly	*1980*
Roger Staubach	*1985*
Tom Landry	*1990*
Tex Schramm	*1991*
Tony Dorsett	*1994*
Randy White	*1994*
Mel Renfro	*1996*

Events at the Cowtown Coliseum

1908   First exhibition round-up of cattle ever held under a roof in the United States

1908   First horse show in the Unites States held at night

1909   Comanche Chief Quanah Parker appeared with 36 braves

1911   Theodore Roosevelt addressed a crowd of 5,000

1918   World's first indoor rodeo

1923   World's first live radio broadcast of a rodeo

1920   Enrico Caruso performed before a crowd of 8,000

1947   Bob Wills performed

1949   Bob Hope and Doris Day performed

1956   Elvis Presley performed before a crowd of 7,000

The Cowtown Coliseum has been the performance venue for groups from the Russian Ballet to the Chicago Grand Opera, and the location for movies, television shows, and music videos. When it opened in 1908, the then North Side Coliseum was billed as "the most opulent and dynamic livestock pavilion in the entire Western Hemisphere."

centers, since its opening in 1988. The world-class facility hosts more than 25 horse shows each year, including the National Cutting Horse Association Super Stakes, the American Paint Horse World Championship Show, the Appaloosa Horse Club World Championship Show, and the American Quarter Horse Youth Association World Show. The complex includes two show arenas with 1,946 and 1,100 seats, respectively, and accommodations for hundreds of horses. & (Southwest Fort Worth)

Football

DALLAS COWBOYS
Texas Stadium

TRIVIA

Texas Stadium has 52 full concession stands, 40 specialty stands, 115 drinking fountains, and 86 restrooms.

2401 Airport Freeway
Irving
972/438-7676
Ticket Information 972/579-5000
www.dallascowboys.com
Since its beginning in 1960, "America's Team" has been to the Super Bowl eight times and was the first team to win five Super Bowl championships. Not bad for a team that went 0-11 their first season. Following the departure of their first and long-time coach, Tom Landry, the Cowboys have seen numerous changes. But the loyal Cowboy fans still pack Texas Stadium to watch their team —or maybe it's to watch the Cowboys cheerleaders. Irving's home for the Cowboys, has 63,855 covered seats and 388 luxury suites. A unique showcase when it opened in 1971, the famous stadium with a hole in its roof also hosts country-and-western concerts and public tours (see Chapter 5, Sights and Attractions). Tickets $35-50. ♿ (Mid-Cities)

Golf

GTE BYRON NELSON CLASSIC
PGA TOURNAMENT
Four Seasons Resort and Club
4150 North MacArthur Boulevard
Irving
Tickets: 972/717-1200
This celebrated PGA tour event is held and televised each year in mid-May at the spectacular course at the Four Seasons Resort & Club. It draws huge crowds, but shuttle buses run to the tournament site from the parking lot at Texas Stadium. (Mid-Cities)

Loyal fans pack Texas Stadium to cheer the Dallas Cowboys during football season

Dallas CVB

Norm Alden, a former Texas Christian University (TCU) football player, became a well-known actor and the AC/Delco Man on television.

MASTERCARD COLONIAL PGA TOURNAMENT
Colonial Country Club
3735 Country Club Circle
Fort Worth
Tickets: 817/927-4280
More than 50 years old, this prestigious PGA tour event is usually held the week after the Byron Nelson tournament in Irving. A long-time favorite tournament of the touring pros, most of the big names in golf compete at the Colonial. Also televised, the four-day event draws tremendous crowds and is a place to see and be seen. Shuttle buses run from the parking lots at the TCU football stadium and nearby Will Rogers Equestrian Center and Farrington Field. (Southwest Fort Worth)

Hockey

DALLAS STARS
Reunion Arena
777 Sports Street
Dallas
972/868-2890
Tickets: 214/GO-STARS
Okay, so most cowboys didn't grow up playing ice hockey. The sport was originally entertainment for our immigrants from the North. That is, until the Stars became the 1999 NHL Champions and won the Stanley Cup! Now, all of Dallas has gone hockey-crazy. Texas's only National Hockey League team, the Stars play their home games from September through April in Reunion Arena in

Dallas. A new $230-million, 750,000-square-foot downtown arena is scheduled to open in the fall of 2000 that will be their new home. They practice on the rink at their headquarters in the Dr Pepper Star-Center Ice Arena in Irving. ♿ (Downtown Dallas)

FORT WORTH BRAHMAS
Ticket information: 817/336-4423
www.brahmas.com
Now in their third year, the Brahmas have made the Western Professional Hockey League playoffs the past two years. Most games are played at the Tarrant County Convention Center. ♿ (Downtown Fort Worth)

Horse Racing

LONE STAR PARK
AT GRAND PRAIRIE
1000 Lone Star Parkway
Grand Prairie
972/263-RACE (metro) or
800/795-RACE
www.lonestarpark.com
And they're off! Catch the thrill and excitement of world-class live thoroughbred and quarter horse racing. The multi-level, 280,000-square-foot, glass-enclosed grandstand can seat approximately 8,000. It has box seats, penthouse suites, and a European-style saddling paddock. Dining options include the Silks Dining Terrace with 1,200 seats overlooking the track or six themed concession

stands and landscaped outdoor picnic areas. The whole family will enjoy the adjacent Family Fun Park (see Chapter 7, Kids' Stuff) with its picnic pavilion, petting zoo, pony rides, and giant playground. Don't miss the state-of-the-art Post Time Pavilion, a 36,000-square-foot facility where you can see live horse races via simulcast from top tracks around the world. There's a Las Vegas-style race book, sports bar, and casual dining area. & (Arlington/Grand Prairie)

Rodeo

STOCKYARDS CHAMPIONSHIP RODEO
Cowtown Coliseum
121 East Exchange Avenue
Fort Worth
817/625-1025
Built in 1908 to house the Fort Worth Livestock Show, the mission-style Cowtown Coliseum was the largest show arena of its day. It hosted the first indoor rodeo in 1918, where a crowd of 20,000 watched cowboys compete for a $3,000 purse. The Fat Stock Show evolved into the Southwestern Exposition and Livestock Show, subsequently outgrew the arena, and in 1944 moved to the then-new Will Rogers Coliseum. Today Cowtown Coliseum is home to excellent family entertainment every weekend year-round with Championship Rodeo events and Pawnee Bill's Wild West Show. Even if no events are scheduled while you're visiting, stop by because you'll likely see cowboys and cowgirls practicing in the arena. Outside the Coliseum at Rodeo Plaza and Exchange Avenue stands a bronze statue of the black cowboy, Bill Pickett, who originated the rodeo sport of bulldogging. & (North Fort Worth)

MESQUITE CHAMPIONSHIP RODEO
1700 Rodeo Drive
Mesquite
800/833-9339 or 972/285-8777
www.mesquiterodeo.com

Having a Ball with the Mavericks

Since billionaire computer-guru Mark Cuban purchased controlling interest in the Dallas Mavericks in early 2000, the team may never be the same. The young entrepreneur made his money by selling his first company, MicroSolutions, to Microsoft in 1990 and his second company, Broadcast.com, to Yahoo in 1999. Cuban says he has more money than he can ever spend, but is determined to remain a "regular guy." An enthusiastic basketball fan, Cuban is living a dream and having a ball. Literally. He's been seen shooting hoops during practice and heard shouting encouragement from the stands during games. Go, Mark!

The Fort Worth skyline

 attribution (vertical text): Ft Worth CVB

The highly acclaimed Mesquite Championship Rodeo features a full range of pro rodeo events, including bull riding, roping, steer wrestling, barrel racing, and wild bronc riding. One of the world's most famous rodeos, it is broadcast via satellite to Europe, Asia, and South America, as well as on The Nashville Network cable channel. The ultra-modern, fully-enclosed, climate-controlled arena offers comfortable seating, a paved parking lot, and even a barbecue buffet

The Dallas Texans

By Steven A. Jent, author of *The Browser's Book of Texas History*

Texas acquired its first National Football League team in 1952 when the feckless New York Yanks were sold to Dallas millionaire Giles Miller and renamed the Dallas Texans. Miller was sure that fans would support professional football as enthusiastically as college ball, but it would take a better team than the Yanks. The only score in their opening game against the New York Giants was a touchdown scored after a fumbled punt reception by Giants back, Tom Landry. The Texans lost 24-6. The rest of the season wasn't any better, and Miller had to sell the franchise back to the NFL. The Dallas Texans' first season was their last.

(extra cost) before each performance. Come early and browse the Texas-themed shops, enjoy live music, and visit the petting zoo and pony rides for the kids. You can check the schedule of events and purchase advance tickets on the web site. Rodeos every Friday and Saturday night at 7:30 from April-September. Reserved seats $12-25, general admission $10 adults, $7 seniors, $4 children 3-12, children under 3 free. & (East Dallas)

Rugby

DALLAS HARLEQUINS
Glencoe Park (Home Field)
5300 Martel Avenue
Dallas
www.quins.com
Founded in 1971, the Dallas Harlequins Rugby Football Club has risen to its position as one of the top clubs in the United States, and in 1997 became a founding member of the USA Premier Rugby Super League. The club has a varied membership of all ages, professions, and a sprinkling of players from countries around the world. Visiting "ruggers" are always welcome at the pitch and in the pub. Home matches are played at Glencoe Park just east of North Central Expressway at McCommas, and the "Quins" train there each Tuesday and Thursday at 6:30. (Central Dallas)

TRIVIA

Former Dallas Cowboys quarterback Clint Longley's hobby is rattlesnake hunting!

Soccer

DALLAS BURN
Cotton Bowl (Fair Park)
Dallas
214/979-0303
www.burnsoccer.com
The Dallas Burn is a world-class professional outdoor soccer team that plays in the Cotton Bowl from April through September. They have made the playoffs every year since Major League Soccer began play in 1996. The Burn participates in a unique program between the team and local soccer associations. The pro team gives away thousands of free tickets to young soccer players and coaches, visits local game fields, sponsors competitions, and interacts in various ways throughout the year with the players of the future. & (East Dallas)

DALLAS SIDEKICKS
Reunion Arena
777 Sports Street
Dallas
214/653-0200
www.sidekicks.com
Charter members of the Premier Soccer Alliance, Dallas's professional indoor soccer team plays in Reunion Arena from June through October. & (Downtown Dallas)

RECREATION

Bowling

AMF ARLINGTON LANES
1801 East Lamar Boulevard
Arlington
817/276-9898
www.amf.com
With more than one dozen Metroplex locations, AMF bowling cen-

ters offer bumper bowling for kids, automatic scoring, the latest equipment, full-service concessions and/or restaurants, lounges, and group facilities. Xtreme™ Bowling is available at most locations. (Arlington/Grand Prairie)

BRONCO BOWL
ENTERTAINMENT CENTER
2600 Fort Worth Avenue
Dallas
214/943-1777
Part bowling alley, part arcade, part pool hall, part concert venue, part Sports Grill & Bar, the Bronco Bowl is a 140,000-square-foot facility near downtown Dallas. The concert stage hosts performances by local and big-name groups from pop/rock to rhythm and blues to country. (Central Dallas)

DON CARTER'S ALL-STAR LANES
6343 East Northwest Highway
Dallas
214/363-9418
With 52 lanes, automatic scoring, a game room, a coffee shop, and a bar, this is a popular center, especially since it's open 24 hours. Another location, also open 24 hours, with 58 lanes, is located in Dallas at 10902 Composite Drive (Walnut Hill and Stemmons Freeway), 214/358-1382. And in Fort Worth, Don Carter's All-Star Lanes' location is 6601 Oakmont, 817/346-0444 or 800/874-2695. (Central Dallas)

Fitness

THE HEALTH
& FITNESS CONNECTION
6242-A Hulen Bend Boulevard
Fort Worth
817/346-6161
This outstanding facility is an affiliate of the Osteopathic Health System of Texas. You'll find everything from state-of-the-art exercise equipment, an indoor pool, racquetball courts, and an indoor track to water fitness and aerobic classes, seniors pro-

"Hogan's Alley"

It was 1946. World War II had ended, optimism was in full swing, and the Colonial Golf Tournament was born. Local golfer Ben Hogan blazed past some of the biggest names in the sport to win the first Colonial with a course record 65. Little did he know at the time, but he was on his way to becoming a Fort Worth legend. His purse was a whopping $3,000, and tickets to the event were $2. After he won four more Colonial titles, the course was dubbed "Hogan's Alley." The course, the players, and the tournament have changed in the years since 1946, but Ben Hogan still holds the record for the most Colonial tournament wins.

Golfer Ben Hogan grew up in Fort Worth. At the age of 15, he lost a special caddy's tournament in a playoff to another Fort Worth boy—Byron Nelson.

grams, playcare, yoga, and karate. There's even an on-site medical director, and consultation in weight loss, health risk assessment, and nutrition are available, as well as licensed physical therapy. Daily rates are available. (Southwest Fort Worth)

PREMIER CLUB
5910 North Central Expressway at Mockingbird
Dallas
214/891-6600
This full-service facility has cardiovascular equipment, aerobics classes, an indoor swimming pool and track, basketball, racquetball, and squash courts, and a whirlpool/sauna/steam room. A children's nursery is available during the daytime. Daily rates are available. (Central Dallas)

SIGNATURE ATHLETIC CLUB
14725 Preston Road
Dallas
972/490-7777
Thirteen acres of full-service facilities include state-of-the-art exercise equipment, a 25-meter heated indoor/outdoor pool, a basketball gymnasium, four racquetball and three squash courts, a steam room/sauna, a whirlpool, a massage service, and a kids' club and nursery. Daily rates are available. (Far North Dallas)

THE TEXAS CLUB

800 Main Street
Dallas
214/761-6300
This 50,000-square-foot luxury fitness club offers the latest in exercise equipment, an indoor running track, a steam room/sauna, a whirlpool, a massage service, a full-size basketball gymnasium, five racquetball courts, and a cardiovascular training program. Daily rates are available. (Downtown Dallas)

YMCA
4621 Ross Avenue at Akard
Dallas
214/954-0500
Four floors of the YMCA include exercise equipment, three basketball courts, 20 racquetball and volleyball courts, a full-size swimming pool, and two indoor tracks with another on the roof. A steam room/sauna and aerobics classes are offered. A babysitter is available Monday through Saturday during the day. Daily rates are available. (Downtown Dallas)

Golf
Literally scores of golf courses are located in the Metroplex. The cities of Fort Worth and Dallas, as well as Irving, Arlington, Garland, Mesquite, Plano, Grapevine, and others, maintain municipal courses. A full listing can be found in the "Community Pages" in the front of the Fort Worth and Dallas phone directory's Yellow

Top Ten Public Golf Courses in the Metroplex

by Matt McKay, area golf writer for the
Dallas Morning News

1. **Bridalwood**, 4000 West Windsor Drive, Flower Mound, 972/355-4800
2. **Buffalo Creek,** 624 Country Club, Rockwall, 972/771-4003
3. **Ridgeview Ranch,** 2701 Ridgeview Drive, Plano, 972/390-1039
4. **Sky Creek Ranch,** 6000 Promontory Drive, Keller, 817/498-1414
5. **Southern Oaks,** 13765 Southern Oaks Drive, Burleson, 817/426-2400
6. **Tangle Ridge Golf Club,** 818 Tangle Ridge Drive, Grand Prairie, 972/299-6837
7. **Texas Star,** 1400 Texas Star Parkway, Euless, 817/685-7888
8. **Tierra Verde,** 7005 Golf Club Drive, Arlington, 817/478-8500
9. **Tour 18,** 8718 Amen Corner, Flower Mound, 817/430-2000 or 800/946-5310
10. **Woodbridge,** 7400 Country Club Drive, Wylie, 972/429-5100

Pages. Listings here are limited to public courses, although a few semi-private clubs will offer guest privileges. Green fees are the posted ones, although most courses offer senior discounts, twilight rates, and specials throughout the year.

BRIDALWOOD GOLF CLUB
4000 West Windsor Drive
FM 1171
Flower Mound
972/355-4800
Nominated for *Golf Digest*'s Best New Upscale Public Course, this is one of the "top ten." Mon-Thu $60, Fri-Sun $69, includes cart and practice balls. (Mid-Cities)

COYOTE RIDGE GOLF CLUB
1680 Bandera
Carrollton
972/939-0666
Relatively new, this 18-hole championship course has bent-grass greens and a practice range. PGA instruction is available. Mon-Thu $49, Fri-Sun $59, includes cart. (Far North Dallas)

FAMILY GOLF CENTER
AT ARLINGTON
1301 NE Green Oaks Boulevard
Arlington
817/261-6312
This facility offers a tremendous variety of golfing fun. The driving range

has 45 stalls (20 covered) overlooking simulated greens with artificial water hazards. A short game area includes an 800-square-foot chipping green and a 1,500-square-foot putting green, as well as a practice bunker. A complete pro shop and PGA/LPGA instructors are available. The entire family can enjoy the two "resort-style" miniature golf courses. (Arlington/Grand Prairie)

THE GOLF CLUB AT FOSSIL CREEK
3401 Club Gate Drive
Fort Worth
817/847-1900
Arnold Palmer designed this championship course complete with practice facilities, PGA lessons, and a restaurant serving breakfast and lunch. Mon-Thu $49, Fri-Sun $59, includes cart. (North Fort Worth)

HYATT BEAR CREEK GOLF
& RACQUET CLUB
West Airfield Drive
DFW Airport
972/615-6800
There are two 18-hole championship courses at this public facility. Locals have dubbed the West course one of the most challenging courses in the Metroplex. Located at DFW International Airport, it's extremely popular with travelers and businesspeople. Mon -Thu $70, Fri-Sun $88, includes cart. (Mid-Cities)

IRON HORSE GOLF COURSE

NE Loop 820 at Rufe Snow
Fort Worth
817/485-6666
Rated one of the top-ten public courses in Texas by the *Dallas Morning News,* it's also a local favorite. PGA lessons and a driving range are available. Mon-Fri $42, Sat-Sun $52, includes cart. (Mid-Cities)

RIDGEVIEW RANCH GOLF CLUB
2701 Ridgeview Drive
Plano
972/390-1039
One of the best new public golf courses in the Metroplex, Ridgeview Ranch has scenic rolling hills and tree-lined fairways with two meandering natural creeks. Mon-Thu $39, Fri $42, Sat-Sun $49, includes cart. (Far North Dallas)

SOUTHERN OAKS GOLF CLUB
13765 Southern Oaks Drive
Burleson
817/426-2400
Designed and managed by PGA champion Mark Brooks, Southern Oaks is a challenging course with complete facilities. Mon-Fri $50, Sat-Sun $65, includes cart and range balls. (Southwest Fort Worth)

TANGLE RIDGE GOLF CLUB
818 Tangle Ridge Drive
Grand Prairie
972/299-6837
This eight-hole championship golf

TRIVIA

Fort Worth boasts the state's largest purse for professional rodeo competition: more than $100,000. For information on local events, call the Professional Rodeo Cowboys Association at 719/593-8840.

course is situated just south of scenic Joe Pool Lake. Rated the eighth best course in Texas by *Golf Digest,* it resembles a fine country club course even though it's owned and operated by the city. It also has a nice clubhouse and dining room. Mon-Fri $49.50, Sat-Sun $59.50, includes cart. (Arlington/Grand Prairie)

TEXAS STAR
1400 Texas Star Parkway
Euless
817/685-7888 or 800/TEX-STAR
Selected as the "Best New Public Course in Texas" by the *Dallas Morning News* golf panel in 1998, Texas Star features an interesting landscape. Designed around Hurricane Creek, players encounter ancient oak trees, waterfalls, and

native grasses as they play the 18 holes set amid rolling hills and natural woodlands. Raven's Grille (see Chapter 4, Where to Eat) is a great place to eat and relax after a challenging game. Mon-Thu $37, Fri-Sun $53; cart $12 per person extra. (Mid-Cities)

TOUR 18
8718 Amen Corner
Flower Mound
817/430-2000 or 800/946-5310
Described as a "Disneyland for Golfers," Tour 18 is a unique conglomeration of 18 meticulously designed replicas of 18 famous golf holes around the United States. Each is historically significant or renowned in the world of golf. Now you can play that challenging hole

Top Ten Trails Around Dallas
by Henry Chappell, Dallas area outdoors writer

1. **Breckenridge Park Trail:** 4.5-mile loop near Renner and Brand in Richardson
2. **Boulder Trail Park:** 3.8 miles, near Camp Wisdom Road and Boulder Drive in Dallas
3. **Cross Timbers Hiking Trail:** 14-mile backpacking trail at Lake Texoma
4. **Duck Creek/Audubon Trail:** 3-mile loop near Oates and Duck Creek Drive in Garland
5. **Joe Pool Lake Trail:** 4.5 miles at Cedar Creek State Park
6. **L. B. Houston Trail:** 4 miles along the Trinity River at Wildwood Road
7. **Northshore Trail:** 10-mile trail at Lake Grapevine
8. **Ray Roberts Greenbelt:** 12 miles at Ray Roberts State Park
9. **White Rock Trail:** 19 miles around White Rock Lake
10. **Dallas Nature Center:** various trails

at Sawgrass like the pros. The state-of-the-art facility has global positioning systems (GPS) and communications equipment on the golf carts, upscale yet casual dining, and 90-day advance tee-time bookings. Mon-Thu $65, Fri-Sun $75, includes cart and range balls. (Mid-Cities)

Hiking/Biking
Unlimited opportunities to enjoy the great outdoors exist in this fitness-conscious metropolitan area. A few popular trails are listed as follows, but see also Chapter 8, Parks, Gardens and Recreation Areas.

The city of Dallas maintains more than five hundred miles of bike trails. Trail maps are available at City Hall or most bike shops in the area for about two dollars.

Dallas County:
- Cedar Hill State Park
- Dallas Nature Center
- Duck Creek Greenbelt Trail
- White Rock Lake Park

Tarrant County:
- Loyd Park, Joe Pool Lake
- Northshore Trail, Lake Grapevine
- River Legacy Parks, Arlington
- Trinity River Trails

Ice Skating

AMERICA'S ICE GARDEN
700 North Pearl Street
Dallas
214/720-8080
Located in the Plaza of the Americas in the Dallas Arts District, this large rink offers public skating and lessons for all ages. Some of the innovative programs include be-

ginning hockey lessons, summer camps, field trips, and freestyle training. You can even rent the rink for private birthday parties. (Downtown Dallas)

DALLAS ON ICE
700 Munger (in the West End)
Dallas
214/969-RINK
This outdoor skating rink is open from the Friday after Thanksgiving through February. Open for public skating, the rink also hosts entertaining ice shows. $6 admission, $3 skate rental. (Downtown Dallas)

DR PEPPER STARCENTER ICE ARENA
211 Cowboys Parkway
Irving
214/GO-SKATE
This facility has two full-sized ice rinks. In addition to being the practice rink for the Dallas Stars, it is also home to the Dallas Junior Hockey Association, a senior hockey league,

Skating at the Galleria Ice Rink

Dallas CVB

The Fort Worth Cats were the scourge and glory of the Texas minor league. They were a dynasty with seven consecutive league championships (1919-1925). Fans spent days reading stories of this once omnipotent team, but only the old-timers remember that the Cats were really the Fort Worth Panthers. "Cats" fit better in newspaper headlines than "panthers," and the nickname stuck.

a figure skating club, and a speed skating club. Lessons are given, and public skating is available when the rink is not otherwise booked. Call for schedule. (Mid-Cities)

GALLERIA ICE SKATING CENTER
13350 Dallas North Tollway at LBJ
(in the Galleria)
Dallas
972/392-3363
Located on the lower level of the Galleria, this popular rink offers free beginner lessons on Saturdays. Lessons are available for all ages, as are party packages and a full-service retail shop. Restaurants with patios overlooking the rink surround it and provide ready-made audiences. (Far North Dallas)

ICE CHALET
5301 Belt Line Road
Addison
972/980-8575 (Metro)
Lessons are available at this skating rink in Prestonwood Mall. Public skating times vary. $5 admission, $2 skate rental. (Far North Dallas)

ICEOPLEX
15100 Midway Road
Addison
972/991-7539
IceOPlex gets a special nod because of the "EZ Skater" program for beginners. Providing a bar at waist level, it's a wonderful way for tiny tots to begin to get their bal-

ance on skates. Broomball is another way to enjoy skating without filling moms with as much terror as hockey seems to elicit. IceOPlex offers lessons for all ages and skill levels. (Far North Dallas)

THE ICE
Fort Worth Outlet Square
100 Throckmorton
Fort Worth
817/415-4800
Its location in Fort Worth Outlet Square, surrounded by shops and restaurants, makes this skating rink popular for skaters and observers alike. Public skating sessions are available throughout the day, with special lunchtime and evening prices. There's a full-service Pro Shop, and lessons can be arranged to fit most schedules. Park free in the Tandy lot and ride the Subway (see Chapter 5, Sights and Attractions). Open daily. $3.75 admission, $1.25 skate rental. (Downtown Fort Worth)

Polo

DALLAS POLO CLUB
2906 Maple Avenue
(Corporate office)
Dallas
214/979-0300
The Dallas Polo Club is located at the 85-acre Bear Creek Polo Ranch about 30 minutes south of the Metro-

plex near Red Oak. It's the most active polo club in North Texas, with three leagues running simultaneously throughout the summer and arena leagues in the winter. Facilities include three match fields, a practice field, an arena, a club barn housing more than one hundred horses, and a polo school for new members. (East Dallas)

Tennis

Hundreds of parks throughout the Metroplex and in all of the suburbs have a combination of indoor, outdoor, or covered tennis courts. Call the city Parks and Recreation Departments listed on page 167 for specific information. The facilities, including tennis courts, for each of the Fort Worth city parks, are listed in the "Community Pages" in the front of the Fort Worth telephone directory. In addition to neighborhood parks, Dallas has several well maintained city-owned Tennis Centers that offer lessons, a pro shop, and ball-machine rentals: Fair Oaks (7501 Merriman Parkway, 214/670-1495; 16 lighted courts), Fretz (14700 Hillcrest, 214/670-6622; 15 lighted courts), Kiest (2324 West Kiest Boulevard, 214/670-7618; 16 lighted courts), L. B. Houston (11225 Luna Road, 214/670-6367; 16 lighted

courts), and Samuell-Grand (6200 East Grand Avenue, 214/670-1374; 20 lighted courts).

ARLINGTON TENNIS CENTER
500 West Mayfield Road
Arlington
817/557-5683
Located in south-central Arlington, this modern 12-lighted-court facility includes instruction for all ages. Certified professional instructors, lighted courts, a full-service pro shop, and a clubhouse are available. (Arlington/Grand Prairie)

HIGH POINT TENNIS CENTER
421 Spring Creek Parkway
Plano
972/461-7170
This center has 22 lighted courts. (Far North Dallas)

HYATT BEAR CREEK GOLF AND RACQUET CLUB
Hyatt Regency DFW Airport
Grapevine
972/615-6808
A nice facility with four outdoor lighted tennis courts and three indoor courts plus nine racquetball courts. (Mid-Cities)

MARY POTISHMAN LARD TENNIS CENTER

Top Ten Area Fishing Lakes
by Clell Guest, District Management Biologist, Texas Parks & Wildlife District

1. Lake Ray Roberts
2. Lake Ray Hubbard
3. Lake Arlington
4. Benbrook Lake
5. White Rock Lake

6. Lake Lewisville
7. Grapevine Lake
8. Eagle Mountain Lake
9. Lake Lavon
10. Joe Pool Lake

In 1917, cattlemen met at the Stockyards' Cowtown Coliseum to plan a contest in the arena for cowboys. When it came to naming the competition, one rancher suggested a Spanish word for roundup, went to a chalkboard and wrote the word "rodeo."

**3609 Bellaire North
(on TCU campus)
Fort Worth
817/257-7960**

On the campus of TCU, 16 lighted outdoor courts are recessed into the ground for better wind protection. There are six additional outdoor courts and a first-rate five-court indoor complex. The public is welcome. (Southwest Fort Worth)

Water Sports

Dallas claims more than 60 lakes within a 100-mile radius. Add Fort Worth and now you know what people around here do in the hot summer months.

**GRAPEVINE LAKE
110 Fairway Drive
Grapevine
817/481-4541**

This popular recreational lake covers about 7,400 acres. A visitors center is located off Highway 26/121 near the dam. There are twelve parks and four marinas along its 150 miles of tree-lined shoreline. Complete facilities are available for boating (sail and power), waterskiing, windsurfing, fishing, and swimming. An extensive park system provides courts, diamonds, playgrounds and fields for all imaginable activities. Campgrounds, picnic areas, hiking and

biking trails surround the lake. Fees for some areas. (Mid-Cities)

**JOE POOL LAKE
Two miles south of I-20 at Great Southwest Parkway exit
817/467-2104**

Set amid the rolling hills south of the Metroplex, Joe Pool Lake straddles the Dallas-Tarrant County line. Although the shoreline is still being developed, it has three parks with facilities for fishing, boating, swimming, and waterskiing, as well as picnicking and camping. Lynn Creek Marina has boat and ski rentals, a fishing pier, a restaurant, and a club. Lynn Creek Park has boat ramps, beaches, volleyball courts, restrooms, a playground, and a miniature golf course. (East Dallas)

**LEWISVILLE LAKE
Access via Highway 121, then FM 423 north of The Colony Facilities
972/434-1666
Lake Park
972/219-3550**

Picnic at more than 20 public parks along the 233 miles of scenic shoreline. The lake has an average depth of 25 feet, making it suitable for all kinds of water sports, including windsurfing, sailboating, jetskiing, powerboating, and waterskiing. Lake Park on the south shore has picnic areas, RV and

Trails Around Fort Worth
By Linda Sutphin, Texas Trails Network

• **Fort Worth Nature Center:** *3,500-acre wildlife sanctuary north of Downtown. A 25-mile trail system meanders through prairies and marshes along the Trinity River, amid native plants and wildlife.*

• **River Legacy Park:** *The heart of the Trinity River Greenway through Arlington. The 400-plus-acre city-owned park includes a diverse trail system, picnic facilities, open fields, and parking.*

• **Trinity River Trails/Greenway Fort Worth:** *Approximately 35 miles of river trails now link key local sites such as the Stockyards Historic District, Fort Worth Zoo, Gateway Park, Trinity Park fishing pier, Rockwood Park, Tarrant County Courthouse and Downtown.*

• **The Cotton Belt Line:** *A paved hiking and biking path from downtown Grapevine, along the historic Cotton Belt railroad line through Colleyville. The path is still under construction and ultimately will extend through North Richland Hills, then to downtown Fort Worth. The Tarantula Steam Trail now runs along the old Cotton Belt tracks.*

• **Rails to Trails Conservancy:** *A 20-mile hiking, biking, and equestrian trail that cuts through the heart of the western Cross Timbers region. Managed by Texas Parks & Wildlife at Lake Mineral Wells State Park, the trail goes from Mineral Wells to Weatherford, west of Fort Worth.*

• **Benbrook Lake Nature Trail:** *A 7.3-mile nature and horseback trail on the west side of Benbrook Lake. Traverses diverse topography, plant species, and panoramic views of the lake and countryside.*

• **The Katy Trail (Dallas):** *A 3-mile hiking and biking trail through central Dallas along the abandoned right-of-way of the old MKT (Katy) railroad tracks. The trail winds from near Downtown's West End Historic District through Uptown, Oak Lawn, Turtle Creek, SMU, and Highland Park neighborhoods. Trees and shrubs shade much of the trail; a verdant path connecting residences, restaurants, offices, arts venues, and retail shops.*

tent camping, a 24-hour fishing barge, a swimming beach, and excellent public facilities. Fishing, marinas, boat rentals, and angler's supplies are available. (Far North Dallas)

11

THE PERFORMING ARTS

The Dallas Convention and Visitors Bureau says that on any given night in Dallas, you can choose from more than 110 live performances. From the elegant Morton H. Meyerson Symphony Center in the Dallas Arts District to a Deep Ellum dive, the variety and number of productions is terrific.

Approximately 40 professional and community theaters, 13 symphony and chamber orchestras, 4 ballet groups, and 2 opera associations exist in the Dallas/Fort Worth area. If you're looking for an event or performance to attend, you'll surely find something to your liking.

The Dallas Arts District (www.dallasartsdistrict.org), a 60-acre development at the northern edge of the downtown business district, is the largest urban arts district in the country, anchored by the Dallas Museum of Art and the Morton H. Meyerson Symphony Center. Formed as part of a 1978 downtown revitalization program, the District's centerpiece, the Dallas Museum of Art, opened in 1984, followed by the Arts District Theater, the Black Dance Theater, the Booker T. Washington High School for the Performing Arts, Artist Square, and the spectacular Morton H. Meyerson Symphony Center. The Trammell Crow Center, an office building, exhibits artwork in its lobby and sculpture in the outdoor garden.

Fort Worth's performing arts venues aren't as concentrated in one area. Several are found in the Cultural District just west of downtown, along with many fine museums. Many organizations now perform at the new Nancy Lee and Perry R. Bass Performance Hall in downtown's Sundance Square. Others are scattered throughout the city.

Dallas and Fort Worth, offer the widest selection , but several smaller cities in the Metroplex have surprisingly good performing arts groups and community theaters. They also have numerous performance venues that attract touring groups and musicians of all kinds.

For current and upcoming performance schedules and ticket information, consult the Arts and Entertainment Guide insert in the Friday edition of the Dallas Morning News or the Startime insert in the Friday edition of the *Fort Worth Star-Telegram.*

THEATER

ALLIED THEATRE GROUP
3055 South University Drive
Fort Worth
817/784-9378
www.alliedtheatre.org
The Allied Theatre Group brings together two critically acclaimed Fort Worth theater companies: Stage West and Shakespeare in the Park. For more than 20 years, Stage West has been one of the leading professional theaters in Texas. It presents a wide range of productions, from classic to contemporary. Now it has joined with Shakespeare in the Park to present a year-round schedule of the best in drama, comedy, music, and special events. ♿ (Southwest Fort Worth)

CARAVAN OF DREAMS
312 Houston
Fort Worth
817/429-4000
www.caravanofdreams.com

T
I
P
The Dallas Morning News Arts and Entertainment Hotline: 214/522-2659 (recorded information)

One of the first attractions in Sundance Square, this multipurpose entertainment complex features a nightclub and concert venue on the street level, a 212-seat theater on the second floor, and a rooftop grotto bar overlooking downtown. The stage is often the site of live theater and dance performances featuring a wide variety of entertainment. ♿ (Downtown Fort Worth)

CASA MAÑANA
3101 West Lancaster
Fort Worth
817/332-CASA
This geodesic-domed theater-in-the-round has brought locally produced musical comedies, plays, concerts, and touring shows to Fort Worth since 1958. The oval stage, surrounded by 1,800 seats, was one of the first permanent theaters designed to present musicals-in-the-round.

Although most of the big stage shows are now produced at the Bass Performance Hall, Casa still hosts well-known entertainers in concert. It's the venue for an outstanding series of Children's Playhouse productions and an all-ages theater school. ♿ (Southwest Fort Worth)

CIRCLE THEATER
230 West Fourth Street
Fort Worth
817/877-3040
www.circletheatre.com
The basement beneath the historic downtown Sanger Building houses this intimate, 125-seat theater. The lively arts organization offers an enticing mixture of contemporary works, including premieres of new plays. ♿ (Downtown Fort Worth)

DALLAS SUMMER MUSICALS
P.O. Box 710336
Fair Park Music Hall
Dallas
214/691-7200 (office); 214/373-8000 (tickets)
www.dallassummermusicals.org
This nonprofit organization has brought touring companies of Broadway shows to Fair Park Music Hall every season (May-October) since 1941. Now it also presents a variety of other productions in the fall and winter months. ⅊ (East Dallas)

DALLAS THEATER CENTER/ARTS DISTRICT THEATER
2401 Flora Street
Dallas
214/922-0422
www.dallastheatercenter.com
Across Artists Square from the Morton H. Meyerson Symphony Center, the Dallas Theater Center presents a medley of performances, including an annual production of *A Christmas Carol,* at the 700-seat Arts District Theater. ⅊ (Downtown Dallas)

DALLAS THEATER CENTER/KALITA HUMPHREYS THEATER
3626 Turtle Creek Boulevard
Dallas
214/526-8210; Tickets: 214/522-8499
The only circular theater designed by Frank Lloyd Wright hosts a full season of professional theater productions, from musical comedies to the classics. Special studios accommodate classes for the Children's Theater. If no plays or rehearsals are taking place, fascinating, behind-the-scenes tours, led by volunteers of the Guild, may be arranged by appointment. The attractive theater nestles among the ancient trees in a picturesque setting along beautiful Turtle Creek. ⅊ (Central Dallas)

DEEP ELLUM OPERA COMPANY
501 Second Avenue
Dallas
214/823-2907
This offbeat company performs "al-

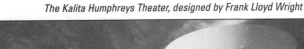

The Kalita Humphreys Theater, designed by Frank Lloyd Wright

Dallas CVB

Casa Mañana

Fort Worth's domed theater-in-the-round in the Cultural District is not the original Casa Mañana. History tells us the original housed the largest revolving stage and café in the world, accommodating four thousand diners and dancers. It was a product of neighborly rivalry with the city to the east. In 1936, Dallas was chosen as the site for the celebration of the 100th anniversary of Texas independence. This recognition, of course, infuriated Fort Worth booster Amon Carter, who then signed the famous Broadway producer Billy Rose to produce the "show of shows" for Fort Worth. Citizens were shocked when he brought in Sally Rand, an exotic fan dancer, as the headline performer. According to the history books, it was quite a spectacle! In 1958, Fort Worth built the year-round, air-conditioned facility you see today.

ternative theater" at the Hickory Street Annex Theater from August to May. (East Dallas)

FORT WORTH THEATRE
4401 Trail Lake Drive
Fort Worth
817/921-5300
Fort Worth's oldest theater company performs a wide variety of plays year-round and is widely known for its Hispanic series. ♿ (Southwest Fort Worth)

HIP POCKET THEATRE
1620 Las Vegas Trail North
Fort Worth
817/246-9775
A highly original theater group, Hip Pocket presents an eclectic mix of musical theater, comedy, and drama, regularly showcasing works of regional playwrights. Performances are held from June through October. (Southwest Fort Worth)

JUBILEE THEATRE
506 Main Street
Fort Worth
817/338-4411
www.jubileetheatre.org
The only African American community theater group in Texas presenting a year-round season, Jubilee has risen to a prestigious status in the region. Operating in an intimate, 100-seat downtown playhouse, it focuses on African American heritage in drama and song. ♿ (Downtown Fort Worth)

ONSTAGE
Trinity Arts Theater
2821 Forest Ridge Drive
Bedford
817/354-6444
The Trinity Arts Theater, on the

grounds of the Bedford Boys Ranch Park, is home to this ambitious, volunteer community theater group. Their weekends-only performances run the gamut from drama to melodrama to children's plays. ♿ (Mid-Cities)

PLANO REPERTORY THEATER/ARTCENTRE THEATRE
1039 East 15th Street
Plano
972/422-7460
This community theater group presents a year-round season of classic dramas, musicals, and comedy. Its summer schedule includes a booing-hissing melodrama and a children's program. ♿ (Far North Dallas)

POCKET SANDWICH THEATER
5400 East Mockingbird
Dallas
214/821-1860
Just off North Central Expressway in a small strip shopping center, this popular neighborhood theater is known for professional-quality productions, mostly of comedies and melodramas. It has launched several local and regional playwrights toward successful careers. The annual Christmas production of *Scrooge* has become a local tradition. Most performances are suitable for families, and you can buy sandwiches, as well as nachos, pizza, quiche, and other snacks. ♿ (Central Dallas)

SHAKESPEARE FESTIVAL OF DALLAS
Sammons Center for the Arts
3630 Harry Hines Boulevard
Dallas
214/559-2778 (office)
The second-oldest free Shakespeare festival in the United States (only New York City's is older) draws huge crowds with two outdoor plays in Samuell-Grand Park Amphitheater, 6200 East Grand, for six weeks each summer. Take a lawn chair and insect repellent. During the rest of the year, acclaimed actors perform Shake-

---

To Buy Tickets

Bass Performance Hall: Ticket outlet depends on event, call 817/212-4280

Central Tickets: 817/335-9000

Caravan of Dreams/Ticketline: 817/877-3000

Dillard's Ticket Outlet: 800/654-9545

Encore Tickets: 800/460-4500

First Row Tickets: 214/750-7555

Ticketmaster: Tickets may be ordered by phone at 972/647-5700 or 214/373-8000. Ticketmaster locations in Foley's, Kroger, Fiesta, and Cowtown Coliseum. Service charges vary.

---

speare's works at the Majestic Theater and other venues around town. (East Dallas)

TEATRO DALLAS
1925 Commerce Street
Dallas
214/741-1135
http://web2.airmail.net/teatro
Established in 1985, Teatro Dallas is the only theater dedicated to presenting the works of classical and contemporary Latino playwrights. They present quite a variety of plays and dance productions (even Cabaret-style shows and puppetry) that reflect the area's rich Hispanic heritage. They perform year-round at various venues around the city, represent the United States at international festivals, and hold classes for children. ♿ (Downtown Dallas)

THEATER ARLINGTON
305 West Main Street
Arlington
817/275-7661
Technically a community theater, this troupe frequently achieves professional-caliber productions. Both play selection and performance quality has grown impressively in recent seasons as the group has taken on more challenges. The theater presents about six productions a year, ranging from musicals to award-winning plays. ♿ (Arlington/Grand Prairie)

THEATRE THREE
2800 Routh Street
Dallas
214/871-3300
The oldest and second-largest professional theater in Dallas, this theater-in-the-round presents a wide variety of productions from musical revues and plays to an occasional children's program. Begun by Dallasite Norma Young in 1961 with a $2,000 inheritance, the theater prospered, winning six Dallas Theater Critics Forum Awards in 1997. Mrs. Young passed away in 1998, but her husband, Jac Alder, continues as executive producer and director. ♿ (Central Dallas)

MUSIC AND OPERA

DALLAS OPERA
Fair Park Music Hall
909 First Avenue
Dallas
214/443-1000
www.dallasopera.org
The nationally known Dallas Opera Company has performed classic productions from November to February at the Music Hall in Fair Park for more than 40 years. The history of opera in Dallas goes back to the nineteenth century, but most people remember the starting point as 1957 when Maria Callas sang to open the Dallas Civic Opera's first season. She returned in 1958 and again in 1959. That was only the beginning of exceptional visiting stars, including a 19-year-old Placido Domingo in 1961, making his American debut. ♿ (East Dallas)

DALLAS SYMPHONY ORCHESTRA
Morton H. Meyerson Symphony Center
2301 Flora Street
Dallas
214/692-0203
www.dallassymphony.com
The Dallas Symphony celebrates its 100th anniversary in 2000. Its schedule of programs includes pops and classical series, both featuring guest artists and conductors. Most series

performances are held at the Morton H. Meyerson Symphony Center. The summer months will find the orchestra giving free concerts in city parks and playing at various festivals and events. & (Downtown Dallas)

DALLAS WIND SYMPHONY
Morton H. Meyerson Symphony Center
2301 Flora Street
Dallas
214/528-5576
The only professional civilian wind band in the country performs at the Morton H. Meyerson Symphony Center. & (Downtown Dallas)

FORT WORTH OPERA COMPANY
Nancy Lee and Perry R. Bass Performance Hall
525 Commerce Street
Fort Worth
817/731-0200 (box office)
A full season of fine opera is presented in grand scale at the Nancy Lee and Perry R. Bass Performance Hall in Sundance Square. Most company members are local professionals, but renowned visiting artists frequently perform lead roles. & (Downtown Fort Worth)

FORT WORTH SYMPHONY ORCHESTRA
330 East Fourth Street
Fort Worth
817/665-6000
www.fwsymphony.org
Under the leadership of music director John Giordano, the Fort Worth Symphony offers a classical and pops subscription series at the Nancy Lee and Perry R. Bass Performance Hall and an outdoor summer series at the Fort Worth Botanic Garden. The concert series is broadcast across North Texas over WRR Classical Radio, 101.1 FM. The professional symphony orchestra, founded in 1925, also travels extensively. & (Downtown Fort Worth)

Entertainers from Fort Worth

Betty Buckley: *TV, movie, and Broadway actress/singer*

Larry Hagman: *born in Fort Worth (son of Mary Martin of Weatherford), but moved on to become best known as J. R. Ewing of* Dallas *fame*

Dan Jenkins: *Sports journalist and novelist* (North Dallas Forty *and* Semi-Tough)

Delbert McClinton: *legendary blues musician*

Gary Morris: *One of the best voices in country music, now crossed over to Broadway*

Liz Smith: *America's premier gossip columnist*

GRAPEVINE OPRY
Palace Theater
308 South Main Street
Grapevine
817/481-8733
Every Saturday night there's a hand-clappin', foot-stompin' country-and-western show in the restored Palace Theater. It's great family entertainment featuring a variety of regional performers. Several well-known singers have performed here throughout the years, including Willie Nelson, Faron Young, the Judds, Jeanie Pruitt, and Bill Anderson. Famous headliners still occasionally perform in the 500-seat auditorium. The Palace Theater was opened in 1940 as a movie theater, fell into disrepair after World War II, and was partially restored in 1975. The Grapevine Heritage Foundation acquired it in 1991 and is continuing restoration efforts. Ticket prices vary, but are usually reasonable. Sat 7:30 p.m. & (Mid-Cities)

JOHNNIE HIGH'S COUNTRY MUSIC REVUE
Arlington Music Hall
224 North Center Street
Arlington
817/226-4400 (metro)
or 800/540-5127
Now at a new home in Arlington, Johnnie High's Country Music Revue entertained thousands of fans for decades in Fort Worth. Highly entertaining performances featuring singers, instrumentalists, comedians, and cloggers are good, clean family fun. Consistently offering veteran entertainers and new talent, this revue has been voted the best live country music show of the year by several organizations. Special gospel shows and holiday performances are also given seasonally. Friday and Satur-

day at 7:30 p.m. $12-14 adult, $6-7 children. & (Arlington/Grand Prairie)

SAMMONS JAZZ
3630 Harry Hines Boulevard
Dallas
214/520-7788
This ongoing jazz performance series features local and regional jazz artists playing everything from swing to dixieland music at the Sammons Center for the Arts (see listing in Concert Venues section) the first Wednesday of each month at 7 p.m. from February through December. $12-16. & (Central Dallas)

TEXAS BOYS CHOIR
Fort Worth
817/924-1482
Since its founding in 1946, the Texas Boys Choir has built an international reputation, made 35 records, and won two Grammys. One of the world's leading boys choirs, it trains young singers from age 8 and offers a fully accredited school program for grades 4 to 12 at the school's new facility. The resident choir performs at area festivals and concert venues, while the elite touring choir performs around the United States and in several foreign countries. Call for information on local performances. (Southwest Fort Worth)

TEXAS GIRLS CHOIR
Fort Worth
817/732-8161
Not to be outdone by the boys (see previous listing), about 200 girls ages 8 to 16 have been an active performance group for more than 30 years. They receive musical training in the Fort Worth-based ensemble and perform about one hundred local concerts annually as well as tour nationally and internationally. Call for

information on local performances. (Southwest Fort Worth)

Symphony Center. (Downtown Dallas)

TURTLE CREEK CHORALE
Morton H. Meyerson Symphony
Center
2301 Flora Street
Dallas
214/526-3214
Comprised of two hundred voices, the all male chorus presents a wide variety of performance concerts at the Morton H. Meyerson

DANCE

BALLET FOLKLORICO
4422 Live Oak Street
Dallas
214/828-0181
This Hispanic arts group traces its roots to neighborhood children in a recreation center on the west side

---

How Many Angels in the Bass Performance Hall?

Nobody knows. Not even the architect. But the ethereal theme is carried out extensively throughout the magnificent Nancy Lee and Perry R. Bass Performance Hall. Begin with the pair of angels, each standing nearly 50 feet tall and weighing 250,000 pounds, suspended on the entrance to welcome you. Created by Hungarian-born sculptor Marton Varo, the sculptures are two of the largest in the world. Varo was carefully selected as the artist capable of designing and creating the heavenly beings from mammoth blocks (weighing 15 tons) of Cordova Crème limestone from the Texas Quarries near Austin. The angels have a wing span of 18 feet and hold 13-foot brass trumpets. Inside, the great dome of the auditorium is encircled with white wings, which are 80 feet in diameter. Feathers appear on the tops of lobby columns, on the sides of the auditorium seats, in the elevator doors, and in the wood grain of the bar on the main level. And 155 angels grace the women's restroom on the gallery level. Another heavenly body is found in the evening sky of the west dome—the Hale-Bopp comet. The murals were being painted during the time the comet was visible, and an enthusiastic patron offered to donate a substantial sum to the performing arts if the artists would add the comet.

Ballet Folklorica celebrates Mexican Heritage through song and dance

of Dallas in 1975. The ballet group produced its first professional dance season in 1990 with dancers from the United States and Mexico. Now it is one of Texas's leading Folklorico troupes, with a tradition rooted in the Mexican heritage of its performers. Two major annual productions (one in May, the other in mid-September) are performed at the historic Majestic Theater in Downtown Dallas, and they perform at various events and festivals throughout the year. (Downtown Dallas)

DALLAS BLACK DANCE THEATRE
214/871-2376
Not to be mislead by the theater group's name, the troupe consists of dancers from a variety of ethnic backgrounds, not only African American. The modern contemporary dance company performs an eclectic mixture of modern, ethnic, jazz, and spiritual works by renowned choreographers. They dance at the Majestic Theater and

other performance venues around Dallas as well as around the world. They do a tremendous amount of work with children of the community, encouraging, teaching, and entertaining them. A great tribute to this fine troupe is that they were invited to perform at the 1996 Olympic Games in Atlanta, Georgia. Call for a schedule of performances. (Downtown Dallas)

FORT WORTH DALLAS BALLET
6845 Green Oaks Road
Fort Worth
817/763-0207 or 888/597-7287
The Fort Worth Ballet expanded to include Dallas when the Dallas Ballet dissolved in 1988. The company presents a mixture of new and traditional works, performed at the Bass Performance Hall in Fort Worth and the Music Hall at Fair Park in Dallas. In addition, the company performs across Texas and tours internationally. One of the most spectacular programs is the annual Christmas presentation

Dallas CVB

Dallas Black Dance Theatre's repertoire is as ethnically diverse as the troupe

of the *Nutcracker*. & (Downtown Fort Worth and East Dallas)

CONCERT VENUES

BATH HOUSE CULTURAL CENTER
521 East Lawther Place
Dallas
214/670-8749
On the western shore of White Rock Lake, this former bathhouse, built in 1930, was used by generations of swimmers. Opened in 1981 as Dallas's first neighborhood arts center, it's now a small, city-owned theater that hosts a variety of performances and art exhibits. & (Central Dallas)

DALLAS CONVENTION CENTER
650 South Griffin
Dallas
214/939-2700
One of the largest convention centers in the country, this excellent facility supports Dallas as one of the top major convention cities in the nation. The facility is also the site of meetings, concerts, trade shows, and numerous special events. & (Downtown Dallas)

ED LANDRETH AUDITORIUM
Texas Christian University
University Drive at West Cantey
Fort Worth
817/921-7810
On the TCU campus, the Ed Landreth Auditorium is considered one of the finest acoustical halls in the area. Containing 1,200 seats and a world-class concert organ, it serves as a concert venue for dozens of performances. & (Southwest Fort Worth)

FAIR PARK MUSIC HALL
909 First Avenue
Dallas
214/565-2226
This splendid hall is home to the Dallas Summer Musicals, the Dallas Opera, the Fort Worth Dallas Ballet, as well as a variety of concerts and other productions throughout the year. & (East Dallas)

THE MAC
3120 McKinney Avenue
Dallas
214/953-1212
www.themac.net
The MAC opened in 1994 as North Texas's first venue where contemporary arts in all forms are presented under one roof. Located in an 18,000-square-foot renovated building in the uptown area of Dallas, the facility offers two exhibition galleries, a theater, a small cinema, a coffee shop, a bookstore, and the Cyber Café. Offerings include a variety of classes, lectures, poetry readings, musical and dramatic performances, and art exhibits. The cutting-edge Kitchen Dog Theater

(214/953-1055) performs five plays a season at The MAC, offering an evening of excellent entertainment for about $15. ♿ (Downtown Dallas)

MAJESTIC THEATRE
1925 Elm Street
Dallas
214/880-0137
This exquisitely restored 1920s-era theater features state-of-the-art sound and lighting, and every seat has a good view of the stage. It's a favorite venue for a variety of performing arts groups during the year, so call for the current performance schedule. ♿ (Downtown Dallas)

MORTON H. MEYERSON
SYMPHONY CENTER
2301 Flora Street
Dallas
Box office: 214/692-0203
www.dallassymphony.com
Opened in 1989, the centerpiece of the Dallas Arts District is the only symphony center designed by world-renowned architect I. M. Pei. Acclaimed for its architecture and world-class acoustics, the Morton H. Meyerson Symphony Center is home to the Dallas Symphony Orchestra, the Dallas Wind Symphony, and the Turtle Creek Chorale. One of its treasures is a $2-million, hand-built Fisk organ, one of the largest ever built for a concert hall. For a donation of $12 million, Dallas billionaire Ross Perot was given the honor of naming the hall after his business colleague, Morton H. Meyerson. ♿ (Downtown Dallas)

NANCY LEE AND PERRY R. BASS
PERFORMANCE HALL
525 Commerce Street
Fort Worth
Information hotline: 817/212-4325
www.basshall.com
The Nancy Lee and Perry R. Bass Performance Hall is the crown jewel in a city boasting one of the most successful downtown revitalization efforts in the country. Built en-

Van Cliburn

Although many Texans assume the much-honored pianist has a two-word last name, Van (short for Lavan) is his middle name and Cliburn is his last (his first name is Harvey). The acclaimed Van Cliburn International Piano Competition is considered one of the most esteemed music competitions in the world. Held every four years at the Nancy Lee and Perry R. Bass Performance Hall, the prestigious event was organized after the young pianist won the Tchaikovsky International Piano Competition in Moscow in 1958. He did much to convince the rest of the nation that Texas not only understood but could actually produce and even advance culture. Van Cliburn makes his home in Fort Worth.

tirely with private funds, the $67.5-million facility is the permanent home of the Fort Worth Symphony Orchestra, the Fort Worth Dallas Ballet, the Fort Worth Opera, and the Van Cliburn International Piano Competition.

A showpiece as well as a showcase, the 2,056-seat, multipurpose hall is characteristic of the classic European opera house style, with a Great Dome and 48-foot-tall angels sculpted from Texas limestone, gracing the Grand Façade. Every aspect of the hall's design has focused on superb acoustics, exceptional sight lines, and ambience on a level with the great halls of Europe and America. It features two piano boxes, which exist in no other performance space in the world. The hall sits on a full city block in the historic Sundance Square district in Downtown Fort Worth. Public tours are given Fridays at 1:30 and Saturdays at 10:30, performance schedule permitting (see also Chapter 5, Sights and Attractions). & (Downtown Fort Worth)

REUNION ARENA
777 Sport Street
Dallas
214/939-2770
Home to the Dallas Mavericks and the Dallas Stars (see Chapter 10, Sports), this arena also hosts pop and country concerts, theatrical events, and the annual performance of the Shrine Circus. & (Downtown Dallas)

SAMMONS CENTER
FOR THE ARTS
3630 Harry Hines Boulevard
Dallas
214/520-7788
This multipurpose facility has a variety of performance and recital halls. It provides a home for small, nonprofit arts groups and is used for workshops and rehearsals by dozens of local music, arts, and cultural organizations. One popular performance series is the Sammons Jazz, featuring regional jazz artists at reasonable prices. & (Central Dallas)

Nancy Lee and Perry R. Bass Performance Hall adorned with limestone angels

Ft Worth CVB

Ginger Rogers grew up in Fort Worth and once won a dance contest at the now-gone Majestic Theater. One of the girls who lost the contest was Mary Martin of nearby Weatherford.

SOUTHERN METHODIST UNIVERSITY
Dallas
214/768-2000
Theater, dance, and music performances can be attended throughout the year at performing arts venues on the SMU campus, including the McFarlin Memorial Auditorium, the Caruth Auditorium, the Bob Hope Theatre, the Greer Garson Theatre, the Margo Jones Theatre, the Charles S. Sharp Performing Arts Studio, and the O'Donnell Lecture/Recital Hall. (Central Dallas)

STARPLEX AMPHITHEATRE
1818 First Avenue (Fair Park)
Dallas
214/421-1111; Automated Concert Line: 214/712-7518
Big-name singers, musicians, and major acts perform at Starplex, a bow-shaped outdoor amphitheater, every summer. Reserve seating under an awning and wraparound lawn seating are available. It's a bring-your-own-blanket-and-cooler kind of place. (East Dallas)

TARRANT COUNTY CONVENTION CENTER
1111 Houston Street
Fort Worth
817/884-2222
The Fort Worth/Tarrant County Convention Center Arena hosts numerous conventions, trade shows, concerts, ice shows, and other performances. It's also the home of the Fort Worth Brahmas Hockey team (see Chapter 10, Sports). The Center's JFK Theater is a full performing arts theater that seats almost three thousand for theatrical performances. & (Downtown Fort Worth)

WILL ROGERS AUDITORIUM
3401 West Lancaster
at University Drive
Fort Worth 76107
817/871-8150
The auditorium is part of the Will Rogers Memorial Center (see Chapter 5, Sights and Attractions). Part of the original 1936 complex, the 2,850-seat auditorium isn't used as much since newer and larger performing venues have been built, but it's an intimate, comfortable stage for some classical concerts and touring shows. & (Southwest Fort Worth)

WILLIAM EDRINGTON SCOTT THEATRE
3505 West Lancaster
Fort Worth
817/738-1938
Opened in 1966, this 480-seat theater was created by Broadway scenic designer Donald Oenslager and features sharply raked seating and technical bells and whistles. It now rents its performing space to various production companies and business and civic groups. & (Southwest Fort Worth)

Dallas CVB

12

NIGHTLIFE

The legal drinking age in Texas is 21. Some areas and towns of the Metroplex are still "dry," and because the "wet/dry" issue is voted by precinct, some places can serve alcoholic beverages whereas the place across the street from it cannot.

Dallas's nightclub scene changes more often than Texas weather, so the best thing to do is literally walk the streets of the entertainment districts and listen to the variety of music drifting from the doors. Yup, you'll hear plenty of country-and-western music, but Dallas also sings the blues, jazz, folk, pop, and rock-and-roll. Hotel lounges and some restaurants have piano bars and quiet music where you can enjoy pleasant conversation in relaxing surroundings.

Lower Greenville Avenue is one of the city's oldest entertainment areas. SMU students and soon-to-be-yuppies crowd the lively restaurants, bars, and clubs. Upper Greenville Avenue features newer, more trendy establishments, ranging from casual to elegant.

Although it is not the "side show" that it used to be, you'll still see plenty of purple hair and pierced body parts in Deep Ellum. The name evolved from the phrase "the deep end of Elm Street." Dallas's first black community was here, near the railroad tracks in an industrial area. It was home to some of the finest jazz and blues speakeasies in Texas until the area declined after WW II. Now revitalized, it's an alternative neighborhood of eclectic art galleries, music venues, bars, and restaurants located only a few blocks from downtown. It's loosely bounded by Elm, Commerce, Oakland, and Good Latimer streets.

The West End (www.dallaswestend.org) is festive at night, with Dallas Alley (seven nightclubs in one), Planet Hollywood, and a Cinema 10 movie theater.

The McKinney Avenue/Uptown area also offers a medley of choices from upscale restaurant lounges to upbeat bars appealing to the slightly-older-than-college crowd.

Fort Worth's clubs and nightspots are also concentrated in areas, although you won't find nearly as many as in Dallas, and a higher percentage feature country-and-western entertainment.

You'll find almost any kind of music in Sundance Square's bars, clubs, and restaurants. A variety of contemporary, eclectic, and alternative music will be heard coming from the spots scattered around TCU on the city's south side. More subdued music can be found in the upscale restaurants along Camp Bowie Boulevard on the city's west side. The scene in the Stockyards Historic District will be rowdy, boot-scootin' country-and-western, no doubt about it.

Many area hotels have fine lounges with piano bars or live music for a conversation-oriented crowd. One of the latest trends in the Metroplex is the Sport Bar with outrageously gigantic TV screens, billiard/pool tables, darts, and video games.

For current and upcoming performance schedules and ticket information for music clubs, comedy clubs, and movie theaters, consult the Startime insert in the Friday edition of the Fort Worth Star-Telegram or the Arts and Entertainment Guide insert in the Friday edition of the Dallas Morning News.

DANCE CLUBS

BILLY BOB'S TEXAS
2520 Rodeo Plaza
Fort Worth
817/624-7117 or 817/589-1711 (metro)
www.billybobstexas.com
The World's Largest Honky-Tonk is located in the heart of Fort Worth's Stockyards Historic District. If you don't know what a honky-tonk is, then you've just got to see it! Billy Bob's boasts Texas-sized dance floors and stages, more than 40 bars, pool tables, pinball and arcade games, restaurants, the Dry Goods General Store with gifts galore, and live bull riding every Friday and Saturday night in the rodeo arena. You can also ride a "photo bull," which is a replica of a real one set against an authentic-looking backdrop to fool the folks at home. Such well-known performers as Willie Nelson, Waylon Jennings, George Jones, Merle and Haggard, have performed on this stage at one time or another. Live music is featured every night, and top-name entertainment is not always country-and-western; rock groups and even big bands draw huge crowds to the 100,000-square-foot facility. (North Fort Worth)

COUNTRY 2000
10580 North Stemmons Freeway at Northwest Highway
Dallas
214/654-9595
www.country2000.com
Modern country music is the rage here, where nobody looks old enough to remember life before George Strait. The space-age décor makes it look more disco than honky-tonk, but the folks who come in droves are urban cowboys and cowgirls. Nominated for the 1998 Academy of Country Music's "Country Club of the Year" award, Country 2000 boasts more than 40,000 square

feet of entertainment, a capacity of nearly 3,400, a 3,500-square-foot main dance floor, dance instructors (free lessons are given several times a week), two VIP seating areas, and state-of-the-art lighting equipment, sound systems, video cameras, and DDS satellite receivers. Several fully equipped bars are located throughout the club, and a complete kitchen can serve anything from light snacks to elaborate banquets. (Central Dallas)

COWBOYS ARLINGTON
2540 East Abram at Highway 360
Arlington
817/265-1535
Cowboys Arlington is the ultimate urban honky-tonk, with pure-country atmosphere, wood décor, and gaudy neon-framed bars. Not the place for intimate conversation (read: it's LOUD), this place is strictly for dancing. The Texas-sized dance floor is great for two-stepping and the Cotton-Eyed Joe. You can see the stage from almost anywhere, and when a celebrity performs, the parking lot overflows with pickups and the inside overflows with fans. (Arlington/Grand Prairie)

COWBOYS RED RIVER DANCE HALL AND SALOON
10310 West Technology Boulevard
Dallas
972/263-0404
The large, racetrack-style dance floor is the centerpiece here. This 1980s-style club is a local favorite of two-steppers and offers live music Wednesday through Sunday and dance lessons on Sundays from 4 to 7 p.m. The saloon also has pool tables and a huge-screen TV for game/fight nights. (Central Dallas)

JOE'S BIG BAMBOO
2800 East Pioneer Parkway
Arlington
817/640-0059
DJs spin the best of the '70s, '80s, and '90s at Arlington's hottest new dance club. Sound and lighting create a tropical ambience. It's a bit on the small side, but it's also pretty new, so it could grow if its popularity continues. (Arlington/Grand Prairie)

KEMPI'S NIGHTCLUB
Hotel Inter-Continental
15201 Dallas Parkway
Addison
972/386-6000
Even though the former Grand Kempinski is now the Hotel Inter-Continental, Kempi's Nightclub is still there. The site of many big band-era dances in the past, the format has changed to DJs spinning Top 40 and progressive music, and a free happy hour buffet Tuesday through Friday. (Far North Dallas)

LIZARD LOUNGE
2424 Swiss Avenue
Dallas
214/826-4768
Part bar, part light show, and part music, the Lizard Lounge is most assuredly a dance club. Live music or DJs play into the night so folks can dance to a wide variety of tunes; two separate rooms may be playing different kinds of music. Gothic nights are pretty weird. (Central Dallas)

RED JACKET
3606 Greenville Avenue
Dallas
214/823-8333
Swing, '70s funk and disco, and '80s retro make the Red Jacket a bit hard to describe. But it's a comfortable, casual place adorned with cheesy

Celebrities from the Metroplex

Linda Darnell, Dallas
Greer Garson, Fort Worth
Larry Hagman, Fort Worth
Jerry Hall, Mesquite

Dorothy Malone, Dallas
Ginger Rogers, Fort Worth
Brenda Vaccaro, Dallas

red velvet walls, a sunken dance floor, pool tables, and a cigar bar. Live music may be anything from new wave to disco. According to old timers, the club is not what it used to be. (Central Dallas)

SONS OF HERMANN HALL
3414 Elm Street
Dallas
214/747-4422
Located in Deep Ellum, this club has been open since 1911, where the stately white building housed the Sons of Hermann German fraternal organization until it opened to the public in 1982. It's a local favorite of "Texas country" fans, and according to some, one of the best-kept secrets in Dallas. Upstairs, an elegant ballroom with a high ceiling and the original wooden dance floor is perfect for boot-scootin' and occasional big band/swing performances. Lots of reminiscing takes place on those nights. The whole place is like a step back in time. The downstairs bar has a great '50s ambience and serves burgers and snacks, too. Open Wed-Sat. (East Dallas)

TOP RAIL
2110 West Northwest Highway
Dallas
972/556-9099
Open since 1935, the Top Rail is one of the oldest ballrooms in the state.

A somewhat older clientele seems more interested in dancing than searching for singles, although many young and single people kick up their heels here, too, as their parents did years ago. Locals rate it high for friendliness, good drinks, good music, and less smoke than some other establishments. Open seven days a week with live country music and a spacious dance floor, the Top Rail is packed when similar places are closed on Mondays or Tuesdays. You can learn the push, line dancing, or the two-step on Sundays. (Central Dallas)

MUSIC CLUBS

Jazz

BALCONY CLUB
1825 Abrams Road
Dallas
214/826-8104
Classy and relaxed, cozy and intimate, this popular neighborhood club draws an eclectic clientele from students to lawyers. Located next to the historic Lakewood Theater, the Balcony features high-quality live music, often jazz, seven nights a week. Dan Hoden, a classical guitarist, plays often, and occasional quiet piano music makes it a favorite place for lovers. (Central Dallas)

CARAVAN OF DREAMS
312 Houston
Fort Worth
817/877-3000
The first floor of this performing arts venue is the intimate, dimly lit live music club. Once one of the most notable jazz spots around, it has hosted such artists as Dizzy Gillespie and Harry Connick Jr. The format has changed now to offer an eclectic mix of jazz, blues, folk, rock, and whatever else comes along. With pin-drop-clear acoustics and plush décor, it's a great place to hear good music and to be in the center of the Sundance Square scene. (Downtown Fort Worth)

MOOSE & VINNY'S
2301 North Collins
Arlington
817/461-2027
Located near the University of Texas in Arlington, Moose & Vinny's gets great marks from local folks. It's open every day and features live music, mostly jazz or blues. (Arlington/Grand Prairie)

SAMBUCA MEDITERRANEAN JAZZ CAFÉ
2618 Elm Street
Dallas
214/744-0820
Sambuca is one of those places that can be listed as a great restaurant (see Chapter 4, Where to Eat) as well as a great jazz club. Creative executive chef Pete Nolasco put Sambuca on the map with his outstanding Mediterranean fare. The Aegean Pasta Salad is a delectable choice, or try the Bistecca sandwich made from beef tenderloin tips. A second Sambuca is located at 15207 Addison Road (972/385-8455) in Addison. It's much larger but has the identical menu and features live jazz nightly. (East Dallas)

SIPANGO
4513 Travis at Knox Street
Dallas
214/522-2411
The restaurant is California-Italian. The décor is sleek designer. The bar/club is cool and hip. A live jazz pianist performs, a crooner sings, and the elite smoke in the hip cigar bar. A nightclub/dance club in the back is open on weekends with disco and funk music. (Central Dallas)

Blues

BLUE CAT BLUES
2612 Commerce Street
Dallas
214/744-CATS
www.bluecatblues.com
Deep Ellum's only full-time blues bar features blues artists and groups performing live music Wednesday through Saturday. Owner Doug Henry searches out the best musicians from around the block to

---

TRIVIA

The frozen margarita, a drink made of tequila, lime juice, and triple sec, was supposedly invented in Dallas. The frozen concoction can be ordered anywhere that drinks are served.

Music and Food

Many restaurants in the Metroplex also offer musical entertainment and could easily be listed here instead of in Chapter 4, Where to Eat. Conversely, some restaurants listed here could also be listed there because they serve full menus of excellent fare along with the music. Sometimes, it's just hard to separate them.

around the world; such greats as ZuZu Bolin, Big Daddy Kinsey, James Cotton, Johnny Clyde Copeland, and Lonnie Brooks have performed at the Blue Cat. The walls display posters, photos, and memorabilia, and the club features state-of-the-art sound and lighting systems. When the club moved to a larger location in 1999, it added a gourmet kitchen. In popular polls, the Chicago-style blues bar is consistently voted one of Dallas's best. (East Dallas)

THE BLUE MULE
1701 North Market
Dallas
214/761-0101
This place caters to tourists similar to the West End Entertainment District where it's located. Open daily, it features live music, nearly always blues or rhythm and blues. The ambience is above hole-in-the-wall, and the food is reliably good, from Mule Burgers to fajitas to a great selection of finger food. (Downtown Dallas)

HOLE IN THE WALL
11654 Harry Hines
Dallas
972/247-2253

Now here is a place to observe local color-a relaxed, friendly, diminutive dive with autographed-photo-and-bar décor. Live music is played almost every night, usually jam sessions during the week and renowned blues artists on weekends. If you're claustrophobic, sit on the large backyard patio or deck and listen to the music and munch on classic burgers and fries. (Central Dallas)

J&J BLUES BAR
937 Woodward Street
Fort Worth
817/870-2337
For more than 15 years this bar has been the top blues club in the city. Tons of folks have played here, including legends such as Albert King, Koko Taylor, James Cotton, and Pinetop Perkins. In addition to touring artists, J&J hosts the best in local talent and jam sessions. Dave the bartender often jams with 'em on harmonica. Live music is played most nights. (Downtown Fort Worth)

KEYS LOUNGE
5677-H Westcreek Drive
Fort Worth
817/292-8627
Located in a strip shopping center,

this neighborhood bar is not much on personality or character, but the friendly regulars don't seem to mind. Musical offerings are usually local blues musicians with jam sessions on Sundays and Thursdays, an "unplugged" night on Wednesdays, and jazz or blues artists on Fridays and Saturdays. (Southwest Fort Worth)

MUDDY WATERS
1518 Greenville Avenue
Dallas
214/823-1518
This outpost on Lower Greenville is a dinky, funky bar/honky tonk and a good spot to listen to the blues. Assorted blues bands, singers, and musicians perform while the customers drink beer. The casual place contains an Elvis clock, a small dance floor, and a pool table in back. (Central Dallas)

POOR DAVID'S PUB
1924 Greenville Avenue
Dallas
214/821-9891
www.poordavidspub.com
It may be a no-frills club, but it must have something going for it because it's been here more than 20 years. The no-frills menu offers sandwiches and nachos. Vinyl chairs and exposed rafters make up the no-frills décor. There are no video games, pinball machines, or juke boxes either. There's just good music! Some of the greatest folk and blues musicians have played

Teen Scene

Just because you're not old enough to drink doesn't mean you can't have a good time. Check out the following places that cater to the under-21 crowd:

- *Venice Beach, 1621 Lamar Boulevard, Arlington, 817/469-6696, www.venicebeachteen.com; Teens aged 13 to 19 can enjoy DJs or live entertainment, a multilevel dance floor, two full-sized volleyball courts, a basketball court, pool tables, a game room, and free sodas. Fri-Sat 7 p.m.-1 a.m. $10 (Arlington/Grand Prairie)*
- *"Young Guns" at Cowboys Red River, 10310 Technology Boulevard, Dallas, 214/352-1796, www.cowboysdancehall.com; This spacious honky-tonk (see listing under Dance Clubs section) reserves Sundays from 5 to 11 p.m. for young people ages 13 to 20. Enormous crowds learn to line dance and have plenty of boot-scootin' fun! Some nights are for ages 18 and over. (Central Dallas)*

here, and the pub continues to draw a crowd. (Central Dallas)

Rock/Pop

AARDVARK
2905 West Berry Street
Fort Worth
817/926-7814
Founder John Davis built a solid reputation as one of the best music venues in Fort Worth. Near TCU, Aardvark combines the best local bands with a first-rate sound system, low cover charges, and good management. Packed with the young crowd, it's a popular place where you can almost always hear good contemporary music. (Southwest Fort Worth)

CLUB DADA
2720 Elm Street
Dallas
214/744-DADA
Another eclectic Deep Ellum music club, this one leans toward blues and rock. The tree-shaded back patio is a nice place to enjoy a drink and the music in good weather. Live music is usually played nightly on one of three stages (two indoor and one outdoors). Happy hour starts at 5 p.m. (East Dallas)

DALLAS ALLEY
2019 North Lamar
Dallas
214/720-0170
In the West End Marketplace, this establishment is actually a multi-nightclub complex. One low cover charge allows entrance to seven diverse nightclubs, including a piano bar, a karaoke bar, disco, rock, dance music, and country boot-scootin'. Sculptures in the Alley honor Texas pop and blues legendary performers The Big Bopper, Blind Lemon Jefferson, Lefty Frizzell, Buddy Holly, Scott Joplin, Lightnin' Hopkins, Roy Orbison, Tex Ritter, T-Bone Walker, and Bob Wills. (Downtown Dallas)

GALAXY CLUB & GAMES
2820 Main Street
Dallas
214/742-5299
The Galaxy has gotten better in recent years and now boasts that it is the first stop in Dallas for touring bands. It may well be because the quality of bands that play on weekends is quite good. During the week, local bands often perform, and several have credited the Galaxy with giving them their first big break. It's a friendly place that is usually not overcrowded. The cover charges and audience vary with the bands. Open Wed.-Sat. (Downtown Dallas)

MOOSE & VINNY'S
2301 North Collins Street, #150
Arlington
817/461-2027
A popular hangout for University of Texas at Arlington (UTA) students, this club brings live music to Arlington. With great live bands, a big-screen TV, pool tables, and a full menu of munchies, this establishment allows smoking throughout the club. (Arlington/Grand Prairie)

RIDGLEA THEATER
6025 Camp Bowie Boulevard
Fort Worth
817/738-9500
A 1940s Art Deco theater has been converted into a hip live-music venue, where bands play along to laser light shows. Concerts begin at 10 p.m. on weekends. (Southwest Fort Worth)

Bronco Bowl Entertainment Center

Part nightclub, part bowling alley, part arcade, part pool hall, part concert venue, part Sports Grill & Bar, the Bronco Bowl (2600 Fort Worth Avenue, Dallas, 214/943-1777) is a 140,000-square-foot facility near Downtown Dallas. The concert stage hosts performances by local and big-name groups from pop/rock to rhythm & blues to country.

Country-and-Western

BIG BALLS OF COWTOWN
302 West Exchange Avenue
Fort Worth
817/624-2800
This dance hall and saloon claims to be the "Home of Western Swing" in the Stockyards Historic District. Along with live music entertainment, they boast indoor plumbing. (That's a joke, folks!) Owner Gary Beaver is doing a great job of reviving Cowtown's Western swing heritage for today's youth. (North Fort Worth)

THE RIVER NIGHTCLUB
1541 Merrimac Circle
Fort Worth
817/336-3764
This club offers a variety of programs, including happy hours, free dance lessons, ladies' night, and talent searches on various nights. (Southwest Fort Worth)

WILHOITE'S
432 South Main Street
Grapevine
817/481-2511
A home-cooking restaurant during the day, this spot is a popular bar and entertainment venue at night. The bands are usually country or rock on weekends; Tuesdays and Thursdays are karaoke nights. (Mid-Cities)

WHITE ELEPHANT SALOON
106 East Exchange Avenue
Fort Worth
817/624-1887
People don't get shot here anymore, but Fort Worth's last gunfight occurred in the street in front of the White Elephant in 1887. The famous shootout took place between the gambler Luke Short (owner of the Elephant) and the former marshal "Long Hair" Jim Courtright. Today's saloon still evokes the memory of the Old West with its long wooden bar and brass footrail. Live music is played nightly, and the cozy dance floor and the big, friendly bar are exactly what most people expect a Texas cowboy bar to be. The adjacent White Elephant Beer Garden has live music and dancing on weekends April through October. (North Fort Worth)

PUBS AND BARS

BARLEY HOUSE
2916 North Henderson Avenue

Dallas
214/824-0306
This comfortable, casual, friendly bar is located in the trendy Knox-Henderson neighborhood, adjoining the East Side Grill. It offers lots of beer, a great munchie menu, a huge-screen TV visible from almost anywhere inside, two pool tables in the back, and an outdoor patio in front. Local bands entertain with live music on weekend nights. (Central Dallas)

BLARNEY STONE
904 Houston Street
Fort Worth
817/332-4747
Tucked away down a flight of stairs, The Blarney Stone serves beer, and gallons of it. An old-fashioned, friendly-bartender kind of place, it's off the beaten track enough to draw a relaxed crowd not trying to "see and be seen." (Downtown Fort Worth)

THE CAVERN
1914 Lower Greenville Avenue
Dallas
214/841-9091
Beatles memorabilia decorates this intimate, tucked-upstairs funky bar. But the music in the low-red-lighted neighborhood bar is eclectic '90s, ranging from jazz to rock to alternative. Live music is played Wednesday through Saturday. (Central Dallas)

CHELSEA CORNER
2822 McKinney Avenue
Dallas
214/521-8780
It's a British-style pub with an excellent beer and ale selection as well as a delicious and diverse menu offering giant burgers, homemade

pizza, and other selections from traditional to upscale yuppie. The 25-35 year-old crowd use it as an aferwork destination. Open daily, often with live music on weekend nights.

CORNER TAP
2101 Lower Greenville
Dallas
214/827-0999
Unlike most smelly and dingy waterin' holes, this bar has a huge mirrored bar with shiny wood trim and a row of bright, windowed booths. It's supposed to represent the Chicago-style neighborhood/sports tavern, and it does a darned good job. The older clientele seems to appreciate the single-malt scotches and Italian sausages. The menu offers a nice variety of sandwiches. (Central Dallas)

DAVE & BUSTER'S
10727 Composite Drive
Dallas
214/353-0620
Dave & Buster's has been called "an amusement center for big kids," which is a pretty apt description. Big kids can visit two full bars, a cutting-edge video game room, a karaoke room, several pool tables, a small performance theater, and a great restaurant. Little kids are welcome, too, but they must be accompanied by an adult while in the club and must leave promptly at 10 p.m. It's a big, fun place for a date or to meet a group of friends. Open daily; happy hour weekdays. (Central Dallas)

THE DOME LOUNGE
Reunion Tower
300 Reunion Boulevard
Dallas
214/651-1234
Located on the third and highest

level of Reunion Tower (see Chapter 5, Sites and Attractions), The Dome offers dancing nightly and spectacular views of Dallas. Enjoy cocktails and hors d'oeuvres as you gently revolve above the city. (Downtown Dallas)

THE DUBLINER
2818 Lower Greenville Avenue
Dallas
214/818-0911
A true Irish pub—owned and operated by two Dublin transplants—offers a fine selection of imported ales, stouts, and whiskeys. Cozy, with attentive bartenders, it's a local favorite. (Central Dallas)

FILTHY MCNASTY'S
114 West Exchange Avenue
Fort Worth
817/624-1401
In the Stockyards Historic District, this place is one of many western saloon-style bars lining Exchange Avenue. It serves up yummy frozen margaritas and country-and-western music. (North Fort Worth)

FOX & HOUND
1001 NE Green Oaks Boulevard
Arlington
817/277-3591
Arlington has jumped on the trendy bandwagon with this English-pub-sounding neighborhood bar with a large pool room. The Fox & Hound has become a popular after-work hangout for all ages. A comfortable dining/lounge area features a full menu of American favorites. (Arlington/Grand Prairie)

FLYING SAUCER
DRAUGHT EMPORIUM
111 East Fourth Street
(Sundance Square)

Fort Worth
817/336-PINT
A great beer and cigar pub in Sundance Square, the Flying Saucer claims to have 100 beers from around the world on tap, plus domestic and microbrews from all over the country. This Fort Worth location has more of a Euro-pub ambience with a bar on each level, whereas the Dallas location (1520 Greenville Avenue, 214/824-7468) has an outdoor patio and separate smoking area. Both are popular after-work hangouts and feature a variety of sound-blasting music from blues to rock to soul. The menu is mostly killer sandwiches and wurst plates and snacks like Buffalo wings, nachos, and quesadillas. (Downtown Fort Worth)

GRAPE ESCAPE
500 Commerce Street
Fort Worth
817/336-9463
This popular, trendy establishment offers a great wine selection and light food offerings and snacks. (Downtown Fort Worth)

JACK'S PUB & VOLLEYBALL CLUB
5550 Yale Boulevard
Dallas
214/360-0999
Located not too far from SMU, this popular hangout has two outdoor sand volleyball courts, pool tables, dartboards, foosball, pinball, and other games. It serves hamburgers and has happy hour Monday through Saturday. (Central Dallas)

LONGHORN SALOON
121 West Exchange
Fort Worth
817/626-1161
What's to say about a saloon in the

Get in the Spirit of the Old West

In order to truly experience the spirit of the Old West, try the following activities:

- *Attend a rodeo.*
- *Watch the Herd.*
- *Shop for Western apparel, boots, hats, and souvenirs.*
- *Go to the Cattle Raisers Museum.*
- *Take a tour of the Stockyards National Historic District and the Stockyards Museum.*
- *Ride the mechanical bull at Billy Bob's.*
- *Have your picture taken on the "photo" bull at Billy Bob's.*
- *Go to a Cowboy Gathering or a Cowboy Poet's reading.*
- *Sip a cool one at the White Elephant Saloon and people-watch.*
- *Ride a horse on the equestrian trails along the Trinity River.*

Stockyards Historic District in Fort Worth? Enjoy a longneck and soak up the flavor of a "gin-u-wine" saloon right out of an Old West movie. (North Fort Worth)

MICK'S BAR
2825 Greenville Avenue
Dallas
214/827-0039
Mick's live jazz is gone and has been replaced by a DJ. It's a dark and cozy place, which is quiet in the early evenings. A former bartender at Terilli's, the long-time popular jazz restaurant next door, Mick knows how to create custom cocktails. He has also added a selection of premium cigars. (Central Dallas)

MILO BUTTERFINGER'S
5645 Yale Boulevard
Dallas
214/368-9212
Near SMU, this place of nearly 30-years' duration is almost an institution. Enjoy the foosball and pool tables, pinball machines, darts, or just watch the ballgames on TV. Munch on burgers and sandwiches and killer cheese fries. Cold beer is served by a friendly bartender at this neighborhood sports bar. Part of Oliver Stone's *Born on the Fourth of July* was filmed here. Daily drink specials are offered. (Central Dallas)

THE OLD MONK
2847 North Henderson Avenue
Dallas
214/821-1880
This Euro-pub on trendy Henderson Avenue serves about any kind of beer or liquor imaginable. Watch a game on two TVs at the long, mahogany bar, play darts, or relax with your drink and a friend on the

outdoor patio. Friendly folks staff this comfortable bar. (Central Dallas)

OUI LOUNGE
3509 Bluebonnet Circle
Fort Worth
817/927-9209
Far from trendy, this neighborhood bar has been on Bluebonnet Circle, near TCU, since Harry Truman was president. A second generation of students gather in the game/sports rooms while the old-timers congregate in the bar. (Southwest Fort Worth)

PALM BEACH CLUB
2807 Commerce Street
Dallas
214/742-4743
This funky place just spent $60,000 for a facelift and now sports palm trees, painted parrots, and Egyptian murals. With a little imagination (and a few drinks), you could be in a tropical paradise. An eclectic crowd listens to a diverse array of music with live reggae music on Saturday nights. (Downtown Dallas)

PYRAMID LOUNGE
The Fairmont Hotel
1717 North Akard Street 75201
Dallas
214/720-2020 or 800/527-4727
www.fairmont.com
An outstanding hotel lounge has happy hours in elegant surroundings Monday through Saturday 5-7 p.m. In addition to an admirable selection of beverages, they feature a tempting special each day; for example, soft California cheeses with pinenut crackers on Tuesdays. (Downtown Dallas)

ROCK BOTTOM BREWERY
4050 Belt Line Road

Addison
972/404-7456
In addition to the house brews, this spacious brewpub/restaurant serves excellent food and tasty appetizers such as Buffalo wings and huge nachos. The chef prepares a wide variety of entrees, including steaks, grilled fish, pasta dishes, ribs, and some Southwestern fare. Listen and dance to jazz or rock on weekends and sometimes during the week. (Far North Dallas)

ROOFTOP GROTTO BAR
Caravan of Dreams
312 Houston Street
Fort Worth
817/877-3000
www.caravanofdreams.com
On top of the Caravan of Dreams, the truly unique Rooftop Grotto Bar features a domed terrarium and cactus garden as well as a great view of Sundance Square. Weather permitting, it's a grand place to enjoy the scenery. (Downtown Fort Worth)

ROUTH STREET BREWERY
3011 Routh Street
at Cedar Springs Road
Dallas
214/922-8835
Routh Street Brewery's focus on traditional European ales and beers sets it apart from the trendy here-today-gone-tomorrow pubs. The food here is excellent, and the menu even recommends beer choices to accompany the entrees. In Dallas's Uptown neighborhood, the building began as an 1890s-era house; a grocery store was added to the front in the '40s; it has been extensively expanded and remodeled to house the Brewery, which is now reminiscent of a hunting lodge with a fireplace and antler

The City of Arlington prohibits smoking in public buildings unless the establishment has installed a special filter and exhaust system. Most small places found that cost prohibitive, so if this issue is important to you, ask first.

chandeliers. Sit on the spacious stone patio during nice weather, although you can watch the brewing operation (visible behind glass) from the inside tables. The kids can enjoy the home-brewed root beer. (Downtown Dallas)

SCHOONER BREWERY
1701 Market Street
Dallas
214/651-0808
This popular West End brewpub offers a nice variety of brews and is considered by many to be the finest brewpub in Dallas. During the holiday season, they offer a special Rudolph the Rheinbeer. The pub also offers a wide variety of munchies and a better-than-decent meal menu. (Downtown Dallas)

SHIP'S LOUNGE
1613 Greenville Avenue
Dallas
214/823-0315
If you like theme bars, visit this funky, neighborhood bar with its pseudo-nautical décor. It's tiny (or cozy, if you prefer) and appeals to a slightly older crowd, probably because it lacks the ear-shattering live music and no hard liquor is served. There's a jukebox and a small selection of munchies. (Central Dallas)

SNEAKY PETE'S
Two Eagle Point
Lewisville

972/434-2500
If you find yourself on or near Lake Lewisville, a visit to Sneaky Pete's is worth your while. At Eagle Point Marina, it's a long-time local hangout for the lake crowd. Decorated with tasteful nautical décor and aquariums with colorful fish, it's a casual, friendly place with cold beer and big-screen TVs. You can play volleyball, swim, or watch the sunset from the dock. If you're looking for something a little out of the ordinary, you can rent the houseboat and tour the lake. (Far North Dallas)

TIPPERARY INN
5815 Live Oak
Dallas
214/823-7167
The Tipperary Inn is a great place to enjoy your pint of Guinness Stout or other Irish beers or ales. A DJ spins old and new CD favorites in the friendly pub in the eclectic Lakewood neighborhood. Tuesday night is Trivia Night and draws huge crowds of all ages to test their knowledge of useless information. (Central Dallas)

THE VELVET ELVIS
1906 McKinney Avenue
Dallas
214/969-5568
You'd never guess from the name that this eclectic bar is housed in a restored 1874 building with 22-foot ceilings and was once a house of ill

repute. Drink your choice of more than 50 draft beers and 30 single-malt scotches on one of three patios in nice weather. There's usually live blues or swing on weekends, and Italian food is available from Grace & Tony's in the same building. (Downtown Dallas)

THE WRECK ROOM
3208 West Seventh Street
Fort Worth
817/870-4900
Although small, this cozy bar has become hugely popular with Fort Worth's younger crowd. The selection in the jukebox constantly changes with tunes from private collections of staff members. Live rock music blasts on weekends; the beer is cold, and the people are friendly. (Southwest Fort Worth)

COMEDY CLUBS

AD-LIBS
2613 Ross Avenue
Dallas
214/754-7050
Since 1986, Ad-Libs Improvisational Comedy Troupe has entertained and amazed crowds with its fresh, energized blend of improvisational comedy and audience participation. Each show is completely unrehearsed, and the subject matter comes directly from the audience. The troupe performs more than three hundred shows per year at the Dallas club and travels around the country performing at special events. Performances are Fridays and Saturdays at 7:30 and 10:00 p.m. $15 (Downtown Dallas)

HYENA'S COMEDY CLUB
604 Main Street
Fort Worth
817/877-5233
Enjoy performances by nationally recognized comedy and variety entertainers, mostly on weekends. A second location is at 2525 East Arkansas Lane, Arlington, 817/226-5233. The early show on Saturday night at the Arlington location is smoke-free. (Downtown Fort Worth)

DINNER THEATERS

MEDIEVAL TIMES DINNER & TOURNAMENT
2021 North Stemmons Freeway (I-35E)
Dallas
214/761-1800 or 800/229-9900
www.medievaltimes.com
Pretend you are guests in the castle of a royal family in the eleventh century. Admission includes a Middle Ages-style, four-course dinner and a live performance of knights in authentically reproduced costumes waging battle, competing in games of skill, jousting, and riding Andalusian stallions. Cheer the knights of the realm to victory while feasting

Several movie theaters have "dollar days," usually during the week or on Sunday afternoons.

on the bill of fare. The castle is air-conditioned and wheelchair accessible. (Central Dallas)

MOVIE HOUSES OF NOTE

Most of the movie houses in the Metroplex are of the chain, multi-theater variety. AMC, UA, Loews, and General Cinema have dozens of locations throughout the area.

BRAZOS DRIVE-IN
1800 West Pearl Street
Granbury
817/573-1311
Located 35 miles southwest of Fort Worth in Granbury, this drive-in is one of the few remaining 1950s-era movie theaters. It shows first-run movies, so pile the family in the car and enjoy the show (see Chapter 13, Day Trips).

CINEMARK IMAX® THEATRE
I-635 (LBJ) at Webb Chapel Road
Dallas
972/888-2629
www.cinemark.com
Advertising the only 3-D IMAX® experience in Dallas, this giant-screen picture is enhanced by six-channel surround sound. It's all designed to make you feel as if you're part of the show. Call for features and showtimes. (Central Dallas)

GRAPEVINE MILLS 30
3000 Grapevine Mills Parkway at Highway 121 North
Grapevine
972/724-8000
This huge theater complex in Grapevine Mills Mall features about

half PG or PG-13 films, stadium seating, and all the conveniences and amenities of a sparkling new theater complex. (Mid-Cities)

OMNI THEATRE
Fort Worth Museum
of Science and History
1501 Montgomery Street
Fort Worth
817/255-9300, 888/255-9300
www.fwmuseum.org
Inside the Fort Worth Museum of Science and History (see Chapter 6, Museums and Art Galleries), the Omni Theater is an 80-foot-high domed theater with sophisticated audio and video systems that dazzle your senses with spectacular film experiences. Recent films include *The Great Migrations* (thousands of Monarch butterflies surround you), *Everest* (thrill to the climb), and *The Living Sea* (an underwater adventure experience). (Southwest Fort Worth)

TI FOUNDERS IMAX® THEATER
The Science Place (Fair Park)
Dallas
214/428-5555
www.scienceplace.org
Feel as if you're part of the film experience in the TI Founders IMAX® Theater with its scientifically designed seats and state-of-the-art sound system. (East Dallas)

TINSELTOWN GRAPEVINE
Highway 114 at William D. Tate
Grapevine
972/481-2201
A newer 15-screen movie theater, Tinseltown has all stadium-style seating, a game room, and a large snack bar. (Mid-Cities)

13

DAY TRIPS FROM DALLAS AND FORT WORTH

Day Trip: Athens

ATHENS VISITOR INITIATIVE PROGRAM
124 North Palestine
Athens, TX
903/677-0775
24-hour hotline: 888/249-AVIP
www.athenstx.org

Distance from Dallas: About 75 miles
Distance from Fort Worth: About 110 miles
The drive itself from Dallas to Athens is worth the trip; you travel through rolling hills and hay meadows, which display a rainbow of wildflowers in spring and vibrant foliage in autumn. Here, in scenic East Texas surrounded by Christmas tree farms, you can enjoy the slow, easy pace of a truly Texas-friendly small town. Athens' claims to fame are the Black-Eyed Pea Capital of the World and the birthplace of the hamburger.

Located within minutes of five lakes, Athens is a renowned fishing center. **Lake Athens** is rated third in the state in pounds of bigmouth black bass per acre of water; it also boasts record bass, crappie, bluegill brim, and catfish. Bring your swimsuit and visit the **Athens Scuba Park** (500 N. Murchison, 903/675-5762), home of Aquanut Diving, Inc., and spring-fed, blue water with visibility up to 28 feet.

One of the best outdoor entertainment values for the entire family is the **Texas Freshwater Fisheries Center** (5550 Flat Creek Rd., FM 2495, 903/

676-BASS, www.tpwd.state.tx.us/fish/infish/hatchery/tffc/welcome.htm). Part of the Texas Parks and Wildlife Department, this facility is an innovative aquarium and hatchery complex, the only one of its kind in North America. It's educational—learn about underwater life by viewing the galleries through glass walls: a Texas Hill Country stream, an East Texas farm pond, the wetlands and alligator pond, and the 178,000-gallon Reservoir habitat. It's entertaining—watch the show in a 26,000-gallon tank as a diver hand-feeds fish and answers questions from the audience by way of advanced communications equipment. It's scientific—the lower level of the center contains the state-of-the-art hatchery and scientific laboratory. It's fun—try your luck at the stocked casting pond, or watch your kids from the new deck seating or fishing pier. It's fascinating—explore the history of fishing, view collections of antique reels, spinners, and lures, see replicas of record fish, and read about the legendary anglers Hall of Fame Museum. You'll find everything you need at the Angler's Pavilion, including bait, tackle, knowledgeable instructors, and refreshments. The gift shop is stocked with snacks and a fine selection of Texas Parks and Wildlife gifts and souvenirs.

Downtown, a variety of shops and restaurants surround the **Henderson County Courthouse.** Stop at the **Welcome Center** on the east side of the square for helpful information and a cup of coffee. **Jubilee House Restaurant and Club** serves fine Cajun fare and has daily lunch specials. **Hog Heaven** sells smoked hams and turkeys, as well as serves good sandwiches for lunch. From the downtown square, east on Corsicana Street, visit the **Old Towne Shoppes,** including **Apple Gap** for crafty items and jewelry and **Waldenwood,** a delightful house stuffed with unusual gifts and treasures. **Athens Alley** contains a hodgepodge of antique shops and a tearoom, **Garden of Eatin',** in a renovated warehouse district.

Getting there from Dallas and Fort Worth: *Take I-20 east to the Canton/Highway 19 exit. Follow Highway 19 south into Athens.*

Visitors get up close and personal with fish at the Texas Freshwater Fisheries Center

Texas Freshwater Fisheries Center

DALLAS/FORT WORTH REGION

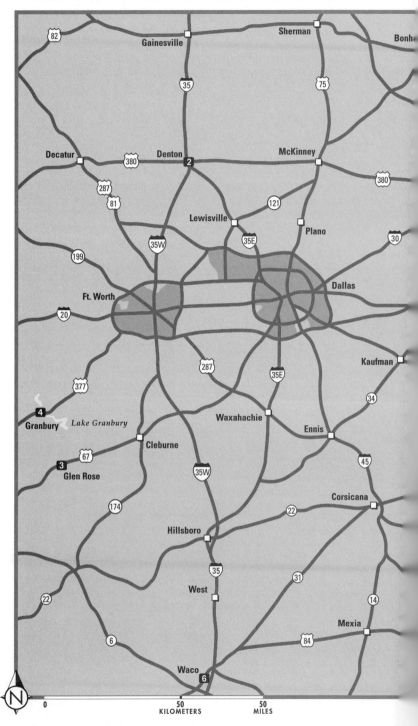

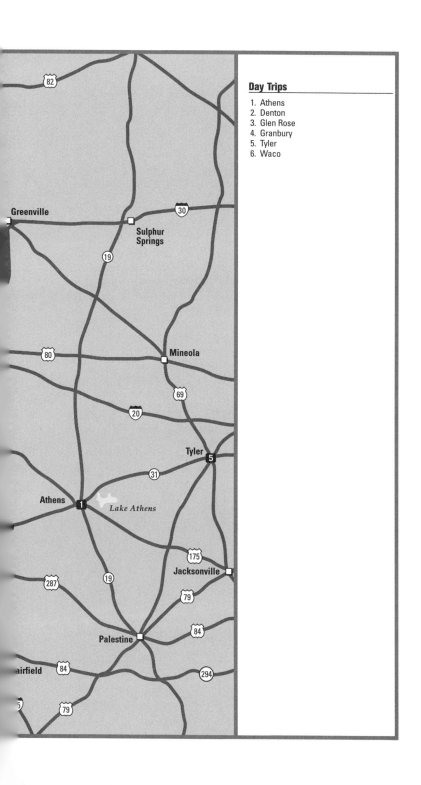

Day Trips

Day Trip: Denton

DENTON CONVENTION & VISITOR BUREAU
414 West Parkway
P.O. Drawer P
Denton, TX
940/382-7895 or 888/381-1818
www.denton-chamber.org

Distance from Dallas and Fort Worth: About 35 miles

Located about 35 miles north of Dallas and Fort Worth where I-35W joins I-35E, Denton blends a proud historic past with the lively international flavor of a university community.

The centerpiece of this Texas Historical Commission Main Street City is the magnificent 1896 **Denton County Courthouse,** now home to the **Courthouse-on-the-Square Museum** (940/565-5667). The historic downtown Oak-Hickory District contains more than 120 renovated structures, a vibrant area of art galleries, antique shops, gift boutiques, eclectic retail establishments, and eateries. Just a few blocks from Downtown, the restaurants, clubs, and businesses of Fry Street cater to university students and the young-at-heart.

As you walk around the town square, which looks much as it did at the turn of the century, visit **Evers Hardware** (109 W. Hickory, 940/382-5513), a family-owned business serving customers since 1885. If you're a bibliophile, plan to spend a good part of the day in **Recycled Books, Records, & CDs** (200 N. Locust, 940/566-5688). Other irresistible shops include **Sleeping Lizards, King Richard's Cat, The Courtyard Collection, Stone Soup, At the Ritz, This Old House,** and **The Garden Gate.** Stop in **Beth Marie's Ice Cream Parlor** for a dip of Old South Fudge ice cream.

Deciding where to have lunch is a problem here because there are actually too many choices. On or near the square are the **Chestnut Tree & Garden Tea Room** (107 W. Hickory), **Rama's Courtyard Café** (222 W. Hickory), **Sweetwater Grill & Tavern** (115 S. Elm), **Texican Grill** (111 W. Mulberry), and **The Loophole** (119 W. Hickory). For fine dining, walk a few blocks to **Giuseppe's Italian Restaurant** (821 N. Locust), which is located on the ground floor of Magnolia Inn, one of the elegant B&Bs of the historical Heritage Inns (940/565-6414; 888/565-6414).

For discount shopping, try **Denton Factory Stores** (I-35 at North

Denton, Texas

Donovan Reese

Female Fishers

An East Texas girl, Sugar Ferris, is the only woman in the Texas Freshwater Fisheries Center's Hall of Fame Museum. In 1972, everyone knew that wives were supposed to play bingo or cards while their husbands fished. Well, Sugar Ferris wanted to fish, too! Some of the other wives agreed. They invaded the "bubba" sport and planned the nation's first all-women bass fishing contest. Ninety-six women showed up at Lake Livingston! Bass 'N Gal was founded as the nation's first female fishing organization and had more than 300,000 members at its peak.

Loop 288), with outlets for Westpoint Pepperell, Dress Barn, Famous Footwear, Lenox, Famous Brands Housewares, and others.

Denton is a gathering place for music and performing arts enthusiasts. The restored **Campus Theater** (214 W. Hickory, 940/382-1915) is a 1940s-era Art Deco masterpiece offering a variety of entertainment productions. The **University of North Texas** (UNT) is world-renowned for its Jazz Studies program, and **Texas Woman's University** (TWU) groups are critically acclaimed for ballet and modern dance. Both universities have art galleries, theaters, and performance halls.

Several interesting displays, unique collections, and museums are tucked away on the two university campuses. The **DAR Museum** (940/898-3201) at TWU exhibits the First Ladies of Texas Collection of inaugural gowns; UNT is known for its Rare Book and Texana Collection (Willis Library, 940/565-2769) and extensive Texas Fashion Collection (Scoular Hall, 940/565-2732).

If you have time for outdoor activities, Denton is only minutes from Lake Ray Roberts, which is considered to be one of the best fishing lakes in the state and a popular recreational lake.

Getting there from Dallas: *Take I-35E north into Denton.*
Getting there from Fort Worth: *Take I-35W north into Denton.*

Day Trip: Glen Rose

GLEN ROSE CONVENTION & VISITORS BUREAU
P.O. Box 2037
Glen Rose, TX
254/897-3081 or 888/DINO-CVB

Distance from Dallas: About 80 miles
Distance from Fort Worth: About 50 miles

Get your official Dinosaur Hunting License and head for **Dinosaur Valley State Park** (254/897-4588, www.tpwd.state.tx.us/park/dinosaur/dinosaur .htm) near Glen Rose. More than 120 million years ago, giant prehistoric beasts walked through the Paluxy River beds; now visitors can see the well-preserved tracks in this unique state park. Exposed rock in the river bottom contains three types of giant dinosaur tracks. The acrocanthosaurus and pleurocoelus tracks are estimated to be 111 million years old. The scenic river and walking trails wander through oaks and cedars in this lovely park, which is now home to beasts such as deer, armadillos, coyotes, raccoons, beavers, and hundreds of birds (a bird checklist is available at park headquarters). Take wading boots (the tracks are in the river) and insect repellent.

The **Texas Amphitheatre** (254/897-4509), an open-air entertainment showplace, features a state-of-the-art light and sound system. Concerts, musicals, plays, and pageants are performed on the tri-level stage. **The Promise** (800/687-2661), a musical drama of the life of Christ, is performed under the stars in the amphitheater on Friday and Saturday nights June through October.

One of the most interesting places anywhere is **Fossil Rim Wildlife Center** (254/897-2960, www.fossilrim.com). Roaming free on three thousand acres of unspoiled countryside are hundreds of endangered and exotic animals, such as black rhinos, cheetahs, Gemsbok antelope, greater kudu, axis deer, and wildebeest, among a plethora of others. Not just another drive-through zoo, Fossil Rim is a world leader in endangered species conservation through its breeding and management programs. The first of its kind accredited by the American Zoo and Aquarium Association, it participates in scientific research, public education, and training of conservation professionals. Fossil Rim was the first U.S. location chosen to breed the highly endangered, beautiful Grevy's zebra. Acclaimed around the world for its successful breeding of cheetahs, white rhinos, and red wolves, Fossil Rim is a fascinating place. Set your own pace along the scenic 9.5-mile drive and enjoy up-close-and-personal looks at the frolicking, uninhibited animals. If you become entranced (a definite possibility), you may extend your "day trip"; they offer an overnight "Wildlife Safari," a variety of educational camps, and extensive behind-the-scenes

TRIVIA

In the 1880s Fletcher Davis served a popular sandwich, a ground beef patty served between two slices of bread with mustard and a slice of onion, at his lunch counter in Athens. "Uncle Fletch" took his invention to the 1904 World's Fair in St. Louis and the rest, as they say, is hamburger history.

Granbury CVB

Shopping on the square in Granbury

tours. At the visitors center, enjoy the displays and petting pasture, as well as the café/snack bar and well-stocked Nature Store. All proceeds from admission fees and visitor services fund the conservation programs. Don't forget your binoculars and camera! Usually open every day, but the park closes occasionally during inclement weather in winter.

There's almost always something going on at Glen Rose's **Expo Center**, whether it's a concert, a rodeo, a car or boat show, a wrestling match, or a cutting horse show. Call 254/897-4509 for schedules.

If you like the "offbeat," visit the unusual **Creation Evidence Museum** (3102 FM 205, 254/897-3200, www.creationevidence.org), a nonprofit establishment formed to excavate and display scientific evidence for creation. Research and experiments involve the world's first hyperbaric biosphere, simulating the pre-flood world environment. Tours are available Tuesday through Saturday 10-4.

Take a free tour of **Comanche Peak** (254/897-5554), an operating nuclear power plant. An introductory slide show, exhibits, and displays explain how electricity is generated using the atom. Then view an exact replica of a control room to understand plant operations.

The beautifully restored 1893 limestone **Somervell County Courthouse** is the centerpiece of the town square. Art works and collections are on exhibit at **Barnard's Mill and Art Museum** (307 SW Barnard St., 254/897-7494). Built in the 1880s, Barnard's Mill is a Recorded Texas Historic Landmark and is listed in the National Register of Historic Places.

Getting there from Dallas: Take Highway 67 southwest directly into Glen Rose. Follow the sign (left on Barnard St.) to historic Downtown.
Getting there from Fort Worth: Take Highway 377 southwest to Granbury, then Highway 144 south until it merges with Highway 67, turn right into Glen Rose. Follow the sign (left on Barnard St.) to historic Downtown.

Day Trip: Granbury

GRANBURY CONVENTION & VISITORS BUREAU
100 North Crockett
Granbury, TX
817/573-5548 or 800/950-2212
www.granbury.org

Distance from Dallas: About 65 miles
Distance from Fort Worth: About 35 miles
Southwest of Fort Worth lies a slice of small-town America nestled on a scenic lake in the Brazos River Valley. Here you can still attend a drive-in movie, order real ice cream sodas, or take a horse-drawn carriage ride. Granbury's courthouse square was the first in Texas to be listed in the National Register of Historic Places in 1974.

Experience a nostalgic visit to the past by walking or driving past dozens of restored turn-of-the-century homes and discovering the more than 40 historical markers. Listen to the legends and lore; ask about John St. Helen, a bartender who claimed to be John Wilkes Booth. Hear tell of Jesse James, who "staged" his death in 1882, then came to Granbury and lived there until he died at the ripe old age of 104. Located just outside Granbury in the tiny town of Acton, the grave of Elizabeth Crockett, Davy's widow, is the smallest State Park in Texas.

Pick up a self-guided walking or driving tour map at the visitors center or hire a horse-drawn carriage from **Granbury Carriage Company** (817/279-6272) on the courthouse square.

Visit the **Old Jail and Hood County Historical Museum** (208 N. Crockett, 817/573-5135) and see the original hanging tower in the 1885 frontier jail.

When the native limestone **Hood County Courthouse** was built in 1891, the surrounding town square consisted of cowboy saloons and bawdy houses. Now more than fifty antique and art galleries, boutiques and gift shops, and eateries fill the area.

The 1886 **Opera House** (116 E. Pearl, 817/573-9191, www.granburyopera house.org), restored by a community-wide effort, presents family-style fun with musicals, plays, melodramas, and original productions most of the year. Call for current performance schedules.

The **Great Race Automotive Hall of Fame** (114 N. Crockett, 817/573-5200, www.greatrace.com) is a more recent addition to the square. This nonprofit museum displays vintage automobiles and memorabilia from the Great North American Race, a transcontinental rally for antique cars. There's also a resource library and Mercantile Shop offering Great Race souvenirs.

Shopping on the square is a treat indeed, where you can browse more than 50 antique and gift shops, boutiques, and art galleries around the courthouse. **The Panhandle** is one of the finest kitchen shops anywhere with a gigantic selection of cookbooks, kitchen items, cookware, gadgets, and gourmet foods. **The Cat's Meow** is great fun; the **Antique Emporium** is chock-full of grandma's-attic-type stuff; and quilters won't want to miss **Houston Street Mercantile. Books on the Square** is a combination book/card/gift/souvenir shop that is worth browsing. The popular **Granbury Sampler** offers cute birdhouses, crafty gifts, jams, sauces, and homemade fudge.

One drawback to a "day trip" to Granbury is that you don't get to stay at one of the town's quaint bed-and-breakfast inns. The second drawback is that you probably only get to eat one meal there. You'll have to choose. On the square, **Hennington's Texas Café** at the Nutt House (121 E. Bridge, 817/573-8400) serves savory dishes such as Shredded Crab Tacos with

Dr. George P. Snyder built a "drugless sanatorium" in 1916 along the banks of the Paluxy River. People came for curative mineral baths, healthy food, and a good dose of pampering for the purpose of rejuvenation. The historic landmark still offers rejuvenation today at the elegant Inn on the River. In the 1950s, a guest wrote a song inspired by the massive oak trees on the landscaped grounds sloping to the river behind the inn. Elvis Presley recorded the song, "The Singing Trees," in 1965.

Chiltomate Sauce and Seafood Cakes with Thai Sesame Mayonnaise. **Pearl Street Pasta Company** (101 E. Pearl, 817/279-7719) has home-style Italian fare with traditional pastas, veal and chicken dishes, and daily specials. It offers good food and service at a moderate price. The **Merry Heart Tearoom** (110 N. Houston, 817/573-3800) is a favorite with women enjoying a shopping spree or for a mothers' day out. It's located in the back part of an antique/gift shop, so browsing while you wait could be dangerous. The salad sampler plate is a good choice, with portions of chicken salad, fruit salad, and spinach salad plus homemade nutbread. **Rinky-Tink's Sandwich & Ice Cream Parlor** (108 N. Houston, 817/573-4323) serves, what else but, sandwiches and ice cream; it is a popular place in the summer, and a quick lunch choice year-round. **The Coffee Grinder** (129 E. Pearl, 817/279-0977) is a fine coffeehouse that keeps late hours and offers a nice selection of Texas wines and coffee gift items.

Lake Granbury offers a wide array of watersports, including fishing, swimming, skiing, or sailing; or you can take a lazy cruise along the shores on a Mississippi Riverboat-style paddle wheeler. Tee off on scenic golf courses that surround Lake Granbury.

The **Brazos Drive-In** (1800 W. Pearl, 817/573-1311), one of the few remaining 1950s-era drive-ins, shows first run movies (see also Chapter 12, Nightlife).

Getting there from Dallas: Take I-20 west through Fort Worth to Highway 377. Take 377 southwest into Granbury. Follow the sign (right exit) into historic Downtown.
Getting there from Fort Worth: Take Highway 377 southwest into Granbury. Follow the sign (right exit) into historic Downtown.

Day Trip: Tyler

TYLER CONVENTION AND VISITORS BUREAU
Visitor Information Centers
407 North Broadway
Tyler, TX
903/592-1661, 800/235-5712
www.tylertexas.com

Distance from Dallas: 90 miles
Distance from Fort Worth: 120 miles
Tyler is located approximately 35 miles from Athens (see Day Trip listing) and can be combined into a long day trip, depending on your interests. The drive is especially pleasant in the spring, with fields of wildflowers along the highways and backroads. Tyler is a prosperous blend of old and new, a thriving town of approximately 80,000 residents, a university, and first-class shops, restaurants, and medical facilities.

In late March and early April, Tyler becomes a sea of red, pink, and white azaleas. During the annual **Azalea Trails,** visitors and residents alike line the streets to gaze at the zillions of spectacular azaleas, dogwoods, redbuds, and spring flowers. The festivities include arts-and-crafts shows, tours of historic homes, a quilt show, and other special events.

In October, the community stages the floral extravaganza, the **Texas Rose Festival.** Three days of festivities pay tribute to the Rose Capital of America. A highlight for many visitors is a tour of some of the commercial rose gardens in the surrounding countryside, which are open only during the festival. The **Tyler Municipal Rose Garden & Museum** (1900 W. Front St., 903/531-1212) is the largest museum of its kind in the nation, with more than 22 landscaped acres of walkways, pools, and more than 38,000 rose bushes (more than 500 varieties). Admission is free. The area's rose industry is one of the oldest in Texas; today nearly one-half of all the commercially grown rose bushes in the country are produced in the area around Tyler.

Caldwell Zoo (2203 Martin Luther King Blvd., 903/593-0121) is one of the most outstanding small-city zoos in America. It began as a backyard menagerie in 1937; today animals live in re-created natural habitats, and the zoo participates in the Species Survival Plan and numerous children's educational programs. Admission has always been free.

Harrold's Model Train Museum (8103 North U.S. 271, 903/531-9404) is a haven for railroad buffs. Trains are always running, and more than two

Are You a Pepper, Too?

Long a favorite in Texas, where it was invented in 1885, Dr Pepper is now the fifth-best-selling soft drink in America. It was concocted by a Waco pharmacist, Charles Alderton, who started out serving it to regulars at Morrison's Old Corner Drug Store. In 1988, Dr Pepper merged with 7-Up Company, and the joint corporation thus formed became the third-largest soft drink company in the United States. It maintains headquarters in Dallas.

thousand pieces of rolling stock, plus scenery and villages are on exhibit. Harrold supplies entertaining stories and a running commentary.

Take the kids to the **Discovery Science Place** (308 N. Broadway, 903/533-8011, http://discovery.tyler.com), a hands-on learning center in a fun-filled atmosphere. **Brookshire's World of Wildlife Museum and Country Store** (1600 WSW Loop 323, 903/534-2169) features more than 250 mounted wildlife specimens from Africa and North America as well as a replica of a 1920s-era grocery/general store.

The **Goodman-LeGrand Home** (624 N. Broadway, 903/597-5304) is open for tours March through October, Wednesday to Sunday 1-5 p.m. Built in 1859 by a wealthy young Confederate officer, the majestic Colonial mansion exhibits an exceptional collection of antebellum artifacts and period furnishings.

Drive along the **Brick Street Historic District** with its magnificent historic homes, shop for antiques on Broadway, and picnic in pastoral **Bergfeld Park.**

If you're in the mood for Mexican food, try **Mercado Mexican Café** (2214 WSW Loop 323, 903/534-1754) for excellent fare and hot, fresh flour tortillas, made while you watch. **Bruno's Pizza** (1400 S. Vine Ave., 903/595-1676) has been serving super pizza since 1976. And **Dub's Texas Bar B Que** (1021 E. Fifth St., 903/596-0222) is a local institution. Danny Cace, owner of **Cace's Seafood** (7011 S. Broadway, 903/581-0744) is the son of Johnny Cace, whose Longview restaurant has been a popular destination since 1949 and which serves excellent, although a bit pricey, seafood. If you have the kids with you, try **Armadillo Willy's** (215 WSW Loop 323, 903/509-0122), a Texas-theme fun place with lots of cowboy décor.

Getting there from Dallas and Fort Worth: Take I-20 east to the Highway 69 exit. Proceed southeast on Highway 69 into Tyler.

Day Trip: Waco

WACO TOURIST INFORMATION CENTER
I-35 at University Parks Drive, Exit 335B
Waco, TX
254/750-8696, 800/WACO-FUN
www.wacocvb.com

Distance from Dallas and Fort Worth: About 90 miles
Approximately 90 miles south of Fort Worth lies the "six-shooter junction" of the Old West. Since the time the Hueco (pronounced Waco) Indians camped along the Brazos River, this area has had its place in history. Home to Baylor University, Waco offers a wide variety of attractions, sports, and entertainment venues.

The **Brazos Trolley** runs from the Tourist Information Center to most of the major attractions, daily in summer and on weekends only September through November and March through May. The air-conditioned trolleys are a great way to see the sights if you're not familiar with the city. Fare is

The Texas Ranger Hall of Fame & Museum offers a glimpse of life on the frontier

50 cents for adults and 25 cents for seniors and students; children under five ride free with their parents, and exact change is required. Pick up a schedule at the Information Center.

Few history-book heroes have ever captured our imagination as much as the notorious Texas Rangers. The **Texas Ranger Hall of Fame and Museum** at Fort Fisher (I-35 at the University Parks Dr. exit , 254/750-8631, www.texasranger.org) commemorates the legends and lore of the Texas Rangers, which is the oldest state law enforcement agency in the nation.

The **Dr Pepper Museum** (300 S. Fifth, 254/757-1024) pays tribute to the fountain drink first mixed in the Old Corner Drug Store. The museum is housed in the original 1906 bottling plant. The first floor has a replica of the drugstore, complete with an animatron of the pharmacist telling about his invention.

Cameron Park Zoo, an outstanding zoo for its size, emphasizes conservation and provides natural habitats for the animals. Enjoy Cameron Park itself by hiking or biking on the scenic nature trail along the Brazos River past ancient cliffs where sea creatures lived 100 million years ago.

Twenty preserved and restored turn-of-the-century buildings, including a church, a livery stable, a school, a hotel, and early Texas houses, portray life in early Texas in the **Governor Bill and Vera Daniel Historic Village** (1108 University Parks Dr., 254/710-1160).

The world-renowned **Armstrong-Browning Library** on the Baylor University Campus (700 Speight, 254/710-3566) is reminiscent of an Italian Renaissance palace, a masterpiece of art with 56 stained-glass windows and massive bronze entrance doors depicting themes from Browning's poetry. The library showcases the world's largest collection of Robert and Elizabeth Barrett Browning memorabilia, including letters and manuscripts, secondary works, and portraits.

The **Texas Sports Hall of Fame** (1108 University Parks Dr., 254/756-1633, www.hallofame.org) pays tribute to such legendary sports heroes as Byron Nelson, Babe Didrikson Zaharias, George Foreman, and Nolan Ryan. View video clips in the Tom Landry Theater, see multimedia presentations and interactive exhibits, and observe endless memorabilia in the five different halls of fame.

Take a look at the **Waco Suspension Bridge** at Washington Avenue and University Parks Drive. Built in 1870, it was the longest single-span suspension bridge west of the Mississippi at the time and the only pedestrian/wagon span across the Brazos River along the Chisholm Trail.

If all of this sightseeing makes you hungry, Waco offers plenty of tasty places to eat. For a bit of nostalgia, try the **Elite Café** on the traffic circle (2132 S. Valley Mills, 254/754-4941), a 1950s-style diner with good American grub.

On the way back to the Metroplex, stop at the little town of **West** about 15 miles north of Waco on I-35. The Czech community has several nice gift shops, including the **Old Czech Corner Antique Shop** (130 N. Main, 254/826-4094), which specializes in Czechoslovakian glassware and antique quilts. Family-owned since 1896, **Nemecek Bros.** (300 N. Main, 254/826-5182) is an old-fashioned meat market offering Czech sausages, hickory smoked hams, and fresh cut beef (take an ice chest). Or if you prefer, have your cabbage rolls or roast pork served to you at the **Czech-American Restaurant** (220 N. Main, 254/826-3008).

Getting there from Dallas: Take I-35E (merges with I-35W at Hillsboro) into Waco.
Getting there from Fort Worth: Take I-35W (merges with I-35E at Hillsboro) into Waco.

APPENDIX: CITY·SMART BASICS

EMERGENCY PHONE NUMBERS

Police, fire, ambulance
911
Poison Hotline
800/764-7661
North Central Texas Poison Center
214/590-5000
Dental Emergency
800/336-8478
AAA Emergency Road Service
800/AAA-HELP

HOSPITALS AND EMERGENCY MEDICAL CENTERS

Dallas Area

BAYLOR UNIVERSITY MEDICAL CENTER
3500 Gaston Ave.
Dallas
Emergency: 214/820-2501

BAYLOR UNIVERSITY MEDICAL CENTER
2300 Marie Curie
Garland
972/487-5000

BAYLOR UNIVERSITY MEDICAL CENTER
1650 W. College
Grapevine
817/481-1588

BAYLOR UNIVERSITY MEDICAL CENTER
1901 N. MacArthur Blvd.
Irving
972/579-8100

CHILDREN'S MEDICAL CENTER OF DALLAS
1935 Motor St.
Dallas
214/456-7000

COLUMBIA MEDICAL CITY DALLAS
7777 Forest Lane
Dallas
972/566-7000

DOCTORS HOSPITAL
9440 Poppy Drive
Dallas
214/324-6100

GARLAND COMMUNITY HOSPITAL
2696 W. Walnut
Garland
972/276-7116

LAS COLINAS MEDICAL CENTER
6800 N. MacArthur Blvd.
Irving
972/969-2000

MESQUITE COMMUNITY HOSPITAL
3500 Interstate 30
Mesquite
972/698-3300

METHODIST MEDICAL CENTER
1441 N. Beckley
Dallas
214/947-8181

PARKLAND MEMORIAL HOSPITAL
5201 Harry Hines Blvd.
Dallas
Emergency: 214/590-8281

**PRESBYTERIAN HOSPITAL
OF DALLAS**
8200 Walnut Hill Lane
Dallas
214/345-6789

**RHD MEMORIAL
MEDICAL CENTER**
7 Medical Parkway
Dallas
972/247-1000

ST. PAUL MEDICAL CENTER
5909 Harry Hines Blvd.
Dallas
Emergency: 214/879-2790

VA MEDICAL CENTER
4500 S. Lancaster Rd.
Dallas
214/742-8387

Tarrant County

ALL SAINTS CITYVIEW
7100 Oakmont Blvd.
Fort Worth
817/346-5700

**ALL SAINTS EPISCOPAL
HOSPITAL**
1400 Eighth Ave.
Fort Worth
817/926-2544

**ARLINGTON MEMORIAL
HOSPITAL**
800 W. Randol Mill Rd.
Arlington
817/548-6100

**BAYLOR MEDICAL CENTER
GRAPEVINE**
1650 W. College
Grapevine
817/481-1588

**COOK CHILDREN'S
MEDICAL CENTER**
801 Seventh Ave.
Fort Worth
817/885-4000

**HARRIS METHODIST
FORT WORTH**
1301 Pennsylvania Ave.
Fort Worth
817/882-2000

HARRIS METHODIST HEB
1600 Hospital Parkway
Bedford
817/685-4000

**HARRIS METHODIST
SOUTHWEST**
6100 Harris Parkway
Fort Worth
817/346-5000

**HUGULEY MEMORIAL
MEDICAL CENTER**
11801 South Freeway
Fort Worth
817/293-9100

JOHN PETER SMITH HOSPITAL
1500 S. Main
Fort Worth
817/921-3431

MEDICAL CENTER ARLINGTON
3301 Matlock Rd.
Arlington
817/465-3241

NORTH HILLS HOSPITAL
4401 Booth Calloway Rd.
North Richland Hills
817/255-1000

OSTEOPATHIC MEDICAL CENTER OF TEXAS
1000 Montgomery
Fort Worth
817/731-4311

PLAZA MEDICAL CENTER
900 Eighth Ave.
Fort Worth
817/336-2100

RECORDED INFORMATION

Time/Temperature
214/844-4444 or 214/844-6611
National Weather Service
214/787-1111
Road Conditions (Texas)
214/374-4100
24-hour Dallas Events Hotline
214/571-1301
24-hour Fort Worth Events Hotline
817/332-2000

VISITOR INFORMATION

Addison
800/ADDISON; www.ci.addison.tx.us
Arlington Visitor Information Center
817/461-3888, 800/342-4305;
www.arlington.org
Carrollton Community Information Office
972/466-3593
Colleyville Area Chamber of Commerce
817/488-7148;
www.colleyvillechamber.org
Desoto Chamber of Commerce
972/224-3565;
www.desotochamber.org
Duncanville Chamber of Commerce
972/780-5099
Euless Chamber of Commerce
817/685-1821; www.euless.org

Farmers Branch Office of Tourism
972/247-3131, 800/BRANCH9;
www.farmers-branch.tx.us
Fort Worth Chamber of Commerce
817/336-2491; www.fortworth.com
Garland Convention & Visitor Bureau
972/205-2749, 888/879-0264;
www.ci.garland.tx.us
Grand Prairie Convention & Visitors Bureau
972/263-9588, 800/288-8386;
www.gptexas.com
Grapevine Convention & Visitors Bureau
817/481-0454, 800/457-6338;
www.tourtexas.com/grapevine
Grapevine Visitor Information Center
817/424-0561
Greater Dallas Chamber of Commerce
214/746-6600; dallascvb.com
Hurst-Euless-Bedford Chamber of Commerce
817/283-1521
Irving Convention & Visitors Bureau
800/2-IRVING; www.irvingtexas.com
Lewisville Visitors Bureau
972/436-9571, 800/657-9571;
www.lewisville.com/lcc
Mesquite Convention & Visitors Bureau
972/285-0211
North Richland Hills
817/581-5652
Plano Convention & Visitors Bureau
800/81-PLANO; www.ci.plano.tx.us
Richardson Convention & Visitors Bureau
972/234-4141, 800/777-8001

ABOUT THE AUTHOR

An inveterate traveler, Sharry enjoys staying in bed & breakfasts and meeting local people on her journeys. She has explored all 50 states, Canada, Mexico, Europe, Russia, New Zealand, and Fiji. Her passions for travel and writing are now combined in her role as the independent inspector/consultant for Historic & Hospitality Accommodations of Texas. Author of numerous magazine and newspaper articles, her

books include *The Great Stays of Texas, A Guide to Texas' Finest Historic Bed & Breakfasts, Country Inns, Hotels, and Guesthouses* and *Exploring Texas with Children*. When not traveling, she and her husband, Al, live in Fort Worth, Texas. Her hobbies include reading, needlework, and gardening.

AVALON
TRAVEL
publishing

AVALON TRAVEL PUBLISHING
and its City•Smart authors are
dedicated to building community
awareness within City•Smart cities.
We are proud to work with the
Texas Center for the Book as we
publish this guide to Dallas and
Fort Worth.

Established in 1987, the Texas Center for the Book at Dallas Public Library has endeavored to stimulate public interest in books, reading, and libraries and to encourage the study of the printed word. One of more than forty state centers affiliated with the Center for the Book in the Library of Congress, the Texas Center is funded by private donations. The Texas Center operates under the auspices of the Dallas Public Library and is guided by an Advisory Council.

The Texas Center sponsors special exhibits, literary programs, creative writing contests, lectures and symposia, and publications. The center promotes the educational and cultural role of the book, the history of books and printing, authorship and writing, publishing and preservation of books, and reading and literacy.

The Texas Center for the Book invites you to join in its mission of working with organizations and individuals across the state to develop and increase public appreciation of, and support for books, reading, and libraries.

For more information, please contact:
Texas Center for the Book
Dallas Public Library
1515 Young
Dallas, TX. 75201
214/670-7808

Dallas Public Library

TEXAS
CENTER
FOR
THE
BOOK

AVALON
TRAVEL
publishing

BECAUSE TRAVEL MATTERS.

AVALON TRAVEL PUBLISHING knows that travel is more than coming and going—travel is taking part in new experiences, new ideas, and a new outlook. Our goal is to bring you complete and up-to-date information to help you make informed travel decisions.

AVALON TRAVEL GUIDES feature a combination of practicality and spirit, offering a unique traveler-to-traveler perspective perfect for an afternoon hike, around-the-world journey, or anything in between.

WWW.TRAVELMATTERS.COM

Avalon Travel Publishing guides are
available at your favorite book or travel store.

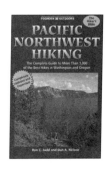

MOON HANDBOOKS

provide comprehensive coverage of a region's arts, history, land, people, and social issues in addition to detailed practical listings for accommodations, food, outdoor recreation, and entertainment. Moon Handbooks allow complete immersion in a region's culture—ideal for travelers who want to combine sightseeing with insight for an extraordinary travel experience in destinations throughout North America, Hawaii, Latin America, the Caribbean, Asia, and the Pacific.

WWW.MOON.COM

Rick Steves shows you where to travel and how to travel—all while getting the most value for your dollar. His Back Door travel philosophy is about making friends, having fun, and avoiding tourist rip-offs.

Rick's been traveling to Europe for more than 25 years and is the author of 22 guidebooks, which have sold more than a million copies. He also hosts the award-winning public television series Travels in Europe with Rick Steves.

WWW.RICKSTEVES.COM

ROAD TRIP USA

Getting there is half the fun, and Road Trip USA guides are your ticket to driving adventure. Taking you off the interstates and onto less-traveled, two-lane highways, each guide is filled with fascinating trivia, historical information, photographs, facts about regional writers, and details on where to sleep and eat—all contributing to your exploration of the American road.

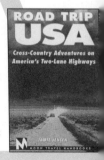

"Books so full of the pleasures of the American road, you can smell the upholstery."
~ BBC radio

WWW.ROADTRIPUSA.COM

TRAVEL ✦ SMART®

guidebooks are accessible, route-based driving guides focusing on regions throughout the United States and Canada. Special interest tours provide the most practical routes for family fun, outdoor activities, or regional history for a trip of anywhere from two to 22 days. Travel Smarts take the guesswork out of planning a trip by recommending only the most interesting places to eat, stay, and visit.

"One of the few travel series that rates sightseeing attractions. That's a handy feature. It helps to have some guidance so that every minute counts."
~San Diego Union-Tribune

Foghorn Outdoors

guides are for campers, hikers, boaters, anglers, bikers, and golfers of all levels of daring and skill. Each guide focuses on a specific U.S. region and contains site descriptions and ratings, driving directions, facilities and fees information, and easy-to-read maps that leave only the task of deciding where to go.

"Foghorn Outdoors has established an ecological conservation standard unmatched by any other publisher." **~Sierra Club**

WWW.FOGHORN.COM

CiTY·SMART™

guides are written by local authors with hometown perspectives who have personally selected the best places to eat, shop, sightsee, and simply hang out. The honest, lively, and opinionated advice is perfect for business travelers looking to relax with the locals or for longtime residents looking for something new to do Saturday night.

There are City Smart guides for cities across the United States and Canada, and a portion of sales from each title benefits a non-profit literacy organization in its featured city.

www.travelmatters.com

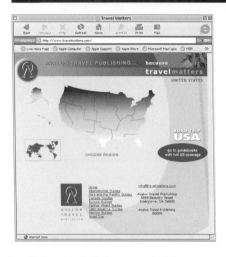

User-friendly, informative, and fun:

Because travel _matters_.

Visit our newly launched web site and explore the variety of titles and travel information available online, featuring an interactive _Road Trip USA_ exhibit.

also check out:

www.ricksteves.com

The Rick Steves web site is bursting with information to boost your travel I.Q. and liven up your European adventure.

www.foghorn.com

Visit the Foghorn Outdoors web site for more information on the premier source of U.S. outdoor recreation guides

www.moon.com

The Moon Handbooks web site offers interesting information and practical advice that ensure an extraordinary travel experience.